Vanquished Nation, Broken Spirit
The Virtues of the Heart in Formative Judaism

JACOB NEUSNER
Brown University

The right of the
University of Cambridge
to print and publish
all kinds of books
was granted by law
in 1534.
The University has printed
and published continuously
since 1584.

CAMBRIDGE UNIVERSITY PRESS

Cambridge
London   New York   New Rochelle
Melbourne   Sydney

Published by the Press Syndicate of the University of Cambridge
The Pitt Building, Trumpington Street, Cambridge CB2 1RP
32 East 57th Street, New York, NY 10022, USA
10 Stamford Road, Oakleigh, Melbourne 3166, Australia

First published 1987

Printed in the United States of America

Library of Congress Cataloging-in-Publication Data
Neusner, Jacob, 1932–
Vanquished nation, broken spirit.
Bibliography: p.
Includes index.
1. Rabbinical literature – History and criticism.
2. Mishnah – Criticism, interpretation, etc.
I. Title.
BM96.5.N483   1987   296.1   86–20768

British Library Cataloguing in Publication Data
Neusner, Jacob
Vanquished nation, broken spirit: the
virtues of the heart in formative Judaism.
1. Judaism
I. Title
296   BM561

ISBN 0 521 32832 2

Vanquished Nation, Broken Spirit

For

WILLIAM SCOTT GREEN

*in celebration
of twenty years of
friendship and collegiality*

Contents

Acknowledgments   xi

Abbreviations   xiii

Introduction   1

I   Emotion, the Individual, and Society: The Affective Aspect
      of Virtue   9

II   Vanquished Nation, Broken Spirit   17

III   The Starting Point   26
      The Mishnah   26
      Where in the Mishnah Matters of the Heart Appear but
         Have No Practical Significance   29
      Where in the Mishnah Matters of Virtue Do Have Prac-
         tical Significance   32
      Where in the Mishnah Attitudes Decide Matters   39
      The Humanity of God: Loving God   41
      Virtues of the Heart in the Law   44

IV   Virtue for Sages   45
      Tractate Abot: The Lessons of Virtue of the Founders
         for the Disciples of Sages   45
      Permissible and Impermissible Attitudes and Affections
         for Sages   55
      The Humanity of God: Loving God   57
      Torah and the Heart   58
      Doctrine, Discipline, Affection, and Virtue   59

V   Virtue in the Extension of the Exegetical Tradition of the
    Law: The Tosefta and the Fathers According to Rabbi
    Nathan   61
    The Tosefta   61
    Supplementing the Mishnah's Rules   61
    The Affection of Shame   68
    Attitude and Event: Hatred Destroyed Jerusalem   71
    The Fathers According to Rabbi Nathan   72

VI The Virtues of the Heart in the Articulation of the Exe-
    getical Tradition of the Law: The Yerushalmi   74
    The Yerushalmi   74
    Supplementing the Mishnah's Rules   77
    The Dimension of Scripture   86
    Torah in the Flesh   91
    Unchanging Virtue   96

VII The Conclusion of the Exegetical Tradition of the Law:
    The Bavli   98
    The Bavli   98
    Supplementing the Mishnah's Rules   100
    The Dimension of Scripture   101
    Torah in the Flesh   117
    Divine Pathos, Human Alienation   125

VIII The Other Torah: Affections in the Exegetical Tradition
    of Scripture   127
    Compilations of Exegeses of Scripture (*Midrashim*)   127
    A Probe of the Earlier Compilations of Scriptural
    Exegeses   130
    A Survey of the Later Compilations   132
    "You Will Love the Lord Your God with All Your
    Heart, with All Your Soul, and with All Your Might"
    in the Rabbinic Compilations of Scriptural Exegeses   137
    Affections as Law   139

IX Constant Affections, Inconstant Heart   141
    Emotion as Tradition   141
    Constancy and Change   145
    Change in the Use of Scripture: Compiling Exegeses   147
    Change in the Definition of the Generative Symbol:
    Torah   150
    Change in the Determination of Destiny: Messiah   153
    Who Is Israel and Why?   157

Bibliographical Essay and Source List   166

General Index   177

Index to Biblical and Talmudic References   180

Acknowledgments

The basic problematic of affections addressed in this book I owe to Paul Lauritzen, a Brown University graduate student. When I started working, I had a theme and data, but no questions. I did not yet know what I wanted to learn from the information I had acquired. Midway through the process of assembling my data – the materials ultimately presented in Chapters III through VIII – I consulted Mr. Lauritzan, sending a draft of part of the preface. With remarkable promptness he gave me a fine critique of my approach and proposed a much better entry into the materials. He wrote, "I think you need to be careful not to make too sharp a dichotomy between emotions and thoughts." He further sent me to the works of Robert Solomon and James Averill, as well as to those of other important scholars in philosophy and psychology. As soon as I had read the works of these considerable figures, I grasped what became the focus of this book, the problem of the interplay between sentiment and society or, as I conclude, *emotion as tradition*, that is, feelings as symbolic behavior at the level we in the Protestant West conventionally regard as most personal and private. The notion of affection as an aspect of symbolic behavior, which I sketch at the end, I owe ultimately to Mr. Lauritzen and those whose work he recommended.

Two other remarkably generous scholars came to my aid: Robert Solomon and James Averill. I wrote to them requesting copies of their résumés and explaining my problem. Both replied within a week. Each sent not only references to his own relevant work but also guidelines on other significant contributions to the topic. In addition each sent parcels of articles, many of which would have been difficult for me to get. I should be proud if Professors Solomon and Averill find in my work a useful footnote to their own, on which the present book depends entirely. I point, also, to the scholarly ethics characteristic of philosophy and psychology, fields in which I found, in my modest exposure, people eager to help one another and to advance the scholarly inquiries of colleagues. I have not always encountered these attitudes, these affections of good will and grace, in the field of Judaic studies. My thanks and debt to Messrs. Lauritzen, Solomon, and Averill are written across every page of this book.

Abbreviations

A.Z.	Mishnah tractate Abodah Zarah
Ar.	Mishnah tractate Arakhin
B.	Bavli
b.	ben, son of
B.M.	Mishnah tractate Baba Mesia
Ber.	Mishnah tractate Berakhot
Chron.	Chronicles
Deut.	Deuteronomy
Er.	Mishnah tractate Erubin
Exod.	Exodus
Exek.	Ezekiel
Gen. R.	Genesis Rabbah
Gen.	Genesis
Hag.	Mishnah tractate Hagigah
Hor.	Mishnah tractate Horayyot
Hos.	Hosea
Isa.	Isaiah
Jer.	Jeremiah
Ket.	Mishnah tractate Ketubot
Kip.	Tosefta tractate Kippurim = Mishnah tractate Yoma
Lam.	Lamentations
Lev.	Leviticus
Lev. R.	Leviticus Rabbah
M.	Mishnah
Mal.	Malachi

M.Q.	Mishnah tractate Moed Qatan
Mak.	Mishnah tractate Makhshirin
Meg.	Mishnah tractate Megillah
Men.	Mishnah tractate Menahot
Mic.	Micah
Ned.	Mishnah tractate Nedarim
Neh.	Nehemiah
Nid.	Mishnah tractate Niddah
Num.	Numbers
Pes.	Mishnah tractate Pesahim
Prov.	Proverbs
Ps.	Psalms
Qid.	Mishnah tractate Qiddushin
Qoh.	Qohelet = Ecclesiastes
R.	Rabbi, "my lord," "sir"
Sam.	Samuel
San.	Mishnah tractate Sanhedrin
Shab.	Misuhnah tractate Shabbat
Sheq.	Mishnah tractate Sheqalim
Sot.	Mishnah tractate Sotah
Suk.	Mishnah tractate Sukkah
T.	Tosefta
Ta.	Mishnah tractate Taanit
Ter.	Mishnah tractate Terumot
Toh.	Mishnah tractate Tohorut
Y.	Yerushalmi, Talmud of the Land of Israel
Yad.	Mishnah tractate Yadayim
Yeb.	Mishnah tractate Yebamot
Zeb.	Zebahim
Zech.	Zechariah
Zeph.	Zephaniah

Introduction

Judaism as we know it took shape in the first seven centuries of the Common Era. Labeled "rabbinic" after the title of its principal authority, the rabbi, or "talmudic" on the basis of one of its authoritative books, the Babylonian Talmud, or "classical" or "normative" because of its authoritative status in later times, the Judaism studied here succeeded all others of antiquity and defined all to come. Its myth and rite governed the religion of Judaism from late antiquity to our own day. "Formative Judaism" is the Judaism that is known to us in authoritative works of Torah, that is, the canon of law and of biblical explanation and theology, that have defined matters ever since their formulation.

The works of law begin with the Mishnah, a law code of deep philosophical interest, completed around A.D. 200, and extend through the Tosefta, a collection of supplements to the Mishnah that was closed some time before A.D. 400. Next comes the Talmud of the Land of Israel, a systematic amplification of the Mishnah, concluded about 400, and the Talmud of Babylonia, an equivalent treatment of the Mishnah, completed about 600. Together, as Judaism has always taught, they comprise the principal parts of the oral, or memorized, Torah revealed by God to Moses at Mount Sinai. The works of theology and biblical explanation, or exegesis – Mekhilta to Exodus, Sifra to Leviticus, Sifré to Numbers, another Sifré to Deuteronomy, Genesis Rabbah, and Leviticus Rabbah – as well as works devoted to Lamentations, Esther, and some other biblical books, form the other part of the same oral, or memorized, Torah that was given written form in late antiquity. These words of exegesis of the Mishnah and of Scripture constitute the definitive canon, or authoritative writings, of Judaism as it emerged from its formative age in late antiquity. If, therefore, we want to know how Judaism defines the virtues of the heart, these are the books to which we turn for the first definitive answer.

1

Ancient philosophers attended to the topic of "virtue," a complex of attitudes encompassing feelings, emotions, and behavior. Virtue embodied one's attitude toward others, one's inner feelings, as well as aspects of public action and individual belief. Hence, virtue constituted not only a personal, but a public and political dimension of individual life. How one showed virtue, what one felt at a critical moment – these exterior and interior expressions of virtue were matters of intense political interest. Merely by invoking the name of a philosophical school, that of the Stoics, we recognize how critical a role attitude played in philosophy. Right attitude – stoic acceptance, in this case – constituted a public expression of inner virtue. The ancient sages of Judaism, in many ways philosophers, taught a doctrine of virtue. Exemplars of civic virtue – right attitude, right emotion, right conduct within the heart – they addressed their nation with a concrete message. The details of the doctrine of virtue, both interior and exterior, would not have surprised other philosophers of their age. What we want to know, in exploring their view of virtue in attitude and action, feeling and relationship, is how their doctrine of virtue was related to their context and circumstance, for as I have stressed, attitudes governing affections (emotions) and actions constituted political factors, not merely private and adventitious whim. And when we understand the interplay between private feeling and public policy, we shall attain our goal: to grasp how sages mended the broken heart of the defeated nation and prepared the people for a long history of hope despite the dire circumstances of their political world. Israel never despaired but always kept the faith, and that attitude of faithfulness and hope, which sustained the Jewish people, was derived, in part, from the sages' doctrine for the virtuous heart.

In this book I trace the unfolding of the sages' doctrine of right attitude, encompassing as much sentiment as sensibility, behavior, and belief: the shape and structure of the heart. But matters of the heart are a fact of society and politics. Therefore, I propose to trace the emergence of teachings about the virtue of the heart in the successive documents of the canon of Judaism, "the one whole Torah of Moses, our rabbi," and to explain how those doctrines are related to the society and politics of Israel, the Jewish nation, in the Land of Israel as well as in Babylonia. As we shall see, a single doctrine of inner virtue predominates over a very long period of time. Here I shall delineate the system and attempt to explain why it endured for as long as it did.

If we wish to know the Torah's definition of a good Jew, we shall find it here. And since, in rabbinic Judaism, to be a good Jew meant to form oneself in God's image and after God's likeness, we realize that, in studying virtue, we enter the heart of God. Thus, the issues of this book are in no way trivial.

What, then, is the Torah's vision of the educated heart? And how will Jews serve God by disciplining affection, as much as intellect and action? These are the questions that define our inquiry in this book. As we shall see, the repertoire of approved and disapproved feelings remains constant through the half-millennium of the unfolding of the canon of Judaism from the Mishnah through the Talmud of Babylonia. I want to know why. The question becomes even more relevant in light of important changes in the treatment of other critical questions in the same books of formative Judaism. In Chapter IX questions of exegetical method, of teleological focus and definition, and of doctrinal and symbolic substance are shown to elicit diverse answers as the literature unfolds. Why should so much have changed while the Torah's message about virtue remained the same? And how, in the formative history of Judaism, shall we account for the distinctive and limited character of the heart's vocabulary taught by our sages as the language of the faith? These two questions flow together into my fundamental theory about why in the history of Judaism some things change and others do not.

In the sages' doctrine the ideal Jew exhibits these virtues: accommodation, congeniality, humility, forbearance, and a spirit of conciliation. Were we to claim that these virtues are the province of emotion alone, we should err, for these matters of deliberation are given expression in our deeds. Thus, a sharp distinction between interior attitude and public action is misleading. If we ignore the emotional foundation of attitudes that lead to actions, pretending that virtue comes to expression only in deed and not in deliberation – right feeling and right action alike – we impose distinctions on what truly forms a union. Accordingly, when we speak of the heart and its virtues we deal with emotions but also with aspects of behavior and demeanor. We address attitude, belief, and behavior as much as feeling and deep sentiment. Sages prescribe not only how Jews are to behave but also how they are to tame and teach the heart to want to behave in the right way: right attitude, right action, resting on the educated heart – virtue. Now, as we shall see, the emotions encouraged by Judaism in its formative age, such as humility, forbearance, accommodation, and a spirit of conciliation, exactly correspond to the political and social requirements of the Jews' condition in that time. The reason that the same repertoire of emotions persisted through the unfolding of the writings of the sages of that formative age was the constancy of the Jews' political and social condition.

To the contemporary debate, in anthropology, philosophy, and psychology, on whether emotions are related to culture and so form social constructions or whether feelings speak for the private individual and so characterize what is particular about the individual, the sages make a modest contribution. They present a suggestive example of how, in their view, emotions fit together with the encompassing patterns of society and culture, theology, and the religious life. Thus, the affective rules are an integral part of the way of life and world view put forward to make sense of the existence of a social group.

My thesis of virtue, accordingly, is that how I am supposed to feel in ethos matches what I am expected to think. In this way, as an individual, I link my deepest personal emotions to the cosmic fate and transcendent faith of that social group of which I am a part. Emotions lay down judgments. They are derived from rational cognition. The individual Israelite's innermost feelings, the microcosm, correspond to the public and historic condition of Israel, the macrocosm. What Judaism teaches the private person to feel links his or her heart to what Judaism states about the condition of Israel in history and of God in the cosmos.

Why? All form one reality, in supernatural world and in nature, in time and in eternity wholly consubstantial (so to speak). In the innermost chambers of deep feelings, the Israelite therefore lives out the public history and destiny of the people, Israel. The genius of Judaism, the reason for its resilience and endurance, lies in its power to teach Jews in private to feel what in public they also must think about the condition of both self and nation. The world within, the world without, are so bonded that one is never alone. The individual's life is always lived with the people. Virtue encompasses the whole of the matter.

In the texts we shall examine here, in the literature of feeling as much as in that of philosophy, virtue remains the same. The canon of Judaism, the Torah, refers not only to principles of metaphysics and laws of philosophical weight. It also speaks of attitudes, for example, intention; of feelings, for example, joy and sorrow; of virtues of the heart and hearth, for instance, humility, loyalty, and integrity. The canon confers on those actions and attitudes, feelings and emotions, a religious status, a place in the larger system.

Therefore, how Jews feel, as much as what they think, may fall within the realm of the Torah. In some contexts, approval extends to feelings, in others, disapproval. Despair, for example, contrasts with hope, treachery with loyalty, steadfastness and loyal love with betrayal. All of these aspects of virtue, though ultimately expressed in concrete actions, are important by themselves. Each of them, whole and real, consequential but important on its own, demands description, analysis, and interpretation.

In invoking the correct theological term, "religious affections," therefore, I mean to speak of the phenomenon of emotion in its public aspect, as a matter of philosophical or theological consequence, hence susceptible to sustained analysis, not something individual and principally psychological, lacking systemic standing in the public discourse of philosophy or theology.

Where was one to find the law of love, the rule of despair, in the system of regularity and order? The answer is clear. One found it in the interstices of singular emotions, private feelings, unpredictable attitudes. In the private person, these converged with the rules, beliefs, and regular patterns of public behavior. Those private and public matters together constituted virtue. To both inner feeling and exterior attitude rules applied. The canon and its system granted full cognizance to each by legislating for the affective life of virtue. The regular and the routine, the individual and the spontaneous affection together formed the whole. The one defined the system. The other made it work. Since the formula of faith hinged on love of God ("You will love the Lord your God"), the system had no choice but to define affections and find the correct place for them.

What in particular I want to know is where and when documents in the canon of formative Judaism invoke feelings and emotions, virtuous attitudes and demeanor, in a systemic (thus consequential) setting – hence, religious affections. I seek evidence on the role a person's virtue plays in the religious life. I make special reference to such feelings as humility versus arrogance, love versus hate, attitudes of anger or acceptance, demeanor of loyalty or treachery, hope or fear. When do the sages of a given document invoke, not principles of law or theology, rules of order, form, and proportion, but issues of virtue, of heart and soul? Whose feelings matter, when do they matter, and what are the consequences of systemically significant emotions? What is the range of affections recognized by a given document and by the system as a whole, and (in a phenomenological framework) what range of omitted or ignored affections can we in theory propose? Finally, what this-worldly expression of emotion or affection or virtue do we find in the literature, with special attention to where and how feelings rise to the surface of religious texture and context? These are the questions to be explored in Chapters III through VIII.

One critical component of my argument is that the program of approved and disapproved emotions and attitudes remains constant from the beginning to the end. Let me explain precisely what I mean. Otherwise the historical claim on which all else rests, involving Chapters II and IX, will be a puzzle to the reader. In order to understand the method of this book, reading the canon in order, document by document, we must recognize the character of the evidence presented. The sources constitute collective, and therefore official, literature. I claim to expound the collective and official account of a principal idea contained in that literature. All of the documents took shape in succession and attained a place in the canon of the rabbinical movement as a whole. None of them was written by an individual in such a way as to testify to personal choice or decision. Accordingly, we cannot provide an account of the theory of a given individual at a particular time. We have numerous references to what a given individual said about the topics at hand, but these references do not reach us through the authorship of that person, or even in his (never her) language. They come to us only in the setting of a *collection* of sayings and statements, some associated with names, others unattributed or anonymous. The collections by definition were composed under the auspices of rabbinical authority, a school or a circle. They tell us what a group of people wished to preserve and hand down as authoritative doctrine about the meaning of the Mishnah and Scripture. The compositions have reached us because the larger rabbinical estate chose to copy and hand them down. Accordingly, what in fact *do* we know? We know only the state of doctrine at the stages marked by the formation and closure of the several documents.

An alternative to the method of this book, as just described, is to assume that, if a given document ascribes an opinion to a named authority, the opinion was actually stated in that language by that sage. On this assumption, the history of an idea as individuals shaped it, and not merely of the literary evidences of that idea, may be described. Within this theory of evidence, we have the history of what individuals thought about a common topic, because the text contains the record of his exact words.

It is obvious why I cannot outline the sequence of ideas solely on the basis of the sequence of sages to whom ideas are attributed: I cannot demonstrate that a given authority really said what has been attributed to him in a given document. What I cannot show I do not know. We *do* know, however, that the Mishnah predates the Tosefta and that the Talmud of the Land of Israel follows it; the earliest compilations of scriptural exegeses come somewhat after the closure of the Talmud of the Land of Israel, and the Babylonian Talmud still later. Hence, we can trace, as the sequence of ideas, not their history but their canonical unfolding.

Let me lay out the range of uncertainty that necessitates this canonical approach. First, we do not know whether the canonical history corresponds to the actual history of the relevant ideas in sages' circles. Second, if we could demonstrate that a rabbi really spoke the words attributed to him, then, as I explained, a given idea would be shown to have reached expression within Judaism before the redaction of the document. By dividing ideas up by documents we give a later date, thus a different context for interpretation, to opinions that might have been held earlier than we now are able to demonstrate.

Third, we focus on the literature produced by a particular group, so we have no clear notion of what people were thinking outside that group. We do not know how the opinions of other groups or of the Jewish people in general came to shape the vision of rabbis.

Accordingly, I here trace the history of a particular doctrine of virtue as it unfolds in a sequence of documents – that alone, nothing more. I do not claim that the documents represent the opinion of the sages, the people, or the synagogue. I do not know whether the history of the idea in the unfolding official texts even corresponds to the history of the idea among the people who framed those documents. Still less do I claim to speak about the history of the program of accepted feelings outside rabbinical circles, among the Jewish nation at large. All of those larger dimensions lie beyond the perspective of this book. The reason is that the evidence at hand is of a particular sort. It permits us to investigate one category of questions and not another. That category, as I have stressed, is defined by established and universal conventions about the order in which the canonical writings reached completion.

We therefore trace the way in which approved feelings and associated matters emerge in the sequence of writings followed here: first the Mishnah, then the exegesis of the Mishnah written down in the Talmud of the Land of Israel, then, more or less in the same period, the exegesis of Scripture. The last was generated by the exegesis of the Mishnah, shaped in the model of that exegesis, and written down in the earliest collections of scriptural exegeses, called *midrashim*, alongside exegesis of the Mishnah as written down in the Talmud of Babylonia. When we follow this procedure, we discover how, within the formation of the rabbinical canon of writings, the repertoire of affections, with its associated conceptions, came to literary expression and how it was then shaped to serve the larger purposes of the canonical system as a whole.

The outline of the book is simple. In the first chapter, I briefly review the anthropological, philosophical, and psychological context in which I propose to frame and answer my questions. In the second chapter, I lay out the historical, literary, and religious context of the study. Then, in Chapters III through VIII, I survey the canon of formative Judaism and present the relevant facts. In the last chapter, I offer the conclusions that seem to me to follow from those facts. Thus, in the simplest structure, I present (1) a theoretical or methodological proposal, (2) the context of the documents, (3) the relevant facts, and (4) the results.

We Jews have always understood that we are what we do. But we have also hoped, or sometimes feared, that we are also what we feel. To bring these deep and conflicting convictions into balance is the task for those of us who aim to build a Judaism both to sustain us and to call on us to surpass ourselves. If we are what we do, we do not have to be merely what we are. With all humanity, we are "in the image, after the likeness" of God, and this not alone in mind and soul, but also in heart. In how we feel, too, we are meant to be like God. And what can that mean?

CHAPTER I

Emotion, the Individual, and Society

The Affective Aspect of Virtue

The religious life takes shape in the personal life of the individual in the emotions or affections – so Protestant theologians have maintained, in the tradition of Jonathan Edwards, for two hundred years. Schleiermacher, for example, saw the individual as (in Niebuhr's words) "an integral and independent being, standing over against the community in a genuine polarity." The selfhood of the individual attains expression in feeling. As Niebuhr wrote, "Feeling is the vehicle of this special quality of existence, of this given, irreducible individuality, this inner unity of the self that underlies all the temporal moments of the self's existence but that never issues into a direct and complete outward manifestation in any one of them."[1] According to one important stream of contemporary theological thought, therefore, the emotions are what mark a person as an individual. Theology sees in affections a critical expression of religion.

For a long time, long before the Protestant position was known, for the purposes of psychology and of philosophy emotions bore the burden of characterizing the individual. Emotions fell into the category of passions, not actions; they were private, therefore personal and individual. Emotions are, according to Darwin, James, and Freud, derived from the life of the biological organism. To be sure, though spontaneous and personal, they may find concrete definition in social transactions, as Dewey, Gerth, and Mills maintain. But at the heart of matters, in theology, philosophy, and psychology alike, emotions are a measure of the individual. The life of religious affections, in particular, testifies to the inner being – "the heart," in metaphorical language – of the private person. The introspective conscience of the West, the celebration of the individual and the individual's freedom to make distinctive choices – these define the religious as much as the philosophical and psychological dimensions of our reading of emotions.

Thus, it is commonplace for religion, psychology, and theology to

9

maintain that what makes the individual distinctive are the emotions, which are private and personal, rather than reason, which is public and social. Feelings, isolated from objects, testify to the person. Grace under stress or fierce temper, capacity to relate and to love, suspicion and anger are emotions that define, that *characterize* in the exact sense, the individual. If, then, in the Protestant tradition, we wish to study the religious life, we seek evidences of hope, joy, fear, zeal, compassion, and love. And these evidences will come to the surface in the personal life of the individual. Thus, religious affections are derived from the lives of individuals. The authentic dimension of true religion will find its measure in the undivided heart, rich in love, hope, joy, fear, zeal, and compassion.

The position that what defines the dimensions of religion is the life of the individual, the condition of the heart, with emphasis on the individual's private emotions, does not characterize theology alone. From the beginnings of philosophy in ancient Greece, almost to the present day, and through most of the history of psychology as well, some thinkers have generally concurred. To know what a person really is, to know that person's virtue, one must look at those things that are truly personal and unmediated by social norms or intellectual considerations. These turn out to focus on individual emotion, which is, I stress, what is taken to mark the person as an individual. In the long history of philosophy, psychology, and theology alike, essentially a single theme has been repeated: The inner life, the part of the person separate from society and remote from history, kept private from the shared markings of common culture, is where the true individual lives, alone, introspective, unique.

In the recent past psychologists and philosophers have called into question the certainty that private emotions define the individual. Deep speculative thought on the part of philosophers concerning the definition and nature of emotions corresponding to systematic psychological experimentation and inquiry produces a fresh perspective. From this new viewpoint emotions, like values and beliefs, cultural preferences and social rules, attitudes and other aspects of virtue, come to us from the world outside ourselves. They form aspects of cognition and judgment, society and culture. They are learned. Hope, joy, anger, love, zeal – these as much as believing in one God, preferring one kind of food over another, or voting for a candidate of the Republican party constitute expressions of social life rather than radically isolated individual life. Emotions are acquired. Feelings represent judgments and intentionalities. Thus, they form part of a shared and continuous life, an aspect of culture, something learned, handed down, and therefore constructed, not private, not personal, not individual. Emotions are traditions, defined by rules, just as much as are food preferences.

Let us pay closer attention to the position that emotions constitute social constructions, not purely private or distinctively individual categories. The beliefs people hold and the ideas they maintain stand in intimate relation to the emotions that fill their heart or spleen, to use familiar metaphors. To state the position most simply, emotions represent judgments and so constitute social constructions. The argument of this book is that the sages' repertoire of recommended or conventional emotions in the canon of formative Judaism constitutes nothing more than a statement, in the medium and terms of emotions, of their fundamental social, theological, and political policies. Examining this position is therefore critical to the study that follows. I propose to argue that the emotional aspect of virtue in Judaism constitutes a social construct and expresses in terms of emotions that same fundamental theory of Israel's life that emerges in every other aspect of the highly integrated system – the Judaism – expressed in the sages' canon of late antiquity. To begin with, that fundamental thesis must be shown to be basically plausible. Therefore, before I can argue about the social foundations in Judaism of what is supposed in general to be individual and private, I have to review the thought of important advocates of the view that social foundations define and sustain in emotional life, as much as other matters of culture or politics.

Let us start with the principal philosopher of this view: Robert C. Solomon. Solomon summarizes history in the apothegm "Emotions are judgments."[2] He thereby rejects radical differentiation between emotion and reason and opens the question of whether emotions are part of a larger social construction. Why? If emotion exists side by side with reason, and passion with logic, then the shared life of community, society, and nation intervenes. Emotion no longer denotes what is singular to the individual. Shared and subject to social judgment, emotion will testify, like any other aspect of shared and social culture, to the character of context, condition, and circumstance.

Solomon phrases all of this in the following way:

Emotions are not the brutish, unlearned, uncultured, illogical, and stupid drives that they are so often argued to be. To the contrary, they are extremely subtle, cunning, sophisticated, cultured, learned, logical, and intelligent. There is more intelligence in resentment than in the routine calculations of syllogizing; and there is far more strategy in envious Iago than in thoughtful Hamlet. The cunning of reason, when you see what Hegel means by it, is almost always the cunning of emotion.[3]

Solomon is careful to define as judgment something other than what is merely deliberative. Judgment may be spontaneous, but emotions do constitute judgments and do express intentionality.

What marks emotions is their engagement of self-esteem – a point critical to my argument later on – as expressed in the notion of "taking things personally." Accordingly, Solomon maintains, emotions should not be seen as "disturbances, breaking the calm of contented objectivity."[4] They are modes of expression and, as we noticed, of judgment as well. Still more to the point: "Every emotion, no matter how specific, structures our world and has definitive influences on the whole of our experience."[5]

Parallel to the movement in philosophy represented by Solomon is the "constructivist view of emotion" in contemporary psychology.[6] Specifically, James R. Averill argues that emotions may constitute learned, not merely "natural," modes of expression. He sees love, for example, as a social construction and has studied stress reactions through their social origins and functions. By no means alone, Averill finds support in works like that of Arlie Russell Hochschild, *The Managed Heart: Commercialization of Human Feeling*. She advances a social theory of emotion to show how institutions "control us not simply through their surveillance of our behavior but through surveillance of our feelings." Hochschild sums up her theoretical view as follows:

I am joining three theoretical currents. Drawing from Dewey, Gerth and Mills, and Goffman within the interactional tradition, I explore what gets done to emotion and how feelings are permeable to what gets done to them. From Darwin, in the organismic tradition, I posit a sense of what is there, impermeable, to be "done to," namely, a biologically given sense related to an orientation to action. Finally, through Freud, I circle back from the organismic to the interactional tradition, tracing through an analysis of the signal function of feeling how social factors influence what we expect and thus what feelings "signal."[7]

To place Hochschild alongside Averill, whose position is somewhat more narrowly psychological, I cite Averill's clearest statement of his views:

Traditionally, the emotions have been viewed from a biological perspective; that is, the emotions have been seen as genetically determined and relatively invariable responses. The present chapter, by contrast, views the emotions as social constructions. More precisely, the emotions are here defined as socially constituted syndromes or transitory social roles. A role-conception does not deny the contribution of biological systems to emotional syndromes; it does, however, imply that the functional significance of emotional responses is to be found largely within the sociocultural system. With regard to subjective experience, a person interprets his own behavior as emotional in much the same way that an actor interprets a role "with feeling." This involves not only the monitoring of behavior (including feedback from physiological arousal, facial expressions, etc.), but also an understanding of how the emotional role fits into a larger "drama" written by society.[8]

Solomon, Hochschild, and Averill call into question long-standing positions in philosophy, sociology and psychology.

Yet a fourth discipline, anthropology, comes under analysis, again by Solomon, in an article that draws us to the threshhold of the problem of this book. Pointing out that anthropology's universalists impute to all peoples "essentially the same emotional make-up," Solomon insists on the contrary view. He points out that the platitude that people are basically the same "has comfortably coexisted with the seemingly contrary belief that emotions are essentially personal and private and that no one can ever really know what anyone else is feeling."[9] Solomon rejects the view that an emotion is "feeling, something that one and only one person can experience, which has virtually no conceptual ties and perhaps minimal causal ties to other aspects of his or her experience."[10] Emotion, he maintains, represents substantially more than feelings. Let me now rely on a sizable abstract of Solomon's article to present the issue critical to this book:

On my theory, an emotion is a complex system of judgments, about the world, about other people, and about ourselves and our place in our world. We simplify these complexities by giving them simple names, for example, anger; and then fall into the lazy pattern of thinking as if the simple names referred to equally simple entities. It has recently been argued, by psychologists and social scientists as well as by philosophers, that emotions have distinctive cognitive connections and properties; the emotions-as-judgments theory explains this straightforwardly, for obviously judgments are cognitive and have all sorts of conceptual and logical connections with other judgments and beliefs.

An emotion is not an isolated judgment, but a system of judgment which is in turn a sub-system of the whole of our way(s) of viewing the world. This means, among other things, that the distinctions we make between emotions, as if they were discrete mental entities, is unjustified. But this means that, quite the opposite of the view that emotions are isolated from the rest of our experience and beliefs and therefore problematic if not impossible to know in other people, emotions are part of an elaborate web of experience and belief, tied to other judgments (for example, explicit moral, scientific and aesthetic judgments) by various logical relationships. To understand another person's emotional life requires nothing less than an understanding of the view(s) of the world as a whole. Each emotion is, so far as it can be isolated from the rest of the experience, a particular focusing of judgmental structures through which the person constructs his or her view of the world and gives it significance.[11]

Here we see how Solomon relates his theory of emotions to the issues of interpretation of social life and culture raised by anthropological study. Solomon therefore builds the bridge to the study of emotions in religious life (as in any other social and cultural circumstance). If how I feel expresses what I think ("a complex system of judgments"), then, as people tell me how I am supposed to feel, they also prescribe what I am expected to think. But they do so in so subtle a manner, in so profound a layer of consciousness, that I am able unaffectedly to link my innermost feelings with vast issues of society and history. My heart turns inward – but therefore draws downward and into my being those large structures of politics, history, and national destiny that lie far outside and beyond me as an individual. The power of emotions harnessed to the forces of history is the ultimate issue I propose to address. If I can show that emotion, a system of judgment, is part of a larger construction of the world, I can discover that missing link between the individual (the personal and the private) and the nation (the social and the public). That is the fusion that gives the system, rabbinical Judaism, its explosive and sustained power. But of this more below. Let me for the moment merely underline the main point: Emotions are part of a larger system, a system of virtue but also a social system, composed of how people live their lives, on the one side, and how they explain themselves and their way of life, on the other. In the context of Judaism, emotions are an integral part of virtue.

In turning to Solomon and Averill and their colleagues in philosophy, psychology, and sociology, I seek a framework in which to interpret the data to be presented in this book. I do not claim to prove that their theories are right or even that they explain more adequately than other theories the data I shall examine. My problem is a simple one. I have selected a category for study, namely, sayings and stories that, to a greater or lesser extent, deal with the heart, or the virtues of the affective life of Judaism. I seek a theory within which to analyze data about how people spoke about their emotions. I turn for such a theory to contemporary philosophers and psychologists who raise the issue of the social foundations of the inner life. I find their theories congenial, indeed, self-evident, because they help me to put into perspective the facts constituted by the sayings and stories that we shall examine. They also frame for me questions that illuminate these sayings and stories. But the facts at hand also illuminate the theoretical inquiries of philosophy and psychology that I have invoked. So although I cannot claim to demonstrate the soundness of what I find to be a congenial theory, I can show how the theory of emotions as constructions, as judgments, makes sense of what seem to me important, but otherwise opaque and discrete facts.

What is at stake is no small matter. The classical and canonical writings of Judaism, defining the norms of the Judaic religious life and world view for Israel, the Jewish people, speak not only of behavior and belief but also of virtue, including emotions. Numerous sayings specify how I should feel. Defining the correct attitude and affective life, these sayings attribute to God precisely that approved affective life that the Israelite is supposed to live. Any conception that how I feel is my personal business, defining me as *distinct* from everyone else and allowing me a private religious life, contradicts what I shall show to be the public and prescriptive position of the authoritative writings of Judaism in late antiquity. These sources take for granted that how I feel – whether I love or hate, mourn or celebrate – constitutes a primary dimension of my life in the holy community of Israel, the Jewish people. Emotions are subject to rule and constitute traditions. Virtue is a public aspect of theology.

Jonathan Edwards and Schleiermacher would not know what to make of such a premise concerning the affective life. The philosophical tradition that treats emotions as brutish, unlearned, uncultured, illogical, and stupid could scarcely cope with the premise of the Judaic system, for that premise treats emotions as learned, logical marks of civility and civilization, expressions of culture, and therefore vehicles of sanctification. If I am commanded not to hate my brother in my heart but to love God with all my heart, soul, and might, then how I *feel* – and this by definition – constitutes a fundamental fact, an irreducible dimension, of what I am, as part of holy Israel, serving the God of all creation.

Thus, as Solomon would put it, emotion indeed is judgment. As we shall see, love invariably has an object and undergoes differentiation because it forms a judgment. To state matters in a secular way, as Averill has done, love or hate, mourning or joy forms a social construction. The emotions I feel, as well as the food I eat, the clothing I wear, the manner in which I tend my fields or do business in my shop, the way in which I pray to God, testify, each in its medium and circumstance, to one thing. I accordingly propose to prove two propositions. First, for holy Israel, as the sages of Judaism in the formative age saw Israel, at issue in how I feel is what is at stake in what I do and think. Second, the historical condition of Israel is related to that affective life that fully expresses both the way of life and the world view framed by the sages who created the Judaism we have known for two thousand years. To put matters simply, my emotions, too, constitute judgments on Israel in God's world, a mighty claim indeed.

Notes

1   Richard R. Neibuhr, *Schleiermacher on Christ and Religion: A New Introduction* (New York, Scribner's, 1964).
2   Robert C. Solomon; see his several works cited in the Bibliographical Essay.
3   Solomon, "The Logic of Emotion," *Nous* 11 (1977), 41–9.
4   Solomon, *The Passions: The Myth and Nature of Human Emotions* (Garden City, N.J., Archer/Doubledary, 1977), 130.
5   Ibid., 172.
6   James R. Averill, "A Constructive View of Emotion," in *Emotion: Theory, Research and Experience, Vol. 1: Theories of Emotion* (Orlando, Fla., Academic Press, 1980), 305.
7   Arlie Russell Hochschild, *The Managed Heart: Commercialization of Human Feeling* (Berkeley, Calif., 1983), 218, 222.
8   Averill, "Constructive View," p. 305.
9   Solomon, "Emotions and Anthropology: The Logic of Emotional World Views," *Inquiry* 21 (1978), 181.
10   Ibid., 185.
11   Ibid.

CHAPTER II

Vanquished Nation, Broken Spirit

Israel in the Land of Israel for nearly a thousand years celebrated God's grace in the Temple in Jerusalem. Once destroyed, in 586 B.C., and then rebuilt, the Temple laid forth the lines of Israel's social and political structure, with the Temple's priestly caste dominant. Also suspended and then resumed, the priests' regular preparation of animals, grain, oil, and wine for God's service, accomplished with precision and punctilious routine, corresponded on earth to the passage of the moon and the stars in the heavens, the seasons in their solar cycle. As the moon and sun made their way across the skies, the sacred meals, shared by the priests and placed on the bonfires of the alter, made their way upward, in smoke, to God in heaven. Scripture, the Torah that people universally believed God had given to Moses at Mount Sinai, laid forth God's rules for this ritual. What the secular eye might see as a caste system, with daily barbeques supporting privileged men, most Israelites celebrated as the point at which heaven met earth, the moment at which all life gained renewal through the return to heaven of God's share in heaven's blessings.

Destroyed, prophets said, because of Israel's sins, then rebuilt, other prophets claimed, because of Israel's reform and regeneration, the Temple was a focus of the life of the nation, near and far. When, therefore, in August of the year 70, the building was burned, the city ruined, the priests scattered, the cult suspended, people found solace in Scripture. There they read the lesson of the past, recalling how, after the Temple had met an earlier calamity in 586 B.C., God had imposed a penance of three generations' exile and suffering, but then in grace had restored to the city the rite, and with it, the nation to its land. Accordingly, the people resigned themselves to a life of suffering, anticipating renewal once three generations had passed. When sixty-five years later, in 132, the war against Rome led by Bar Kokhba turned into catastrophe, the ancient paradigm betrayed the hopes placed in it. Then no precedents guided.

17

But the people endured. The land in substantial measure resided in the people's hands. Scripture, the priests and other castes, the deep order of nature and of supernature, the records and rules of the distant past, and the message of God's love – all these had crossed over the caesura. The survivors of seven decades of calamity, after 140, carried good seeds for future sowing.

The defeated people, badly led in two vast and hopeless wars, had substituted courage for good counsel, appealing to dreams of glory to give them guidance in coping with an incongruous reality. Many expected anointed, that is, divinely appointed, leadership, even imputing to leaders in both wars the status of messiah. If we had to limn a portrait, after the catastrophic defeat, of the inner being of the nation as a whole, we would draw heavily on the dark colors of the affective spectrum, defeat, despair, despondency. Evidence from diverse sources, both Jewish and otherwise, from rabbis' rites of national mourning as much as from Justin's portrait of a Jewish refugee, Trypho, points in a single direction. Israel was a vanquished people and now acknowledged defeat. Israel in its land, the nation of broken spirit, would now offer up one last sacrifice, lasting for how long no one knew, the contrite spirit, the broken heart alone.

The vanquished nation of broken spirit began, in the second century, a whole new history – a history that stretched over an age not yet run its course even to our own day. Surviving one enemy after another, enduring in indomitable hope, the nation not only constructed for itself a new politics and effective mode of public life. Its sages accomplished, also, a reconstruction of the inner life, encompassing a broad range of emotions. For one thing, the entire heritage of the nation came under revision, with parts discarded but larger parts renewed and reworked for the age of restoration. For another, a way of life and world view, claiming beginnings at Sinai, recast the national life in patterns congruent with the new condition. For a third, and most important, people learned so to educate their hearts as to feel in private precisely those emotions that, translated in public into judgments, public policy, modes of behavior, and propositional belief, proved quite appropriate to the condition of the heroic and enduring people. So in heart and in will the defeated people defeated its enemies, not in the second century alone but for all recorded time to come.

The definitions of the second century, unfolding and sustaining refinement and articulation long afterward, laid forth those lines of structure that would uphold Israel's social order. In politics and culture, in matters of the sacred and convictions about the holy, a construction took shape that would stand firm through storm and change. And, as I have said, individuals, seeing themselves as private individuals, were taught to feel for themselves all of those emotions to which, in the way of life and world view of the larger society, the system as a whole gave full expression. In consequence, how individuals felt in their hearts, their virtuous attitudes, turned out to correspond exactly to how the nation lived as a whole, in its politics and social culture.

In a word, the vanquished nation, meant to endure in subjugation, able to go forward only by accepting its condition of weakness, educated the individual to the virtues of the broken heart. Teaching restraint and not rebellion, genial acceptance and not defiance, concern for the feelings of others and not unrestrained self-expression, above all humility and not arrogance, the nation translated its politics into prerequisites for the virtuous affective life. These expressed in terms of emotions what in fact conformed to the unchanging contingencies of national political existence. Circumstances demanded restraint. An accommodating, accepting counsel alone guaranteed survival for weak people who could change little and had to swallow much. Thus, virtue for the individual would consist of moderated expectations. Instruction on correct emotions would emphasize how God favored those who sought the approval of others. Public policy imposed narrow limits on socially sustained forms of rebellion and demanded the power of endurance, the force of patience; hence, the favored individual would cultivate feelings of acceptance, going along so as to get along.

No space remained for the full expression of impulses to strike out or to follow brute instincts, at least none for Israel. The instinct to do evil, as much as the instinct to do good, must pass through the crucible so as to emerge purified in God's service. In these and other ways, the life of feelings, the affairs of the heart constituted judgments (in Solomon's language) on the condition of the group, not solely on the affective character or conscience of the individual out of all cultural or social context. The affections, then, were meant to correspond, in the heart of the individual, or in what we should now call the private counsel and conscience, to those national and historical facts that, as I said, defined the intelligent and sane policy of society as a whole. In reshaping feeling into a counterpart to political culture, the nation would so nurture its coming generations as to guarantee for each individual a stake in correct public policy.

In consequence, the nation lived. True, it was a life favoring restraint and accommodation, discouraging immoderate affection, on the one side, rebellious spirit, on the other. The approved repertoire of feelings may strike some as one suitable for slaves. It assuredly conformed to the condition of weakness. A system that taught, for example, that strength lies in winning over one's enemy, riches in accepting what one has, well served to reconcile the weak to weakness, leaving strength to others. But Israel *was* vanquished. The hearts of the people (so we surmise, and the evidence is strong) were broken. Teaching the virtue of what had to be accepted, training the heart to feel what the mind acknowledged, the system drew remarkable resilience precisely because it educated feeling and disciplined the heart's emotions.

And that fact, one may fairly claim, explains the astonishing strength of Judaism and the extraordinary endurance of the Jews. It lay in their power to accommodate powerlessness not only in politics but in ethos and in ethics. The strength to accommodate and accept not only as an exercise in shrewd and necessary policy but especially as a deeply felt necessity of the heart accounts for Israel's power to endure in this construction, which was therefore, one of affections as much as of politics and theology, the person of virtue will have a Jewish heart (to use an anachronism) as much as a Jewish head. In all rationality to feel as much as to think, in full control of passions as much as actions, was the counsel of the vanquished people's sages. In time, the drawing together of policy and passion, emotion and ethos would heal the broken heart of Israel. But the remedy consisted of accommodation, restraint, self-denial, humility, and reconciliation. That is to say, the broken heart would never find healing. Life now would find sustenance in such life blood as a broken heart could pump.

Having stated matters in an abstract way, let me now provide a concrete example of what I conceive to be the systemic correspondence, counseled by sages, among the components of sound public policy, theological doctrine, ethical teaching, and, consequently, appropriate emotion. Since Israel's engagement in the great wars of the late first and second centuries, it is generally supposed, derived from the peoples' broad expectation that, by fighting, Israel would provoke the coming of the Messiah, we turn to the way in which sages dealt with the messiah theme in constructing their larger system, their Judaism. As I said, what we wish to ask is where and how sages brought into congruence their public policy about men who claimed to be messiahs, their theological doctrine on the coming of a (or *the*) messiah, their ethical teaching about proper conduct in general, and their catalogue of acceptable and unacceptable emotions. In line with the theses of Solomon and Averill, we should anticipate a single and integrated system, of which emotions constitute a cogent part.

Restricting ourselves to one representative statement of the system's messiah doctrine, we turn to the Talmud of the Land of Israel. The reason is that it is here that the matter reaches its first conclusive version, the statement of views characteristic of the system from that time onward. Examining the doctrinal issue first, we ask what makes a messiah a false messiah? In this Talmud (as in the later one), it is not his claim to save Israel. *It is his claim to save Israel without the help of God.* The meaning of the true Messiah is Israel's total submission, through the Messiah's gentle rule, to God's yoke and service. God is ot to be manipulated by Israel's humoring of heaven in rite and cult. The notion of keeping the commandments so as to please heaven and force God to do what Israel wants is totally incongruent with the Talmud. Keeping the commandments as a mark of submission, loyalty, and humility before God is the sages' system of salvation. Israel does not save itself. Israel never controls its own destiny, either on earth or in heaven. The only choice is whether to cast one's fate into the hands of cruel, deceitful men or to trust in the living God of mercy and love. We shall now see how this critical position is spelled out in the setting of discourse about the Messiah in the Talmud of the Land of Israel.

Bar Kokhba, above all, exemplifies arrogance against God. He lost the war because of that arrogance. In particular, he ignored the authority of sages:

[X. J]. Said R. Yohanan, "Upon orders of Caesar Hadrian, they killed eight hundred thousand in Betar."

K. Said R. Yohanan, "There were eighty thousand pairs of trumpeteers surrounding Betar. Each one was in charge of a number of troops. Ben Kozeba [= Bar Kokhba] was there, and he had two hundred thousand troops who, as a sign of loyalty, had cut off their little fingers.

L. "Sages sent word to him, 'How long are you going to turn Israel into a maimed people?'

M. "He said to them, 'How otherwise is it possible to test them?'

N. "They replied to him, 'Whoever cannot uproot a cedar of Lebanon while riding on his horse will not be inscribed on your military rolls.'

O. "So there were two hundred thousand who qualified in one way, and another two hundred thousand who qualified in another way."

P. When he would go forth to battle, he would say, "Lord of the world! Do not help and do not hinder us! 'Hast thou not rejected us, O God? Thou dost not go forth, O God, with our armies' (Ps. 60:10)."

Q. Three and a half years did Hadrian besiege Betar.

R. R. Eleazar of Modiin would sit on sackcloth and ashes and pray every day, saying, "Lord of the ages! Do not judge in accord with strict judgment this day! Do not judge in accord with strict judgment this day!"

S. Hadrian wanted to go to him. A Samaritan said to him, "Do not go to him until I see what he is doing, and so hand over the city [of Betar] to you. [Make peace . . . for you.]"

T. [The Samaritan] got into the city through a drain pipe. He went and found R. Eleazar of Modiin standing and praying. He pretended to whisper something into his ear.

U. The townspeople saw [the Samaritan] do this and brought him to

Ben Kozeba. They told him, "We saw this man having dealings with your friend."

V. [Bar Kokhba] said to him, "What did you say to him, and what did he say to you?"

W. [The Samaritan] said to him, "If I tell you, then the king will kill me, and if I do not tell you, then you will kill me. It is better that the king kill me, and not you.

X. "[Eleazar] said to me, 'I should hand over my city' ['I shall make peace.....']."

Y. He turned to R. Eleazar of Modiin. He said to him, "What did this Samaritan say to you?"

Z. He replied, "Nothing."

AA. He said to him, "What did you say to him?"

BB. He said to him, "Nothing."

CC. [Ben Kozeba] gave [Eleazar] one good kick and killed him.

DD. Forthwith an echo came forth and proclaimed the following verse:

EE. " 'Woe to my worthless shepherd, who deserts the flock! May the sword smite his arm and his right eye! Let his arm be wholly withered, his right eye utterly blinded!' (Zech. 11:17).

FF. "You have murdered R. Eleazar of Modiin, the right arm of all Israel, and their right eye. Therefore may the right arm of that man wither, may his right eye be utterly blinded!"

GG. Forthwith Betar was taken, and Ben Kozeba was killed.

Y. Ta. 4:5

We notice two complementary themes. First, Bar Kokhba treats heaven with arrogance, asking God merely to keep out of the way. Second, he treats an especially revered sage with similar arrogance. The sage had the power to preserve Israel. Bar Kokhba destroyed Israel's one protection. The result was inevitable.

The theory of this Yerushalmi passage is stated very simply. In the sages' view Israel had to choose between wars, either the war fought by Bar Kokhba or the "war for Torah." "Why had they been punished? It was because of the weight of the war, for they had not wanted to engage in the struggles over the meaning of the Torah" (Y. Ta. 3:9.XVII). Those struggles, which were ritual arguments about ritual matters, promised the only victory worth winning. Then Israel's history would be written in terms of wars over the meaning of the Torah and the decision of the law.

Before returning to the question with which we began, let us ask how the authors of materials gathered in the Talmud of the hand of Israel tell us when the Messiah will come and what Israel must do to bring him:

[X] J. "The oracle concerning Dumah. One is calling to me from Seir, 'Watchman, what of the night? Watchman, what of the night?' " (Isa. 21:11).

K. The Israelites said to Isaiah, "O our Rabbi, Isaiah, what will come for us out of this night?"

L. He said to them, "Wait for me, until I can present the question."

M. Once he had asked the question, he came back to them.

N. They said to him, "Watchman, what of the night? What did the Guardian of the ages tell you?"

O. He said to them, "The watchman says: 'Morning comes; and also the night. If you will inquire, inquire; come back again' (Isa. 21:12)."

P. They said to him, "Also the night?"

Q. He said to them, "It is not what you are thinking. But there will be morning for the righteous, and night for the wicked, morning for Israel, and night for idolaters."

R. They said to him, "When?"

S. He said to them, "Whenever you want. He too wants [it to be] – if you want it, he wants it."

T. They said to him, "What is standing in the way?"

U. He said to them, "Repentance: 'Come back again' (Isa. 21:12)."

V. R. Aha in the name of R. Tanhum b. R. Hiyya, "If Israel repents for one day, forthwith the son of David will come.

W. "What is the scriptural basis? 'O that today you would hearken to his voice!' (Ps. 95:7)."

X. Said R. Levi, "If Israel would keep a single Sabbath in the proper way, forthwith the son of David will come.

Y. "What is the scriptural basis for this view? 'Moses said, "Eat it today, for today is a sabbath to the Lord; today you will not find it in the field" ' (Exod. 16:25).

Z. "And it says, 'For thus said the Lord God, the Holy One of Israel, "In returning and rest you shall be saved; in quietness and in trust shall be your strength." And you would not' (Isa. 30:15)."

Y. Ta. 1:1

We must not lose sight of the importance of this passage, with its emphasis on repentance, on the one side, and the power of Israel to reform itself, on the other. The Messiah will come any day that Israel makes it possible. If all Israel will keep a single Sabbath in the proper (rabbinic) way, the Messiah will come. If all Israel will repent for one day, the Messiah will come. "Whenever you want," the Messiah will come.

Two things are apparent here. First, the system of religious observance, including the study of Torah, is explicitly invoked as having salvific power. Second, the persistent hope of the people for the coming of the

Messiah is linked to the system of rabbinic observance and belief. In this way, the austere program of the Mishnah develops in a different direction, with no trace of a promise that the Messiah will come if and when the system is fully realized. Here a teleology lacking all eschatological dimension gives way to an explicitly messianic statement that the purpose of the law is to attain Israel's salvation: "If you want it, God wants it too." The one thing Israel commands is its own heart; the power it yet exercises is the power to repent. These suffice. The entire history of humanity will respond to Israel's will, to what happens in Israel's heart and soul. With the Temple in ruins, repentance can take place only within the heart and mind.

The Messiah myth is thus recast in a philosophical mode of thought and stated as the teleology of an eternally present sanctification attained by obedience to patterns of holiness laid out in the Torah. The version of the Messiah myth incorporated into the rabbinic system through the Talmuds simply restates the obvious: Israel's sanctification is what governs. Thus, if Israel will keep a single Sabbath (or two in succession), the Messiah will come. If Israel stops violating the Torah, the Messiah will come. If Israel acts with arrogance in rejecting its divinely assigned condition, the Messiah will not come. Everything depends, then, on the here and now of everyday life. The operative category is not salvation through what Israel *does* but sanctification of what Israel *is*. The fundamental convictions of the Mishnah's framers, flowing from the reaction against the apocalyptic and messianic wars of the late first and early second centuries, here absorbed and redirected precisely that explosive energy that, to begin with, had made Israel's salvation through history the critical concern. The Messiah became precisely what the sages of the Mishnah and their continuators in the Talmud most needed: a rabbi-messiah who would save an Israel sanctified through Torah. Salvation then depends on sanctification and is subordinated to it.

Yet Israel's condition, moral and social, must govern Israel's destiny – in accordance with the Torah's rules, but also precisely as biblical prophecy and Mishnaic doctrine had claimed. What then could Israel do about its own condition? How could Israel confront the unending apocalypse of its own history? Israel could do absolutely nothing. But Israel could become holy. That is why history was relegated to insignificance. Humble acceptance of the harsh rule of Gentiles would render Israel worthy of God's sudden intervention, the institution of God's rule through a king-messiah.

To return to the main point, let me emphasize that the repertoire of approved emotions and attitudes, particularly self-abnegation and humility, corresponded to the political policy imposed by necessity, that is, submission. Affective and virtuous life within expresses social and cultural policy beyond; a feeling and attitude of humble acceptance within matches obedience to the Torah beyond. The Messiah will come not when Israel *does* something, but when Israel *is* that holy society, living in full obedience to the Torah, that Israel is meant to be. What is called for? In theology, repentance; in politics, submission; in the national ethos, conciliation and accommodation; in one's inner emotions and in relationship to God, humility. These are the diverse modal principles of a single system.

That is why what one feels in the heart matches what one contemplates in the mind and dictates how all Israel conducts its national life in the life of the nations of the world. Israel's condition encompasses all dimensions of Israel's life, defining public policy in history as much as personal passions at home. The individual in the privacy or the emotions then embodies the ethos of the nation, with carefully regulated moments of joy or sorrow and always restrained feelings, with perpetual moderation and persistent self-abnegation to mark the system's perfect match between self and society.

CHAPTER III

The Starting Point

The Mishnah

Concerned with setting forth rules governing various persons, objects, and circumstances, expressing its main point in minutely detailed instructions on the smallest matters, the Mishnah (around A.D. 200) presents few occasions for the expression of feeling or the invocation of virtue. That is so for two reasons. The first is that the composition is a law code. But that consideration hides more than it reveals, for within the law the attitudes of the human actor play an important role; for instance, the actor's plans or intentions decide many matters. Thus, when we recognize that the Mishnah apparently asks little of the heart, we observe a trait of this law code in particular, not necessarily of all such codes. The second reason is that the laws of the Mishnah deal with what is public and routine, not with what must, by definition, prove individual and spontaneous. This draws us back over the ground of the first reason. Philosophical jurisprudents, such as those who wrote the Mishnah, proposed to state the rules taking account of feelings and emotions.

Laws governing rites of mourning treat as routine and ordinary even the most intense and painful trials of the emotions in common life, such as on the occasion of death. Indeed, one task of law is to show the routine in the spontaneous, the orderly rules governing whatever upsets the form and ritual of the workaday world. Treating as a principal ritual the power to love and insisting that the person's first duty was to love God, the philosophers of the Mishnah (within the inherited pattern of Israelite religion) moreover confronted what must be regarded as a major motif in the religious affections of all Judaisms, including the one represented by the canon of the ancient rabbis: loving God.

We cannot ask the Mishnah to tell us what it does not portray, which is a rich and varied emotional life with God and Torah. But neither can

26

we dismiss the Mishnah altogether, excusing its slender, odd testimony on grounds that it does not address the heart's role in the social labor of sanctification and salvation demanded by the Mishnah's authors' reading of God's Torah. What we must learn from this starting point in the formation of the canon of Judaism – this first initiative (in the minds of its authors) beyond Scripture itself, this other Torah, this oral Torah – is simple. It concerns not the Mishnah but our topic. It is a list of words for emotions and how they are used or, more precisely, a catalogue of circumstances for affective participation. We want to find out how and where, in the first formulation of the system of Judaism, religious affections came to full expression and played a substantial role.

If we are to hear the testimony, what we require is a clear view of what we do and do not wish to know. When we speak of affection, we refer to attitudes not defined by reason, feelings not dictated by entirely rational consideration. In consequence of such attitudes and feelings, routine processes of calculation and consideration in speech or even in deed give way to the spontaneous expression of what is in the heart – virtue in a different dimension. We speak of how the soul comes to the surface in feeling unmediated by ratiocination. Clearly, we deal with a species of the genus attitude. An attitude attains rationality when it is formed after reflection on one's purpose and how to achieve it. The species of the genus attitude, namely, purposive or rational attitude, then stands in contrast to the opposing species of the same genus, namely, emotional or affective attitude. The latter does not come about through reflection on goals and how to gain them. It comes from elsewhere than the mind, and it compels distinctive acts, such as weeping or joyful laughter.

The metaphorical language here, appealing to "the heart" as against "the mind," serves quite well to effect the needed contrast. The Mishnaic law takes full account of purposive action, intention, planning. It assigns responsibility to the actor, for example, when the action results from, and attains, the actor's goals. The law in certain circumstances treats as consequential what happens as a result of the human will, and the law dismisses as null what happens merely by accident or not as a result of deliberate deed and considered action. Hence, the attitude before the action may be compared to what is actually done. Then will the law take account of an attitude not joined to an action at all, such as love? Does the law deal with an action, such as weeping; that is not preceded by reflection on a goal or purpose? Finally, can the life of emotion ever reach the surface if impeded by layers of reflection so that we may *decide*, deliberately, to love or to weep? These questions help us recognize the genus and distinguish among its species, thus defining for the first stage in our inquiry the sorts of data that will attract our interest.

In light of this definition, we ask the Mishnah to teach us where and how the law accommodates what in the end law cannot dictate, which is virtue – for example, the rule of love, the way of tears. We recognize that law describes what is routine, and the Mishnaic law proposes to describe an entire world of order and proportion. Thus, we want to know at what points the Mishnah's system of law and order (whatever the object of routinization) brings to center stage not the whole of the human will – that is too large an issue, and not entirely relevant – but feeling alone. What of the thought, word, and deed that realize what (it would seem) is most private and individual in the human being? Were we in search of sociology, we should want to know how the law proposes to treat as social what is personal and individual. I do not mean rites of mourning at death, rejoicing at birth, exaltation at marriage, for example. I refer rather to the feelings, the tears, the private pleasures associated with such events. And having reached that point, I hasten to add, we want to identify the consequences, when there are any, of those same feelings when not associated with such public and social events, but situated out of all relationship with others in common society.

Having framed the question in this preliminary interlocution of the Mishnah, let us answer the question in the way the Mishnah answers questions: The Mishnah commonly lays down its rules by composing detailed lists of facts. The details of items within the list convey the sense of what is important in the whole. It is a process of discovering the general in the particular and distinguishing the distinctive in one particular from the same in another. That method we find routine in modern science too.

The sorts of lists we need for our imitation of the Mishnaic scientific method fall into two categories. First, we require a list of those circumstances, in the entire system of the Mishnah, in which we can identify the heart's virtues, including affections (see Where in the Mishnah Matters of the Heart Appear but Have No Practical Significance below). Second, we want a list of those items within the larger list that enjoy *systemic* standing and importance (see Where in the Mishnah Matters of Virtue Do Have Practical Significance). In other words, we want to ascertain what the Mishnah knows as religious affections, using the word "religious" to stand for things that the system takes seriously, as against things that play no role and so do not matter at all in the system.

In the following two subsections, I list every circumstance in the Mishnah's entire corpus in which the law deals with how or what someone feels (whether or not in connection with an action), without making any reference to what that person thinks, says, or does as a result of rational reflection or consideration of purpose.

Where in the Mishnah Matters of the Heart Appear but Have No Practical Significance

Although paragraphs in the Mishnah make reference to matters of virtue, such as correct emotion, in some cases these references are casual. In what way? The presence or absence of affection has no bearing on concrete decisions, for example, to do or not to do something to invoke or remit sanctions. These passages therefore do not testify to the systemic importance of affections, nor do they tell us where or why a person's feelings by themselves play a role. They simply recite the repertoire of emotions that fall within the system and indicate where these emotions will make their appearance in one's description of the whole.

Two allusions to emotions that play no role in the actual performance of one's obligation follow. In the first there is weeping because of joy, in the second, a reference to joy, and both for the same reason.

M. They voted and decided:

N. Ammon and Moab give poor man's tithe in the Sabbatical year.

O. And when R. Yose, the son of the Damascene, came to R. Eliezer at Lydda, he [Eliezer] said to him, "What new thing have you [learned] in the *bet hammidrash* today?"

P. He said to him, "They voted and decided: Ammon and Moab give poor man's tithe in the Sabbatical year."

Q. R. Eliezer wept, saying, " 'The secret of the Lord is with those that fear him, and he will show them his covenant' (Ps. 25:14).

R. "Go and tell them, 'Do not be anxious about your vote. I have received a tradition from Rabban Yohanan b. Zakkai, who heard it from his teacher, and his teacher from his teacher, a law given to Moses at Sinai,

S. " 'Single quote within double that Ammon and Moab give poor man's tithe in the Sabbatical year.' "

M. Yad. 4:3

Here is a case of weeping and, as in the following case, rejoicing because of finding a fellow for Judah b. Baba. The role of emotion is null. Nothing is affected or decided by feeling. This is simply a report of tears of joy, pure and simple. Were celebration to produce social consequence, it would make a difference in behavior.

Another reference to an emotion that has purely private significance is made in the following:

A.   Said R. Aqiba, "When I went down to Nehardea to intercalate the year, Nehemiah of Bet Deli came upon me. He said to me, 'I heard that only R. Judah b. Baba permits a wife in the Land of Israel to remarry on the evidence of a single witness [to her husband's death].'

B.   "I stated to him, 'That is indeed so.'

C.   "He said to me, 'Tell them in my name –

D.   " 'you know that the country is alive with ravaging bands –

E.   " 'I have a tradition from Rabban Gamaliel the Elder:

F.   " 'They permit a wife to remarry on the testimony of a single witness [to her husband's death].'

G.   "And when I came and laid the matters out before Rabban Gamaliel, he was overjoyed at my report and said, 'We now have found a pair for R. Judah b. Baba.'

H.   "And in the same discourse Rabban Gamaliel recalled that men were slain at Tel Arza, and Rabban Gamaliel the Elder permitted their wives to remarry on the evidence of a single witness."

M. Yeb. 16:7

Here the reference to joy bears no systemic meaning whatsoever. There is happiness simply because the sages succeeded in securing the required evidence on the state of the law. The sages wished to concur with Juda b. Baba (M. Yeb. 16:7A) and found a match for his tradition, so confirming it (M. Yeb. 16:7G). The intrusion of an allusion to affection proves casual and systemically neutral. Why? No decisions or actions based on the presence or absence of the cited emotion are called for.

Another example is an allusion to the truly pious attitude toward praying. People who do not attain such piety nonetheless carry out their obligation to say their prayers, so the emotion is systemically null:

A.   One rises to recite "the Prayer" only in a solemn frame of mind (kbd r'š).

B.   The early saints used to tarry one hour and pray,

C.   so that they could direct their hearts to God (mqwm).

M. Ber. 5:1

Strictly speaking, the passage refers not to an affection but an attitude. Before one recites the Prayer, one has to attain an appropriate attitude of solemnity. I include the item for a simple reason. It is the only place in the entire discussion of rules for reciting the Shema, the Prayer, and the benedictions before, and grace after, meals, in which the attitude of the one who recites the Prayer comes into focus at all. Although the philosophers of the Mishnah cannot have seen prayer to be the same as incantation or endorsed the conception that the mere recitation of words, without comprehension or intention, invariably suffices to fulfill one's obligation, they assuredly remained silent where we might have expected a message. Specifically, they passed over an issue that was highly disputed later on, the issue of whether the performance of one's religious duties, including the recitation of the Shema and the Prayer, requires an appropriate intention.

Another instance of the Mishnah's allusion to emotion without consequence for normative deed is as follows:

A. All seven days they did not hold back food or drink from him.

B. [But] on the eve of the Day of Atonement at dusk they did not let him each much,

C. for food brings on sleep.

A. The elders of the court handed him over to the elders of the priesthood,

B. who brought him up to the upper chamber of Abtinas.

C. And they imposed an oath on him and took their leave and went along.

D. [This is what] they said to him, "My lord, high priest: We are agents of the court, and you are our agent and agent of the court.

E. "We abjure you by him [God] who caused his name to rest upon this house, that you will not vary in any way from all which we have instructed you."

F. He turns aside and weeps.

G. And they turn aside and weep.

M. Yoma 1:4

Here we are in the presence of deep emotion. The high priest weeps, so too the elders, as the high priest prepares for the arduous labor of the Atonement liturgy (described in Leviticus 16). The passage is remarkably reticent about the cause of the weeping, though M. Yoma 1:6 speaks of the priests expounding for the high priest such books as Job, Ezra, and Chronicles. In the context of the narrative, it would appear that the weeping represents a response to the solemnity of the occasion and the responsibility incumbent on the high priest, namely, the fate of Israel should matters go wrong. Obviously, the narrative does not mean to suggest a kind of ritual weeping, because nothing whatsoever suggests that the high priest's failure to weep disqualifies him or the rites he is about to perform. Why, then, the weeping? The passage tells us nothing.

I include the following passage because of the reference in G to Israel's happiness. But the word "happy" here bears not so much an emotional meaning as a factual one. It may mean "fortunate," in that Israel is fortunate that God is the one who renders the people clean of their sins. The word seems not to bear any affective sense whatsoever.

F.   This exegesis did R. Eleazar b. Azariah state: " '*From all your sins shall you be clean before the Lord*' (Lev. 16:30) – for transgressions between man and the Omnipresent does the Day of Atonement atone. For transgressions between man and his fellow, the Day of Atonement atones, only if the man will regain the good will of his friend."
G.   Said R. Aqiba, "Happy are you, O Israel. Before whom are you made clean, and who makes you clean? It is your Father who is in heaven,
H.   "as it says, 'And I will sprinkle clean water on you, and you will be clean' (Ezek. 36:25).
I.   "And it says, 'O Lord, the hope (*miqweh* = immersion pool) of Israel' (Jer. 17:13). Just as the immersion pool cleans the unclean, so the Holy One, blessed be he, clean Israel."

M. Yoma 8:9

Our first list proves uninformative, and that by definition. We wanted to know whether the Mishnah's authors allude to emotions in the course of their exposition of various topics. They do. These allusions are not commonplace. They are not important. But the fact is that, in the narratives, whether a person laughs or weeps may be mentioned.

Where in the Mishnah Matters of Virtue Do Have Practical Significance

In some legal matters a person's attitude and feeling, by themselves and without reference to concrete deeds, govern demeanor and attitude. In such cases the emotional context dictates the legal facts. If a person is happy, one result follows; if sad, the opposite. As I shall explain, moreover, the emotion is specific; "to be happy" is different from acting with intent to produce the result at hand (satisfaction). "To be sad" is different from rejecting the result of a situation (disappointment). We have, finally, to distinguish the present point of analysis from yet another one. In the passages of the following section, affection produces a result, without consequent action and without any external intervention. Here, affection partially defines the context of decision, but the result is not dictated by affection. The presence or absence of a given emotion in the present case constitutes a fact of the matter but not a decisive criterion in determining the outcome. The concerete cases will make quite clear the difference between the two situations.

In the first case, the imposition of anger is part of the penalty for inappropriate action. The case indicates that an affection plays a part in securing proper behavior. Later on we shall find the same word, for rebuke, in the context of heavenly rebuke, indicating a clear correspondence between affections among people on earth and those between God and the individual.

A. He who says, "May the good folk bless you," lo, this is the way of heresy.

B. [He who says,] "Even to a bird's nest do your mercies extend –

C. "May your name be remembered for good –

D. "We give thanks, we give thanks" – they silence him.

E. He who uses euphemisms in the pericope of the prohibited relationships (Lev. 18) – they silence him.

F. He who says, " 'And you shall not give any of your seed to make them pass through fire to Molech,' means 'And you shall not give of your seed to make it pass to heathendom' " – they silence him with a rebuke.

M. Ta. 4:9

What is important here is at M. Ta. 4:9E–F, the increase in the severity of the act of silencing the one who says an unacceptable prayer. The phrase "with a rebuke" is meant to add to the penalty the emotional discomfort of humiliation or embarrassment. Thus, the law takes account of the use of anger as a penalty and humiliation as a form of remorse. But this sanction is uncommon, and the issue is null.

A more interesting case involves the assessment of feelings in determining whether rites may be performed on a given day. Here is a fine instance in which emotions contribute important data to the facts of the case:

A. They do not take wives on the intermediate days of a festival,

B. whether virgins or widows.

C. Nor do they enter into levirate marriage,

D. for it is an occasion of rejoicing.

E. But one may remarry his divorced wife.

M. M.Q. 1:7

At issue is the distinction between public and private feelings. The contrast is not between public rejoicing and private mourning, but between public rejoicing for one reason and public rejoicing for some other. And these two causes of communal happiness, we find, are to be kept distinct from one another. When the community engages in the public celebration of the festival's intermediate days, the people may not in addition engage in the public celebration of a wedding. The considerations are made explicit at M. M.Q. 1:7C–D, with the same implicit at E. Once more the law in its communal prescriptions takes ample account of affections, both individual and collective. One reason, in the present case, is that at issue on the festivals is public celebration, rejoicing in communal life. Accordingly, to generalize, affections serve religious purposes, and just as on the grounds of service to God, one must frame the affection of love, so in the service of the sanctification of the temporal rhythm of Israel's life, one must frame the affection of joy.

The following presents a case of a public and shared affection, serving God through rejoicing:

A.   Flute playing is for five or six days:

B.   This refers to the flute playing on *bet hashsho'ebah*,

C.   which overrides the restrictions of neither the Sabbath nor of a festival day.

D.   They said: "Anyone who has not seen the rejoicing of *bet hash-sho'ebah* in his life has never seen rejoicing."

M. Suk. 5:1

A.   At the end of the first festival day of the festival [the priests and Levites] went down to the woman's courtyard.

B.   And they made a major enactment [by putting men below and women above].

C.   And there were golden candleholders there, with four gold bowls on their tops, and four ladders for each candlestick.

D.   And four young priests with jars of oil containing a hundred and twenty *logs* [would climb up the ladders and] pour [the oil] into each bowl.

M. Suk. 5:2

A.   Out of the worn-out undergarments and girdles of the priests they made wicks,

B.   and with them they lit the candlesticks.

C.   And there was not a courtyard in Jerusalem that was not lit up from the light of *bet hashsho'ebah*.

M. Suk. 5:3

A.   The pious men and wonder workers would dance before them with flaming torches in their hand,

B.   and they would sing before them songs and praises.

C.   And the Levites beyond counting played on harps, lyres, cymbals, trumpets, and [other] musical instruments.

M. Suk. 5:4

What is important here is the use of the word "rejoicing." The word pertains to a particular celebration and connotes public and shared emotion, involving various actions meant to elicit a single, communal affection, a religious one. In this context, "rejoice" seems to me to bear the sense of "celebrate." Hence, if someone has not seen the celebration of *bet hashsho'ebah*, that person does not know the meaning of the word "celebrate." Everything that follows speaks of what is done, not what is felt: lights and bonfires, juggling and dancing, singing and music. This matter far transcends emotions. Although these activities elicit a powerful emotional response, they cannot be classified as emotional activities. Why not? They are not carried out as responses to prior feelings, but only as public modes of shared celebration. The passage refers to an emotion, "rejoicing," but then relates a sequence of actions, leaving unexplained what happens when the throngs see the fires, hear the music, and dance or move to the rhythm of the dancing. Cultic joy is joy, but of what sort and substance we cannot now say. At issue is a correct attitude, one of public weight: virtue.

From joy we turn to sorrow, beginning with the kind that is social and shared – mourning for the deceased – then proceeding to the kind that is private and individual – suffering in a bad marriage. In the first case, an individual's emotion is not allowed to define a situation. When a felon has been executed, his mourning relatives must keep their feelings to themselves. That makes all the more suggestive the numerous laws, which we shall consider presently, in which mourning constitutes a highly public emotion, one that contributes to the determination of what people may or may not do on specified occasions.

A.   When the flesh [has] rotted, they collect the bones and bury them in their appropriate place.

B.   And the relatives [of the executed felon] come and inquire after the welfare of the judges and of the witnesses,

C.   as if to way, "We have nothing against you, for you judged honestly."

D.   And they [do] not go into mourning.

E.   But they observe a private grief, for grief is only in the heart.

M. San. 6:6

The state of mind of the relatives of the executed felon concerns both the institutions of state (M. San. 6:6B–D) and the law at large (M. San. 6:6D,

E). The latter strikes me as the more interesting, since the prohibition of public mourning but the recognition of private grief keeps in balance two contradictory concerns. On the one side, the community cannot be asked publicly to mourn with the family of a felon. On the other, the man's family cannot be asked to refrain. So under the circumstances the grief is kept private. The framers of the law did not try to force people to repress their feelings. Nor did they admit their emotions into the public domain.

Under more common circumstances, by contrast, the feeling of the mourner becomes a factor in the determination of public behavior:

C.   And further did R. Meir say, "A man [on the intermediate days of a festival] may go out and gather the bones of his father and his mother,
D.   "because it is a time of rejoicing for him."
E.   R. Yose says, "It is a time of mourning for him."
F.   A person may not call for mourning for his deceased,
G.   or make a lamentation for him thirty days before a festival.

M. M.Q. 1:5

The intermediate days of a festival, that is, the days between the beginning and end of the Passover and Tabernacles holidays, must serve as occasions of rejoicing. In the present case what is striking is that private affections, not merely public activities, are considered in the assessment of the requirements of the law.

In this we have a contrast to the celebration of the festival of fire, lights, music, and dancing, at M. Suk. 5:1-4. There can be no doubt that at issue now is the celebrant's private emotional condition. The dispute of Meir and Yose concerns the facts of the matter. All concur on the more general circumstances to which M. M.Q. 1:5F-G make reference. The law takes full account of the affective circumstance of private individuals, when they are sad or happy, as much as of the community at large. The issue is mourning as against rejoicing, but other emotions, such as satisfaction as against indifference, pride as against remorse, also come into play. What matters is that in the determination of the laws governing what people may or may not do, the framers of the law take account not only of their attitudes, thoughts, intentions but also of their feelings, whether appropriate or inappropriate to the time or circumstance.

The extended passage that follows raises the same basic considerations:

A.   They do not tear their clothing, bare the shoulder, or provide food for mourners, except the near relatives of the deceased.
B.   And they do not provide mourners food except on an upright couch.

C. They do not bring [food] to a house of mourning on a tray, salver, or flat basket, but in plain baskets.

D. And they do not [in Grace after meals] say the blessing for mourners during the intermediate days of the festival.

E. But [the mourners] do stand in a line and offer consolation and dismiss those that have gathered together.

M. M.Q. 3:7

A. They do not set the bier down in the street,

B. so as not to give occasion for a lamentation.

C. And under no circumstances do they set down the bier of women in the street, on account of respect.

D. Women on the intermediate days of a festival wail, but do not clap their hands.

E. R. Ishmael says, "Those who are near the bier clap their hands."

M. M.Q. 3:8

A. On the celebration of the appearance of the new moon, Hanukkah, and Purim [should a funeral take place] they wail and clap their hands.

B. On none of them do they sing a dirge.

C. Once the deceased has been buried, they do not wail or clap their hands.

D. What is a wail?

E. When all sing together.

F. What is a dirge?

G. When one starts, and then all join in with her,

H. as it is said, "Teach your daughters wailing, and every one her neighbor a dirge" (Jer. 9:19).

I. But in the time that is coming, it says, "He has swallowed up death for ever, and the Lord God will wipe away tears from off all faces, and the reproach of his people he shall take away from off all the whole earth, for the Lord has spoken it" (Isa. 25:8).

M. M.Q. 3:9

Complementing the preceding passages, this rule deals with how public displays of sorrow for the deceased are regulated. Because of the character of the intermediate days of the festivals (M. M.Q. 3:7–8) or the specified celebrations (M. M.Q. 3:9A), one may not go through the routine procedures of mourning. On the other hand, the law recognizes that the dead must be buried, and the burial should follow appropriate procedures. The compromise is to limit the public aspect of the rites of mourning, as at M. M.Q. 3:7D, 3:8A–B, D. Sages take cognizance of the meaning of the conflict in the emotional requirements of the two rites – burial and festival – by effecting a change in the normal procedures for the former. That accounts for such details as M. M.Q. 3:7A–C. The main point is that law mediates between the feelings of the celebrating community and the emotional condition of the mourners, protecting the one, honoring the other.

From mourning for the deceased, a private emotion made strikingly communal, we turn to the humiliation and unhappiness of a wife because of a husband's tyranny and the embarrassment of a husband because of a wife's inappropriate behavior. These are not treated as merely private emotions. Marriage by definition is a social and public institution. What affects it, therefore, including emotions that demand to be sorted out, will come into account. The main point here is that the law takes full account of the affective life of individuals in the community. We see no pretense that such matters are null or trivial. How people feel makes a difference in defining the context of decision.

A.   He who prohibits his wife by a vow from going home to her father's house –

B.   when he [father] is with her in [the same] town,

C.   [if it is a vow] for a month, he may persist in the marriage.

D.   [If it is a vow] for two, he must put her away and pay off her marriage contract.

E.   And when he is another town, [if the vow is in effect] for one festival season he may persist in the marriage. [But if the vow remains in force] for three, he must put her away and pay off her marriage contract.

M. Ket. 7:4

A.   He who prohibits his wife by a vow from going to a house of mourning or to a house of celebration must put her away and pay off her marriage contract,

B.   because he locks the door before her.

C.   But if he claimed that he took such a vow because of some other thing, he is permitted to impose such a vow.

D.   [If he took a vow,] saying to her, (1) "On condition that you say to So-and-so what you said to me," or (2) "What I said to you," or (3) "that you draw water and pour it out onto the ash heap,"

E.   he must put her away and pay off her marriage contract.

M. Ket. 7:5

A.   And those women go forth without the payment of the marriage contract at all:

B.   She who transgresses against the law of Moses and Jewish law.

C. And what is the law of Moses [which she has transgressed]? [If] (1) she feeds him food which has not been tithed, or (2) has sexual relations with him while she is menstruating, or (3) she does not cut off her dough offering, or (4) she vows and does not carry out her vow.

D. And what is Jewish law? If (1) she goes out with her hair flowing loose, or (2) she spins in the market place, or (3) she talks with just anybody.

E. Abba Saul says, "Also: if she curses his parents in his presence."

F. R. Tarfon says, "Also: if she is a loudmouth."

G. What is a loudmouth? When she talks in her own house, her neighbors can hear her voice.

M. Ket. 7:6

The law protects women from emotional pain inflicted on them by mean-spirited husbands. A husband may not make his wife unhappy by trying to sever the bonds between her and her own family (M. Ket. 7:4) or between her and the community at large (M. Ket. 7:5A–B). He may not humiliate her by making public those private sexual matters best left at home (M. Ket. 7:5D). A wife, for her part, must behave in a seemly and modest way (M. Ket. 7:6). None of these rules makes explicit reference to emotions, but the husband's and wife's feelings lie close to the surface. Still, apart from the important inclusion of M. Ket. 7:6E–G, reference to keeping anger within bounds, I see no clear reference to feelings distinct from actions.

Where in the Mishnah Attitudes Decide Matters

From our survey of cases in which emotions define the context in which sages reach a decision, we turn to a far more interesting category: cases settled by emotional factors, entirely by themselves. To understand these cases, let me spell out the law. Then its significance will be entirely accessible, even though the situation is somewhat bizarre.

Reference to the grain owner's emotional condition ("happy") in what follows has to be explained in context. The law interprets Lev. 11:34, 36, to mean that, if produce is dry, it is not susceptible to uncleanness, whereas if it has been deliberately wet down with water, it becomes susceptible. Accordingly, if a dead insect, a source of uncleanness, falls on a pile of wet grain (and the grain is best milled when it has been wet down), it is made unclean. Now the law takes for granted that some Israelites ate their ordinary food in a condition of cultic cleanness, even when eating meals at home consisting of food unconsecrated for priestly consumption. It follows that the market for such guarded produce, preserved under conditions of cultic cleanness, promised a far better return than the market for unclean produce. Hence, the farmer preferred to keep the grain dry as long as possible. At the same time, there were advantages to wetting it down, as the several cases cited here make clear. Now at issue is a critical matter for our inquiry. Does emotion *unconfirmed* by deed make any difference in the law?

So far as the anonymous framer of the passage is concerned, naked emotions do make a difference M. Mak. 3:5G–H; 3:6J–K; 3:7O–P, R–U. In each case merely because there was a feeling of gratification or pleasure in the farmer's heart ("if he rejoiced" or "was happy"), the supernatural status of the grain has shifted, and the grain became susceptible to uncleanness. Why? Because it had been deliberately wet down, in line with Lev. 11:34, 36. How do we know that the action of wetting down was deliberate? Because the man was happy.

Judah, for his part, will not take account of emotion by itself. For the man to indicate his attitude, emotion will not suffice. A concrete deed must confirm the emotion and give it effect. Accordingly, if the farmer kept his cart standing still in the rain (M. Mak. 3:5I), if he kept the olives under the water spout or shook them (M. Mak. 3:6), if he turned the sacks over (M. Mak. 3:7Q), and if the man rinsed off the beast's feet or his own (M. Mak. 3:7V–X), then the application of the water is deemed deliberate.

G. He who brings his grain to the mill and rain fell on them –
H. if he was happy on that account, it is under the law, "If water be put" [as stated at Lev. 11:34, 36].
I. R. Judah says, "It is not possible not to be happy on that account. But if he stood."

M. Mak. 3:5

J. [If] his olives were located on the roof and rain fell on them –
K. if he was happy, it is under the law, "If water be put."
L. R. Judah says, "It is not possible not to be happy on that account.
M. "But if he stopped up the water spout,
N. "or if he shook the olives in it [the rain]."

M. Mak. 3:6

O. The ass drivers who were crossing the river and their sacks fell into the water –
P. if they were happy, it is subject to the law, "If water be put."
Q. R. Judah says, "It is not possible not to be happy. But if they turned over [the sacks, it is under the law, 'If water be put']."
R. [If] one's feet were full of mud –
S. and so the hooves of his beast –

T. he crossed the river –
U. if he was happy, it is subject to law, "If water be put."
V. R. Judah says, "It is not possible not to be happy.
W.

(1) "But if he stood [the animal] still and rinsed off [its feet]
(2) "in the case of man

X. "and in the case of an unclean beast, it is always unclean."

M. Mak. 3:7

Since to begin with the issue of wetting something down is framed in terms of intent, the sense of "was happy" is somewhat awry. "Happy" makes reference not merely to the farmer's feelings, but to his plan or intent. What is striking, therefore, is not the rule, but the formulation of the rule in terms of affections. We already have seen the same word in other passages, in the sense of "rejoice," both in public and in private settings.

Yet I find it difficult to criticize the author of the passage, because Judah's argument is not possible if we do not refer to naked emotions. That is, Judah wishes to say that no farmer can suppress his natural feelings. Hence, intentional deed is unaffected by such feelings. A concrete deed is required to tell us intention, and mere emotion will not inform us about one's prior plan. Accordingly, to accommodate Judah's position, the framer has chosen his word very carefully. The word can mean "be happy" only in the sense of ordinary usage. Thus, the passage as a whole focuses attention on a central issue in the study of the role of affections – not merely intention – in the metaphysics of the law. Emotion by itself governs here.

The Humanity of God: Loving God

In one instance in the Mishnah, God's emotions are compared to those of humanity:

A. Said R. Meir, "When a person is distressed, what words does the Presence of God say? As it were: 'My head is in pain, my arm is in pain.'
B. "If thus is the Omnipresent distressed on account of the blood of the wicked when it is shed, how much the more so on account of the blood of the righteous!"

M. San. 6:5

The clear sense of Meir's statement is that God's emotions correspond to those of the individual. God feels pain, therefore sorrow, just as humans do.

In yet another case the human response must prove appropriate to the divine affection, now anger expressed as a rebuke. The rebuke takes the form of withholding rain. People are expected to respond by taking cognizance of the divine displeasure, subduing their normal activities and affections alike:

A.   [If] these [periods of fasting for rain] too have passed and they have not been answered, they cut down on commerce, building, planting, the making of bethrothals and marriages, and on greeting one another,

B.   like people subject to divine rebuke [displeasure].

C.   Individuals go back and fast until the end of Nisan.

D.   [Once] Nisan has ended, [if] it then rains, it is a sign of a curse,

E.   since it says, "It is not wheat harvest today? I will call unto the Lord, that he send thunder and rain, and you shall know and see that great is your wickedness which you have done in the sight of God to ask a king for yourself" (1 Sam. 12:17).

M. Ta. 1:7

What is interesting in this account of the passage of fasts without divine response in the giving of rain is at M. Ta. 1:7B. Because God is displeased with the people, they have to acknowledge that displeasure. They respond to the rebuke represented by the withholding of rain in appropriate ways both in their deeds – cutting down on exchanges – and in their emotional transactions (if "greeting one another" may be said to fall into that category). The appropriate response is to undertake rites of mourning, that is, rites that embody an emotional condition. Here humans respond to God's emotions, as God responds to theirs at M. San. 6:5.

Finally, we come to the transcendent emotion, the one on which the entire relationship of Israel to God rests, namely, love: "You will love the Lord your God with all your heart, soul, and might" (Deut. 6:5). Clearly, the meaning of the word "love" demands systematic analysis, as we proceed, since that emotion, rather than pain or rebuke, is the one normative for Israel's relationship to God, and, it surely must follow, it also is the one that Israel hopes and expects to characterize God's affections as well. What is this "love"?

A.   One is obligated to recite a blessing over evil as one blesses over good.

B.   As it is said, "And you shall love the Lord your God with all your heart, with all your soul, and with all your might" (Deut. 6:5).

C.   "With all your heart" (lbbk) – with both of your inclinations, with the good inclination and with the evil inclination.

D.   "And with all your soul" – even if he takes your soul.

E.   "And with all your might" – with all of your money.

F.   Another matter: "With all your might" *(m'dk)* – with each and every measure that he measures out for you, thank him much [a play on words: *mydh, mwdd, mwdh, m'd*].

G.   One should not act lightheadedly *(ykl r'šw)* while facing the Eastern Gate [of the Temple in Jerusalem], for it faces toward the Chamber of the Holy of Holies.

H.   One should not enter the Temple Mount with his walking stick, his overshoes, his money bag, or with dust on his feet.

M. Ber. 9:5

I.   And one should not use [the Temple Mount] for a shortcut *(kpndry')*.

J.   And spitting [there is likewise forbidden, as is proved by an argument] *a minori ad majus*.

K.   [At one time] all blessings in the Temple concluded with "from time immemorial" *(mn h'wlm)*."

L.   When the sectarians corrupted [their ways] and claimed: "There is but one world *('wlm)* [and no world to come],"

M.   they ordained that they should say, "from time immemorial and forever."

The evidence proves negative. We note that the commandment to "love" God treats the word for love as equivalent to "serve," as shown in what follows. The "inclination" is to do good or to do evil. One is supposed to love God by harnessing both inclinations to the service of God. That interpretation leaves no room for a view of love that emphasizes mainly attitude, let alone emotion, that is, how one "feels" toward, or about, God.

In M. Ber. 9:5F the author addresses the attitude of gratitude. One is supposed to accept thankfully whatever God metes out. I am inclined to classify "gratitude" as an affection, since it does not entail action, on the one side, or prior reflection, on the other. It is a feeling or an emotion, not a prescription for a particular deed. Yet to identify a feeling of gratitude for whatever God metes out with loving God seems to me to limit the meaning of thanks. It also contradicts what is at issue at M. Ber. 9:5C–E. One is supposed to love God with all of one's inclinations, with one's life, with one's property.

Getting at the heart of matters, it would seem to me, requires that we know what this "love" is. But I cannot find in the passage an explanation of the emotion, if "love" stands for emotion. Still, it is hardly surprising that the recitation of the Shema, of which Deut. 6:5 is a key verse, does place at the very heart of the system composed by the Mishnah what we must regard, by definition, as an attitude and, further, in this context, a distinctively, definitively religious affection.

A clarification at M. Ber. 9:5G–H is related to M. Ber. 5:1A, cited above. The contrast between "lightheadedly" and "reverent" attitude is close, since the one speaks of *YKL* and the other *KBD*, meaning light and heavy, respectively, and both phrases further allude to "the head" *(R'Š)*. The entire passage speaks of actions.

Virtues of the Heart in the Law

To answer the questions with which we began, the law does take account of an attitude not joined to an action at all. It is the attitude of rejoicing, of "being happy," in the context of tractate Makhshirin. Does the law deal with an action not preceded by reflection on one's goal and purpose, such as weeping? Indeed, the law knows of such action. But the Mishnah's authorship treats it mainly when a rule is needed to cover it, in the context of mourning in tractate Moed Qatan. It follows that the law takes for granted that people may decide deliberately to love or to weep or to rejoice, so that emotions constitute a dimension of human deliberation. People bear responsibility for their feelings. Their virtue then comes to expression in their feelings. These do make a difference as to what one must do and produce sanctions. Accordingly, as much as people's intentions, their feelings testify to their character and their judgment. More interesting, these same feelings, imputed to God, make God like human beings or, in the perspective of the sacred, such as in the Mishnah, in their feelings as much as in their deeds, human beings are in the image and after the likeness of God.

CHAPTER IV

Virtue for Sages

Tractate Abot: The Lessons of Virtue of the Founders for the Disciples of Sages

Tractate Abot presents a systematic picture of virtues for sages. What marks the virtuous heart in the view of sages is restraint of emotions, discipline of feelings. Sages set the example for Israel: they seek conciliation, not self-aggrandizement, and therefore nurture an attitude of humility, not arrogance. Emotions in the narrow sense are suspicious to sages, who foster self-control and maintain that God loves those whom people love. Thus, the handbook for the philosophers' life puts emotion at a distance and lays stress on self-discipline. Virtue, good cheer, a generous spirit, subdued feelings, moderation, restraint, balance – these cardinal qualities come to full and rich expression. We shall see later that these qualities persist, unchanged, without much augmentation and without diminution, as the program of virtue for Judaism throughout the subsequent writings of the formative period.

Sixty-one of the Mishnah's sixty-three tractates, all but Eduyyot and Abot, follow an identical program of organization, formulation, and syntactic redaction. All are organized by topics. Within the topical framework, discourse unfolds in accord with an unfolding logic, a problematic, that dictates how problems are to be laid out. All are formulated in exceedingly tight syntactic and stylistic patterns, frequently repeated in groups of three or five repetitions (or multiples thereof). These patterns in their triplets or quintuplets greatly facilitate memorization. Resort to such a high degree of syntactic formalization leads to the conclusion that the framers of the Mishnah expected their writing to be handed down by memorization. These sixty-one tractates find a companion in one of the other two, Eduyyot. The materials in that tractate are organized in accord with a topical program but with names of important authorities. But

45

formally it is one with the rest, and nearly all the materials themselves recur somewhere among the sixty-one standard tractates.

Then there is tractate Abot, the sayings of the founders. That odd tractate ignores all considerations of formal composition, patterning of language, and closely logical and topical organization of materials. Instead, its framers present long lists of authorities, along with free-hand, unpatterned sayings assigned to them. Some of the lists, particularly in Chapters I and II, seem purposeful. M. Abot 1:1–18 lists important authorities from the mythical beginnings, at Sinai, of the group behind the Mishnah through the important figures of the first century A.D. Chapter II then forms an inverted Y, two lists of authorities, one line being major sages of the later first century, beyond A.D. 70, Yohanan b. Zakkai and his disciples. The other line carries forward names of patriarchal authorities, descendants of the final names listed in Chapter I, in particular of the generation of Judah the Patriarch and his sons and associates.

The net effect is to treat as equally authoritative, equivalently linked to the line of sages back to Sinai, the two pillars of Israel as sages saw Israel in the third century. These were, first, the sages' movement, represented by Yohanan b. Zakkai, and second, the patriarchal government, represented, of course, by the patriarch. The former served as clerks and staff to the latter, the ethnarchic authority recognized by the Roman government for the Israelite population of the Land of Israel. Since this one egregious tractate, Abot, contains names of authorities beyond Judah the Patriarch, sponsor of the Mishnah, and since these later names rarely, if ever, occur in the other sixty-two, it seems not unlikely that Abot belongs some time – one might guess a half-century – after the closure of the Mishnah proper, in A.D. 250. The tractate would then serve as a prologue to and apologia for the now-complete Mishnah, listing as authorities in the line of Sinai important figures of the Mishnah itself. Hence, the net effect of Abot is to lay claim to a position, in the revelation of Sinai, for the Mishnah and all that would flow from it.

From this perspective, Abot provides a valuable guide to the ideals of virtue of those sages who inherited the Mishnah and proposed to transform it into Israel's constitution and bylaws, in completion of Scripture. If, therefore, we wish to ask about the definition and place of attitudes and affections in the system generated by the Mishnah, we acquire unusually valuable information in Abot. Because the character of the sayings imputed to the authorities differs from that of the rules of which the Mishnah proper is composed, we can ask another set of questions. Whereas the Mishnah presents bits and pieces of rules on discrete situations of everyday life, real or imagined, Abot provides general rules and sound advice on proper conduct in every circumstance. Its sayings are quite the opposite of the Mishnah's type of law, which ordinarily is specific to circumstance and context. Hence, in Abot we survey what the third-century philosophers, addressing the complete Mishnah, had to say to their disciples about proper attitude and conduct. We can ask not only what they affirm, but also what they reject or ignore.

As a handbook for the disciples of sages, tractate Abot carries us upward to that level of generalization and comprehensive statement to which no other tractate of the Mishnah allows access. Hence, it tells us what we cannot ask of the authors of the Mishnah proper, which is both what is included and also what is omitted. That is to say, when we survey the definition and role of religious affections in the sixty-two normal tractates of the Mishnah, we are justified in pointing to what we find. But we err if we draw conclusions about what we do not find. The obvious reason is that, if the authors of the Mishnah omit reference to the topic of interest to us, we may well argue only one proposition. It is not that they did not find much of interest in that topic. It is only that they wished, in the context of their law code, to which emotions prove only tangentially relevant, to talk about other things entirely. The omission of substantial references to issues of the place and role of emotions in the Mishnah proper tells us only that, in this law code, such issues scarcely come to the fore – not much of a discovery. By contrast, when we deal with a sizable handbook of virtue imparting advice to disciples on how to live and how to perform the labor of learning, we may posit a different premise. It is that this handbook will supply us with a reasonably encompassing composite of values laid down by the sages for their disciples. Not limited by a detailed topical program, the authors may set forth that deep logic, that sense of the whole and of proportion, that (it may be claimed) underlies the entire system and that is presented in the standard tractates only in niggling detail.

Accordingly, we come to Abot to examine how the fundamental philosophy of sages and disciples treated the topic of emotion, the importance accorded to it, the range of permissible disagreement, the perspective on the forbidden topics beyond the frontiers of the system. A religious system that begins with the commandment to frame one's affections so as to love God will assuredly have much to say about the disciplining and defining of emotions, those to be admitted and cultivated, those to be kept out or suppressed. For the purpose of the present inquiry, we do best by reviewing the relevant chapters of the tractate, those assigning sayings to named masters. These are tractate Abot Chapters I through IV, relevant parts of which follow.

A.   Moses received Torah at Sinai and handed it on to Joshua, Joshua to elders, and elders to prophets.

B.   And prophets handed it on to the men of the great assembly.

C.   They said three things:

(1) "Be prudent in judgment.
(2) "Raise up many disciples.
(3) "Make a fence for the Torah."

M. Abot 1:1

A.   Simeon the Righteous was one of the last survivors of the great assembly.

B.   He would say: "On three things does the world stand:

(1) "On the Torah,
(2) "and on the Temple service,
(3) "and on deeds of loving kindness."

M. Abot 1:2

A.   Antigonos of Sokho received [the Torah] from Simeon the Righteous.

B.   He would say,

(1) "Do not be like servants who serve the master on condition of receiving a reward,
(2) "but [be] like servants who serve the master not on condition of receiving a reward.
(3) "And let the fear of heaven be upon you."

M. Abot 1:3

A.   Hillel and Shammai received [it] from them.

B.   Hillel says, "Be disciples of Aaron, loving peace and pursuing peace, loving people and drawing them near to the Torah."

M. Abot 1:12

A.   He would say [in Aramaic],

(1) "A name made great is a name destroyed.
(2) "And one who does not add subtracts.
(3) "And who does not learn is liable to death.
(4) "And the one who uses the crown passes away."

M. Abot 1:13

A.   He would say,

(1) "If I am not for myself, who is for me?

(2) "And when I am for myself, what am I?
(3) "And if not now, when?"

M. Abot 1:14

A.   Shammai says,

(1) "Make your learning of Torah a fixed obligation.
(2) "Say little and do much.
(3) "Greet everybody cheerfully."

M. Abot 1:15

A.   Simeon his son says,

(1) "All my life I grew up among the sages and I found nothing better for a person [the body] than silence.
(2) "And not the learning is the main thing, but the doing.
(3) "And whoever talks too much causes sin."

M. Abot 1:17

A.   He would say, "Make his [God's] wishes into your own wishes, so that he will make your wishes into his wishes.
B.   "Put aside your wishes on account of his wishes, so that he will put aside the wishes of other people in favor of your wishes."
C.   Hillel [his brother] says, "Do not walk out on the community.
D.   "And do not have confidence in yourself until the day you die.
E.   "And do not judge your fellow until you are in his place.
F.   "And do not say anything which cannot be heard, for in the end it will be heard.
G.   "And do not say, 'When I have time, I shall study,' for you may never have time."

M. Abot 2:4

A.   He would say, (1) "A coarse person will never fear sin," (2) "nor will an *amhaares* ever be pious," (3) "nor will a shy person learn," (4) "nor will an intolerant person teach," (5) "nor will anyone too busy in business get wise.
B.   "In a place in which there are no men, try to act like a man."

M. Abot 2:5

A.   Rabban Yohanan b. Zakkai received [it] from Hillel and Shammai.
B.   He would say, "If you have learned much Torah, do not puff yourself up on that account, for it was for that purpose that you were created."

C. He had five disciples, and these are they: R. Eliezer b. Hyrcanus, R. Joshua b. Hananiah, R. Yose the priest, R. Simeon b. Netanel, and R. Eleazar b. Arakh.

D. He would list their good qualities:

E. R. Eliezer b. Hyrcanus: A plastered well, which does not lose a drop of water.

F. R. Joshua: Happy is the one who gave birth to him.

G. R. Yose: A pious man.

H. R. Simeon b. Netanel: A man who fears sin.

I. And R. Eleazar b. Arakh: A surging spring.

J. He would say, "If all the sages of Israel were in one side of the scale, and R. Eliezer b. Hyrcanus were on the other, he would outweigh all of them."

K. Abba Saul says in his name, "If all of the sages of Israel were on one side of the scale, and R. Eliezer b. Hyrcanus was also with them, and R. Eleazar [b. Arakh] were on the other side, he would outweigh all of them."

M. Abot 2:8

A. He said to them, "Go and see what is the straight path to which someone should stick."

B. R. Eliezer says, "A generous spirit."

C. R. Joshua says, "A good friend."

D. R. Yose says, "A good neighbor."

E. R. Simeon says, "Foresight."

F. R. Eleazar says, "Good will."

G. He said to them, "I prefer the opinion of R. Eleazar b. Arakh, because in what he says is included everything you say."

H. He said to them, "Go out and see what is the bad road, which someone should avoid."

I. R. Eliezer says, "Envy."

J. R. Joshua says, "A bad friend."

K. R. Yose says, "A bad neighbor."

L. R. Simeon says, "Reneging on a loan."

M. (All the same is a loan owed to a human being and a loan owed to the Omnipresent, blessed be he, as it is said, "The wicked borrows and does not pay back, but the righteous person deals graciously and hands over [what he owes]" [Ps. 37:21].)

N. R. Eleazar says, "Bad will."

O. He said to them, "I prefer the opinion of R. Eleazar b. Arakh, because in what he says is included everything you say."

M. Abot 2:9

A.   They [each] said three things.

B.   R. Eliezer says, (1) "Let the respect owing to your fellow be as precious to you as the respect owing to you yourself.

C.   (2) "And don't be easy to anger.

D.   (3) "And repent one day before you die.

E.   (1) "And warm yourself by the fire of the sages, but be careful of their coals, so you don't get burned.

F.   (2) "For their bite is the bite of a fox, and their sting is the sting of a scorpion, and their hiss is like the hiss of a snake.

G.   (3) "And everything they say is like fiery coals."

M. Abot 2:10

A.   R. Joshua says, (1) "Envy," (2) "desire of bad things, and" (3) "hatred for people push a person out of the world."

M. Abot 2:11

A.   R. Yose says, (1) "Let your fellow's money be as precious to you as your own.

B.   (2) "And get yourself ready to learn Torah,

C.   "(for it does not come as an inheritance to you).

D.   (3) "And may everything you do be for the sake of heaven."

M. Abot 2:12

A.   R. Hanina b. Dosa says, "For anyone whose fear of sin takes precedence over his wisdom, his wisdom will endure.

B.   "And for anyone whose wisdom takes precedence over his fear of sin, his wisdom will not endure."

C.   He would say, "Anyone whose deeds are more than his wisdom – his wisdom will endure.

D.   "And anyone whose wisdom is more than his deeds – his wisdom will not endure."

M. Abot 3:9

A.   He would say, "Anyone from whom people take pleasure, the Omnipresent takes pleasure.

B.   "And anyone from whom people do not take pleasure, the Omnipresent does not take pleasure."

C.   R. Dosa b. Harkinas says, "(1) Sleeping late in the morning, (2) drinking wine at noon, (2) chatting with children, and (4) attending the synagogues of the ignorant drive a man out of the world."

M. Abot 3:10

A. R. Eleazar the Modite says, (1) "He who treats Holy Things as secular, and" (2) "he who despises the appointed times," (3) "he who humiliates his fellow in public," (4) "he who removes the signs of the covenant of Abraham, our father, (may be rest in peace), and" (5) "he who exposes aspects of the Torah not in accord with the law,

B. "even though he has in hand learning in Torah and good deeds, will have no share in the world to come."

M. Abot 3:11

A. R. Ishmael says, (1) "Be quick [in service] to a superior," (2) "efficient in service [to the state], and" (3) "receive everybody with joy."

M. Abot 3:12

A. R. Aqiba says, (1) "Laughter and lightheadedness turn lewdness into a habit.

B. (2) "Tradition is a fence for the Torah.

C. (3) "Tithes are a fence for wealth.

D. (4) "Vows are a fence for abstinence.

E. (5) "A fence for wisdom is silence."

M. Abot 3:13

A. He would say, "Precious is the human being, who was created in the image [of God],

B. "it was an act of still greater love that it was made known to him that he was created in the image [of God],

C. "as it is said, 'For in the image of God he made man' (Gen. 9:6).

D. "Precious are Israelites, who are called children to the Omnipresent.

E. "It was an act of still greater love that they were called children to the Omnipresent,

F. "as it is said, 'You are the children of the Lord your God' (Deut. 14:1).

G. "Precious are Israelites, to whom was given the precious thing.

H. "It was an act of still greater love that it was made known to them that to them was given that precious thing with which the world was made,

I. "as it is said, 'For I give you a good doctrine. Do not forsake my Torah' (Prov. 4:2)."

M. Abot 3:14

A. "Everything is foreseen, and free choice is given.
B. "In goodness the world is judged.
C. "And all is in accord with the abundance of deed(s)."

M. Abot 3:15

A. He would say, (1) "All is handed over as a pledge,
B. (2) "And a net is cast over all the living.
C. (3) "The store is open," (4) "the storekeeper gives credit," (5) "the account book is open, and" (6) "the hand is writing.
D. (1) "Whoever wants to borrow may come and borrow.
E. (2) "The charity collectors go around every day and collect from man whether he knows it or not.
F. (3) "And they have grounds for what they do.
G. (4) "And the judgment is a true judgment.
H. (5) "And everything is ready for the meal."

M. Abot 3:16

A. Ben Zoma says, "Who is a sage? He who learns from everybody,
B. "as it is said, 'From all my teachers I have gotten understanding' (Ps. 119:99).
C. "Who is strong? He who overcomes his desire,
D. "as it is said, 'He who is slow to anger is better than the mighty, and he who rules his spirit than he who takes a city' (Prov. 16:32).
E. "Who is rich? He who is happy in what he has,
F. "as it is said, 'When you eat the labor of your hands, happy will you be, and it will go well with you' (Ps. 128:2).
G. ("Happy will you be – in this world; and it will go well with you – in the world to come.")
H. "Who is honored? He who honors everybody,
I. "as it is said, 'For those who honor me I shall honor, and they who despise me will be treated as of no account' (1 Sam. 2:30)."

M. Abot 4:1

A. He would say, "Do not despise anybody and do not treat anything as unlikely.

B. "For you have no one who does not have his time, and you have nothing which does not have its place."

M. Abot 4:3

A. R. Levitas of Yabneh says, "Be exceedingly humble, for the hope of humanity is the worm."

B. R. Yohanan b. Beroqa says, "Whoever secretly treats the name of heaven as profane publicly pays the price.

C. "All the same are the one who does so inadvertently and the one who does so deliberately, when it comes to treating the name of heaven as profane."

M. Abot 4:4

C. R. Sadoq says, "Do not make [Torah teachings] a crown with which to glorify yourself or a spade with which to dig.

D. (So did Hillel say [M. Abot 1:13], "He who uses the crown perishes.")

E. "Thus have you learned: Whoever derives worldly benefit from teachings of Torah takes his life out of this world."

M. Abot 4:5

A. R. Ishmael, his son, says, "He who avoids serving as a judge breaks off the power of enmity, robbery, and false swearing.

B. "And he who is arrogant about making decisions is a fool, evil, and prideful."

M. Abot 4:7

A. He would say, "Do not serve as a judge by yourself, for there is only one who serves as a judge all alone.

B. "And do not say, 'Accept my opinion.'

C. "For they have the choice in that matter, not you."

M. Abot 4:8

A. R. Jonathan says, "Whoever keeps the Torah when poor will in the end keep it in wealth.

B. "And whoever treats the Torah as nothing when he is wealthy in the end will treat it as nothing in poverty."

M. Abot 4:9

A. R. Meir says, "Keep your business to a minimum and make your business Torah.

B. "And be humble before everybody.

C.   "And if you treat the Torah as nothing, you will have many treating you as nothing.

D.   "And if you have labored in Torah, [God] has a great reward to give you."

M. Abot 4:10

A.   R. Eleazar b. Shammua says, "The honor owing to your disciple should be as precious to you as yours.

B.   "And the honor owing to your fellow should be like the reverence owing to your master.

C.   "And the reverence owing to your master should be like the awe owing to heaven."

M. Abot 4:12

A.   R. Yannai says, "We do not have in hand [an explanation] either for the prosperity of the wicked or for the suffering of the righteous."

B.   R. Matya b. Harash says, "Greet everybody first.

C.   "And be a tail to lions.

D.   "But do not be a head of foxes."

M. Abot 4:15

A.   He would say, "Better is a single moment spent in penitence and good deeds in this world than the whole of the world to come.

B.   "And better is a single moment of inner peace in the world to come than the whole of a lifetime spent in this world."

M. Abot 4:17

A.   R. Simeon b. Eleazar says, (1) "Do not try to make amends with your fellow when he is angry,

B.   (2) "or comfort him when the corpse of his beloved is lying before him,

C.   (3) "or seek to find absolution for him at the moment at which he takes a vow,

D.   (4) "or attempt to see him when he is humiliated."

M. Abot 4:18

A.   R. Eliezer Haqqappar says, "Jealousy, lust, and ambition drive a person out of this world."

M. Abot 4:21

Permissible and Impermissible Attitudes and Affections for Sages

Because the message of tractate Abot comes to us complete and is stated in generalizations rather than in bits and pieces and only through details, access is much simpler than in the case of the Mishnah. We do not have to rely on key words and phrases expressive of emotion but can describe the sense of the whole. Moreover, we now have a context in which to interpret individual sayings, namely, the impression left by a complete composition. Still, we do well to begin with the smallest pieces of evidence. Affections that make a mark on the framing of sayings make up a modest catalogue indeed: love, fear; generosity of spirit, envy; humility, ambition. One's correct emotions encompass the virtue of love, both for one's neighbor and for the study of Torah. One should fear heaven and its rebuke, human rejection and humiliation.

Where the language of emotions does not play a part, the virtue stemming from what to begin with is emotion is apparent. For example, at M. Abot 1:5, advice to keep one's house open wide to the poor involves that same affection of generosity that is addressed in more general terms elsewhere. So, too, giving everyone the benefit of the doubt (1:6) expresses this same feeling of liberality and absence of ill will. The attitude of hopefulness, a rather general posture, takes on substance and even doctrinal weight when one is told not to give up hope of retribution (1:7). Here the counsel is propositional, namely, that God pays back the evil for what they have done. But the affective side – retaining an attitude of hopefulness, hence exhibiting the affection of hope – is not to be missed. The same is to be said for "love" and "hate" at 1:10: "Love work, hate authority." What follows is that the emotions of loving and hating come into play in the formation of the right attitude, the well-considered life. The same is to be said of loving peace and loving people (1:12). An attitude of prudent generosity and circumscribed selflessness stands behind 1:14 – to be for oneself but not only for oneself.

What then emerges as the cardinal affection? If I had to select one among many, it would be not be good cheer or a generous spirit toward others, but restraint. The repeated emphasis on inner discipline of the emotions is typified at 1:17 – the best thing for someone is silence. Avoiding doubt, waiting to see how things come out, not prejudging matters – all of these prove to be variations on the same theme. Stated in one form or another, the feeling of humility ("Be exceedingly humble," 4:4) and the emotion of submission ("Make his wishes into your own wishes, so that he will make your wishes into his wishes," 2:4) underly any number of concrete pieces of advice on proper conduct. We may therefore say that disciplined emotions define the most general, comprehensive, and desirable affection of all. Whatever one feels, one should not feel it too hastily ("don't be easy to anger," 2:10) or too freely. When we recall that even affections are subject to divine judgment – one is commanded, after all, to love – we see the center and the whole. Once affections take their due part in the service of God, they too are to be humbled and disciplined, as much as actions are to be patterned, reason guided, intellect nurtured – all in God's service, through the Torah.

Therefore, I claim that, before distinct affections stands the principle that the attitudes and affections, as much as the power of ratiocination and the capacity for action, the heart as much as the mind, serve God. But that principle does not close matters. Exactly what emotions are we to nurture, which ones to suppress? We shift forthwith to attitudes. Here we work with a set of matched opposites, as in love–hate. It is fortunate that the framers leave us no doubt about what they choose to match. They have artfully set up their pairs, for example, at 2:9. Among them we find a generous spirit set against envy and good will against ill will. The claim, moreover, that the affections of generosity and good will stand for much else derives directly from the author's express judgment, "I prefer the opinion of . . . because in what he says is included everything you say."

Beyond restraint, the other two principal affective virtues – good cheer and a generous spirit – match one another, the one facing inward, the other outward. One cannot, after all, feel generosity toward others if one does not, through humble acceptance, affirm oneself and one's situation, so the system maintains. The matched opposites in this case are envy and ill will, complementing good will toward others and the inner feeling of self-acceptance and self-affirmation. A species of the genus of liberality is humility over the human condition. One cannot overreach if one re-members where everything is heading, which is to the worm (4:4). An-other species of the same genus is the capacity to honor everyone. One should not despise anyone, because every person has a day and an hour (4:3).

The Humanity of God: Loving God

The permissible affections shape a human being characterized by restraint, a rather generalized amiability, acceptance of others essentially as they are. The result is someone who accepts what he or she has and feels no envy of others, someone of measured feelings and even emotions, some-one of restraint, moderation, and subdued and balanced feelings.

Whether the generality of Israelites exhibited these traits we cannot say. A people capable of mounting two vigorously fought wars against the ruling empire of the age as a nation hardly exhibited the Boston Brahmin traits of cool moderation, restraint, keeping one's own counsel, let alone patience and deliberation. Perhaps that is why, in the end, the sages found it necessary to assign to God in heaven the same traits and to insist that, if the Israelites did what was necessary to keep the peace with their neighbors on earth, then, but only then, would God in heaven find pleasure in them too. Hence, "Anyone from whom people take pleasure, the Omnipresent takes pleasure. And anyone from whom people do not take pleasure, the Omnipresent does not take pleasure" (3:10).

Another way of saying the same thing – "Discipline your feelings and your will" – is to say, "Be like God in your heart": "Make his wishes into your own wishes, so that he will makes your wishes into his wishes. Put aside your wishes on account of his wishes, so that he will put aside the wishes of other people in favor of your wishes" (2:4). Here we have no recipe for altruism but a moderate and sane piece of advice. We know what we want from God and from others. By showing restraint in what we want, we may hope that God will be responsive in the same terms to our will and wants. By giving up what we want for what God wants, we may hope that God will respond similarly in judging our wants in relation to those of others. Thus, restraint and disciplined aspirations, in encompassing feelings, provide the prescription for gaining, in actions involving only the heart, what in concrete ways we cannot otherwise attain.

The upshot of such a view of the power we are supposed to exercise over our attitudes and feelings is simple. If the position of sages is that feelings, as much as deeds, can be restrained, disciplined, moderated, and controlled, then feelings, as much as deeds, are important for a holy way of life. Emotions, no less than opinions, play a role in the drama of salvation. From the simple commandment to love God, much else flows. Once the importance of love is established, other virtues that fall into the same classification as love also take on significance for the religious life. Hence, affections become subject to the evaluation, including the restraints, of the Torah. That is, they become matters of religion because they can be made holy. Since to the world at large how one feels makes a difference mainly when one acts out one's feelings, it must follow that God cares about how we feel. The individual cares only for consequences and effects, not mere affections. And that is made explicit. The heart of the Israelite opens up to God's scrutiny, and the feelings of the Israelite provoke God's response. Such a position imputes to the Israelites in those very intangible matters that they could yet sort out and control on their own a remarkable power indeed.

Torah and the Heart

What validates the system's amazing claim concerning Israel's affective life is the Torah. God's love for Israel is expressed in the simple fact that God informed Israel of his love for Israel. The love without the public expression of it scarcely counts. A human being is precious for having been created in God's image, "but it was an act of still greater love that it was made known to him that he was created in the image of God, as it is said, 'For in the image of God he made man' (Gen. 9:6).'' So too Israel (not only) are called God's children but are informed of that fact (3:14), and at the climax, the Torah, God's precious gift, was not only given but also *declared* to be given as the precious gift. Thus, when Israelites claim that God cares for their love, they rely on the Torah for that information. The Torah then counts as God's most valued gift in expression of his love. Given the system's emphasis on Torah study, one is surprised by its ultimate appeal for validation to the Torah.

The contribution of Abot now proves truly formidable. Why? The philosophers have accomplished the union of their principal symbol, the Torah, with what lies hidden in the distant reaches of the heart. They make explicit what one may suppose had always been implicit. That is the view that the Torah's governance extends to intangible virtues, even to emotions, as much as to concrete deeds. The sages linked the claim that one must discipline emotions as much as actions to the further claim that the Torah's disciplines apply. This they did by alleging two things. First, God responds to human feelings. That must mean that God is like a human being in responding as do women and men to issues of affection. What makes us hateful to others – enmity, pride, and arrogance (4:7), jealousy, lust, and ambition (4:21) – makes us hateful to God. What makes us acceptable to others – cheerfulness (1:15), generosity, and good will (2:9) – makes us acceptable to God (3:10). If we make God's will our own, God will respond in kind (2:4). What makes humanity like God is that (in secular terms) God is like a human being in important ways. And what lends authority to these claims is that God for his part has told us so – the supreme mark of divine love, not the love alone but the exposition, the revelation, of the love in the Torah. Love felt but not expressed makes no difference to the object of love. God not only sympathizes with the human being (using sympathy in the correct sense), but God let the human being know it. More than that one cannot, but also need not, claim.

Doctrine, Discipline, Affection, and Virtue

In framing matters in this way, the authors of tractate Abot emerge as philosophers of considerable skill. For what they have accomplished is to draw together, into an integral whole, both doctrine and discipline, both world view and way of life. This they have done by linking all things to one thing. The one thing, at the superficial and symbolic level, of course, is the Torah. But as we have just noted, the Torah as a symbol is instrumental. Beneath the surface the truth comes out. It is that the

Torah, too, is an expression of God's love, validating the view that God's love is the counterpart to humanity's love. The Torah's instrumental value gives way. And that, in turn, stands for the comprehensive affirmation that the affections of humanity constitute (in our category) a principal dimension of religion, because (in their category) God cares how people respond to one another and responds in the same way and for the same reasons. God, in virtues, including affections, is consubstantial with the individual.

Therefore, knowledge of the Torah (doctrine) and the rules of the way of life (discipline) pertain to our attitudes and demeanor, to how we feel as much as to what we think, say, and do. That is why emotions ultimately constitute traditions and conform to laws. Placing emotions squarely at the heart of matters constitutes not the least of the surprising contributions of the authors of Abot. If they were to have linked deed only to deliberation, the authors of the Mishnah would have left open a final question in their system, the place of affection. By insisting that before deliberation, even more so before deed, God cares for the heart, because God's affections correspond to those of humanity, the successor generation in Abot closed that question and so completed the system.

In linking all three, reflection to action, and the two to affection, those who collected and arranged tractate Abot encompassed the whole of the human condition. That is why, in Yohanan ben Zakkai's words, the heart of goodness encompasses everything good, and envy or ill will, everything bad. Now the Torah has meaning for us because it tells us that God loves us. Study of the Torah makes us, in our heart, what we should be. The life of Torah yields the person of good cheer and good will toward moderated ambition and limited emotion – toward everything God is but the individual commonly is not.

CHAPTER V

Virtue in the Extension of the Exegetical Tradition of the Law

The Tosefta and the Fathers According to Rabbi Nathan

The Tosefta

The compilers of the Tosefta gathered three sorts of material, all of them framed in the Mishnah's topical program and style: first, citations and expositions of passages of the Mishnah; second, autonomous rules that make best sense in the context of corresponding statements of the Mishnah; third, independent sayings with no clear counterpart in the Mishnah. The first two types of material predominate. When the work was done and where the authors obtained their materials – from old tradition? from their own imaginations? – we do not know. The document as a whole extensively cites the Mishnah, so in the form in which we have it, it assuredly derives from the period after approximately A.D. 200. At that time the Mishnah had reached closure and gained status as a focus of exegesis. The Yerushalmi, closed around A.D. 400, makes elaborate reference to passages of the Tosefta, which it subjects to rigorous analysis just as it explains passages of the Mishnah. Hence, a date between 200 and 400 seems appropriate.

Supplementing the Mishnah's Rules

It is not surprising that the authors of the Tosefta stay close to the program of the Mishnah, for it is the Mishnah on which they expound. But at the same time they develop themes not to be found in explicit form or at all in the Mishnah. The one point at which emotions play a role in the actual formation of the law is the same as that in the Mishnah, as in the following:

A. He who brings up bundles of vegetables to the roof so that they will stay fresh –
[Supply: It is not under the law, "If water be put"].

61

B.   [If he gave thought to them] to tie them up –

C.   lo, this is under the law, "If water be put."

D.   And R. Judah says, "It is not under the law, 'If water be put' [until he actually does the deed]."

E.   He who brings [fruit] up to the roof to have it washed in dew and in rain, lo, this is under the law, "If water be put."

F.   [If] he brought them up to keep them free of maggots, and rain fell on them –

G.   if he was happy, it is under the law, "If water be put."

H.   R. Judah says, "It is not possible that he should not be happy. [Supply: But (it is not under the law, 'If water be put') until he turns it over.]"

I.   While the dew or rain is still on them, if he gave thought to it, lo, it is under the law, "If water be put."

T. Mak. 3:1

So far as I can see, the framers of the Tosefta did not add to the slim corpus of the Mishnah's cases in which emotion bears concrete consequences, but as is clear, they did go over the same matters, adding details here and there.

They worked out, in particular, explanations of passages of the Mishnah on celebration and rejoicing as public and communal affections. The concept of "rejoicing" as a public act, deeply embedded in the celebration of the festivals, demanded clarification. If "rejoicing" is to be public, is the affection also private and merely familial? That is the issue addressed in what follows:

A.   "Agents engaged in a religious duty are exempt from the requirement of dwelling in a sukkah" [M. Suk. 2:5],

B.   and [this is the case] even though they have said that it is not praiseworthy of a person to leave his home on the festival.

C.   M'SH B: R. Ilai went to R. Eliezer in Lud. He said to him, "Now what's going on, Ilai? Are you not among those who observe the festival? Have they not said that it is not praiseworthy of a person to leave his home on a festival? For it is said, 'And you will rejoice on your festival' (Deut. 16:14)."

T. Suk. 2:1

The proof text states explicitly that, on the festival of Tabernacles, one is to rejoice. The sense, of course, is twofold: Celebrate, but also feel happy. It is that latter sense that is at issue here. The exegete of the law makes clear that the performance of public duties, which may have a celebratory character, should not impede familiar enjoyment of the festival.

The union of personal and public rejoicing, in the pageant of bonfires, dancing, singing, and juggling of *bet hasho'ebah*, finds amplified description in the following:

A.   At first, when people would witness the rejoicing of *bet hasho'ebah*, the men would watch inside, and the women would watch outside.

B.   But when the court saw that they turned to silliness, they set up three balconies in the courtyard, one on each side, where the women sit and witness the rejoicing of *bet hasho'ebah*.

C.   And [the men and women] did not mix together.

T. Suk. 4:1

A.   "Pious men and wonder workers would dance before them with flaming torches in their hand, and they would sing before them songs of praise" [M. Suk. 5:4A–B].

B.   What did they sing?

C.   "Happy is he who has not sinned. But all who have sinned will he [God] forgive."

D.   And some of them say, "Fortunate is my youth, which did not bring my old age into shame" – these [who say this song] are wonder workers.

E.   And some of them say, "Fortunate are you, O years of my old age, for you will atone for the years of my youth? – these [who say this song] are the penitents.

T. Suk. 4:2

A.   Hillel the Elder says, "To the place which my heart craves, there do my feet lead me.

B.   "If you will come to my house, I shall come to your house.

C.   "If you not come to my house, I shall not come to your house,

D.   "as it is said, 'In every place where I cause my name to be remembered I will come to you and bless you' (Exod. 20:24)."

T. Suk. 4:3

These passages enrich our view of the celebration but do not add to our grasp of the emotions associated with it. The only fresh point is the one assigned to Hillel, who links the feelings of the occasion to the actions in celebration of it. His saying, referring, we may assume, to the Temple as God's house, underlines the religious experience induced by the celebration (as against the more mundane picture of T. Suk. 4:1).

Public celebrations on occasions of both mourning and rejoicing en-
tailed gatherings, including meals. Associations were formed for the purpose of celebration or for mourning, giving concrete form to these
affections. Here again, happiness and sadness were treated as public, and
not only personal, emotions:

D.   Said R. Eleazar b. R. Sadoq, "Thus was the practice of the associations (haburot) that were in Jerusalem: Some were for celebration,
some for mourning, some for a meal in celebration of a betrothal, some
for a meal in celebration of a marriage, some for the celebration of the
week of a son's birth, and some for the gathering of bones [of parents,
for secondary burial]."

E.   [If one has to celebrate] the week of a son's birth and the occasion
of gathering the bones of parents, the celebration of the week of a son's
birth takes precedence over the gathering of the bones of parents.

F.   [If one has the occasion to join in] a house of celebration or a
house of mourning, the house of celebration takes precedence over the
house of mourning.

G.   R. Ishmael would give precedence to the house of mourning over
all other occasions,

H.   Since it is said, "It is better to go to the house of mourning [than
to go to the house of feasting; for this is the end of all men, and the living
will lay it to heart]" (Qoh. 7:2).

T. Meg. 3:15

A.   R. Meir said in the name of R. Aqiba, "What is the meaning of
the verse 'And the living will lay it to heart' (Qoh. 7:2)?"

T. Meg. 3:15

A.   R. Meir said in the name of R. Aqiba, "What is the meaning of
the verse 'And the living will lay it to heart' (Qoh. 7:2)?

B.   [In Aramaic:] "Do [for others], so they will do for you, accompany
[others] to the grave, so they will accompany you, make a lamentation
[for others], so they will make a lamentation for you, bury [others], so
they will bury you."

T. Meg. 3:16 (= T. Ket. 7:6)

The organization of social groups for mourning or celebration presents
no surprises. I see no doctrine of virtue here. The law raises the appropriate questions of classification and precedence. Aqiba's explanation of
the woman's right to attend funerals makes explicit the social concern.
People want to participate so that, in turn, they will enjoy appropriate

honors. In all, emotional life, an aspect of virtue, is treated as social. That fact corresponds to the theological weight imputed to the appropriate, or inappropriate, emotions in relationship to God and to one's fellow human beings.

The authors of the Tosefta included a view I think implicit in the Mishnah's laws, that the community interferes with the private expression of emotion. The Mishnah, we recall, dealt with communal limitations on public rejoicing in times of trouble. The law recognized the need to elicit from individuals shared emotions in response to communal catastrophes of the present, represented by famine or drought. It does not seem a long step to specify limitations on public communal celebrations invoked on account of the destruction of the Temple of Jerusalem, as on other accounts. A general principle comes to expression in the following:

A.   Rabban Simeon b. Gamaliel says, "You have not got a single sort of trouble that comes upon the community, on account of which the court does not annul some form of rejoicing."

T. Sot. 15:6

Specific application to public mourning for the destruction of the Temple comes to the surface in the Tosefta's materials, though I see no reason to claim that the principle was new. The observance of the ninth of Ab, commemorating the destruction of the Temple, included a limitation on greeting friends (T. Ta. 3:12A–B). The balanced emotions, mourning and rejoicing, were joined to the destruction of Jerusalem and the hope for its rebuilding. The fast days observed now will become festival days in the future (T. Ta. 3:14A–B). Those who mourn will rejoice, but we find in the Tosefta the identification of the joy with the world to come:

A.   Said R. Aqiba, "Simeon b. Luga told me, 'A certain child of the sons of their sons and I were gathering grass in the field. Then I saw him laugh and cry.

B.   " 'I said to him, "Why did you cry?"

C.   " 'He said to me, "Because of the glory of father's house, which has gone into exile."

D.   " 'I said to him, "Then why did you laugh?"

E.   " 'He said, "At the end of it all, in time to come, the Holy One, blessed be he, is going to make his descendants rejoice."

F.   " 'I said to him, "Why? [What did you see to make you think of this?]"

G.   " 'He said to me, "A smoke raiser in front of me [made me laugh]."

H.   " 'I said to him, "Show it to me."

I.   " 'He said to me, "We are subject to an oath not to show it to anyone at all." ' "

T. Kip. 2:7

A more striking development, recorded in the Tosefta, is the story of the balance between mourning and rejoicing, again associated with Jerusalem:

A.   After the last Temple was destroyed, abstainers became many in Israel, who would not eat meat or drink wine.

B.   R. Joshua engaged them in discourse, saying to them, "My children, on what account do you not eat meat?"

C.   They said to him, "Shall we eat meat, for every day a continual burnt offering [of meat] was offered on the altar, and now it is no more?"

D.   He said to them, "Then let us not eat it. And then why are you not drinking wine?"

E.   They said to him, "Shall we drink wine, for every day wine was poured out as a drink offering on the altar, and now it is no more."

F.   He said to them, "Then let us not drink it."

G.   He said to them, "But if so, we also should not eat bread, for from it did they bring the Two Loaves and the Show Bread.

H.   "We also should not drink water, for they did pour out a water offering on the festival.

I.   "We also should not eat figs and grapes, for they would bring them as first fruits on the festival of Aseret [Pentecost, Shabuot]."

J.   They fell silent.

T. Sot. 15:11

A.   He said to them, "My children, to mourn too much is not possible.

B.   "But thus have the sages said: 'A man puts on plaster on his house but he leaves open a small area, as a memorial to Jerusalem.' "

T. Sot. 15:12

A.   " 'A man prepares what is needed for a meal but leaves out some small things, as a memorial to Jerusalem.' "

T. Sot. 15:13

A.   " 'A woman prepares her ornaments, but leaves out some small thing, as a memorial to Jerusalem,'

B.   "since it is said, 'If I forget you, O Jerusalem, let my right hand wither! Let my tongue cleave to the roof of my mouth, if I do not remember you, if I do not set Jerusalem above my highest joy!' (Ps. 137:5–6)."

T. Sot. 15:14

A. "And whoever mourns for her in this world will rejoice with her in the world to come,

B. "as it is said, 'Rejoice with Jerusalem and be glad for her, all you who love her; rejoice with her in joy, all you who mourn over her' (Isa. 66:10)."

T. Sot. 15:15

Even though the Tosefta's story refers to public and historical events and emotions associated with them, we note the same emphasis on proportion and emotional order that we considered in tractate Abot. Virtue means moderation in feeling, even under duress. Not too much mourning, rejoicing postponed to the world to come – these moderated emotions were the law's prescription for the affective life even with regard to the loss of the nation's cult.

As we move from the public and communal aspect of the affective life to the individual and personal, we turn once more to what is familiar from the Mishnah's statements. This is the presence of what we may call conventional emotions, such as weeping and laughing, which have no bearing on public life. The following are examples of cases that present conventional sentiments:

A. "Those who are put to death by a court have a portion in the world to come, because they confess all their sins" [M. San. 6:2B].

B. "When he was ten cubits from the place of stoning, they say to him, 'Confess' " [M. San. 6:2A].

C. M^cSH B: There was a person who went out to be stoned. They said to him, "Confess." He said, "Let my death be my atonement for all my sins, but if I did *this* thing, let him [God] not forgive me, and let the Israelite court be free [of guilt for my innocent blood, which they shed now]." Now when this was reported to sages, their eyes filled with tears. They said to them, "To bring him back is not possible, for there will be no end to the matter. But lo, his blood is on the head of those who have testified against him."

T. San. 6:4

Items such as this – and others in the Tosefta (e.g., T. Zeb. 2:17, T. Kip. 2:4, distress; T. Yad. 2:16, weeping for joy) – simply add to the repertoire of instances in which joy or sorrow, laughing or weeping enter into stories and sayings. The Mishnah's accounts have prepared us to expect such details to play a role in stories. In supplementing the Mishnah, the Tosefta simply augments an already clear picture.

The Affection of Shame

The insistence of the compilers of tractate Abot that people take account of public opinion and respond, in particular, to feelings of the community at large recurs in the materials assembled in the Tosefta. That point of emphasis prepares the way for a sanction. If people violate community opinion, they feel embarrassment or shame. Hence, the penalty for the absence of virtue comes to the surface. The Tosefta presents a range of stories recounting how important sages took account of public opinion and accepted a rule more stringent than the actual law required, so as to avoid public shame and to placate contrary sentiment in the community at large:

A.   M ͨSH B: R. Tarfon was going along the way.

B.   A certain old man came across him [and] said to him, "Why do people complain against you? And are not all your rulings true and right? But you accept food in the status of heave offering on the other days of the year [outside of harvest time, wine-pressing or olive-crushing season] from everyone [without regard to the status of the donor as an associate]!!"

C.   Said R. Tarfon, "May I bury my sons, if I do not have a law in my hands from Rabban Yohanan b. Zakkai, who told me, 'You are permitted to receive food in the status of heave offering on the other days of the year [besides the harvest seasons] from any one [not merely an associate].'

D.   "But now that people are complaining against me, I decree for myself that I shall not accept food in the status of heave offering on the other days of the year [besides the harvest seasons] from any one at all,

E.   "unless he will state to me, 'I have set apart in this jug of wine a quarter-*log*, which is in the status of Holy Things.' "

T. Hag. 3:33

A.   M ͨSH B: Rabban Gamaliel took a seat by the chair of gentiles on the Sabbath in Akko.

B.   They said to him, "They were not accustomed to take seats at the chair of gentiles on the Sabbath."

C.   But he did not want to say, "You are permitted to do so."

D.   So he got up and went on his way.

E.   M ͨSH B: Judah and Hillel, sons of Rabban Gamaliel, went in to take a bath in Kabul.

F.   They said to him, "They were not accustomed to have two brothers take a bath together."

G.   They did not want to say, "You are permitted to do so."

H.   So they went in and took a bath one after the other.

T. Moed 2:15

A.   M^cSH B: Judah and Hillel, sons of Rabban Gamaliel, would go out in golden slippers on the Sabbath in Biri.

B.   They said to them, "They were not accustomed to go out in golden slippers on the Sabbath."

C.   They did not want to say to them, "You are permitted."

D.   So they sent them along with their servants.

T. Moed 2:16

What is important here is that Tarfon accepted public norms, not those he knew to be right, so as not to displease the community at large. So, too, Gamaliel's sons accepted public opinion as the norm, even though it involved a more strict rule than in fact applied. The emphasis on shaping a personality that pleases other people as a norm for public office, moreover, is introduced at T. Hag. 2:9R as a qualification for serving as a judge: "Whoever was a sage, modest, humble, sin-fearing, sufficiently mature, and from whom people gain pleasure, do they appoint as a judge in his own town." Here, too, the emphasis we noted in tractate Abot recurs. What we find, therefore, is that the attitude of public acceptance and the feeling of communal approval represented not solely active virtues but qualifications for office. In a context in which public office as a sage marked a man as one approved by God, the deeper message emerges clearly. A web of shared attitudes toward personality and the affective life joined heaven and earth.

Beyond the rather general requirement of pleasing other people, we must ask whether specific affections come into view. A very specific feeling, that of shame, which is implicit in the passage above, is made explicit in what follows:

D.   "The eldest among them makes a speech of admonition" [M. Ta. 2:1D].

E.   "My children, let a person be ashamed before his fellow, but let a person not be ashamed on account of what he has done. It is better for a person to be ashamed before his fellow, but let him and his children not suffer from famine.

F.   "And so it says, 'Why have we fasted, and you see it not? Why have we humbled ourselves, and you take no knowledge of it?' (Isa. 58:3)."

T. Ta. 1:8

A.   M^cSH B: R. Eliezer was arrested on account of *minut* [heresy; in context, sympathy for a teaching of Jesus]. They brought him to court for judgment.

B.   That *hegemon* [official] said to him, "Should an elder of your standing get involved in such things?"

C.   He said to him, "The Judge is reliable in my view [I rely on the Judge]."

D.   That *hegemon* supposed that he referred only to him, but he referred only to his Father in heaven.

E.   He [the *hegemon*] said to him, "Since you have deemed me reliable for yourself, so thus I have ruled: Is it possible that these gray hairs should err in such matters? [*Obviously not; therefore, you are*] *Dimissus* [pardoned]. Lo, you are free of liability."

F.   And when he left court, he was distressed to have been arrested on account of matters of *minut*.

G.   His disciples came to comfort him, but he did not accept their words of comfort.

H.   R. Aqiba came and said to him, "Rabbi, may I say something to you so that you will not be distressed?"

I.   He said to him, "Go ahead."

J.   He said to him, "Perhaps some of the *minim* told you something of *minut* that pleased you."

K.   He said to him, "By heaven! You remind me. Once I was strolling in the camp of Sepphoris. I bumped into Jacob of Kefar Sikhnin, and he told me a teaching of *minut* in the name of Jesus ben Pantiri, and it pleased me.

L.   "So I was arrested on account of matters of *minut*, for I transgressed the teachings of Torah: 'Keep your way far from her and do not go near the door of her house. . . . ' (Prov. 5:8)."

M.   For R. Eliezer did teach, "One should always flee from what is reputable and from whatever appears to be disreputable" [for other versions, see Neusner, *Eliezer ben Hyrcanus* (Leiden, 1973), pp. 400–3].

T. Shehit at Hullin 2:24

The first of the two passages makes explicit reference to accepting public opprobrium or shame. The story ending of the second passage (L) is what is important here. Eliezer was ashamed of his arrest and trial, which were the consequences of his shameful behavior. It follows that one has to avoid what is disreputable. That teaching makes concrete and very specific the generalized attitude noted at the outset. A person should always take account of public opinion and avoid violating public norms. The complementary lesson is that one should avoid endangering one's public standing not only by not doing what others find disreputable but also by not appearing to do so. This seems a very concrete expression of concern for avoiding shame and the penalty of feeling ashamed of oneself. Both lessons deal entirely with public aspects of the affective life: Shame measures a dimension of community affairs, since it exists in relation to other people. The alternative affective sanction, guilt, takes shape between the individual and heaven, not relying on public opinion for its effects.

Attitude and Event: Hatred Destroyed Jerusalem

A second striking passage in the Tosefta assigns to the affection of hatred astounding power in historical affairs. Just as love characterizes the relationship between the individual and God, so hatred defines the condition for the destruction of that relationship as it was embodied in the Temple cult. Although one might claim that that amazing allegation was implicit in the Mishnah's treatment of love and hatred as balanced opposites, still, it represents a considerable development. It takes up the generative notions that virtue includes concern for public opinion and that emotions, with all of their social effects, are part of the normative structure of the law. Those twin principles come to immediate expression in the following:

A. Said R. Yohanan b. Torta, "On what account was Shiloh destroyed? Because of the disgraceful disposition of the Holy Things that were there.

B. "As to Jerusalem's first building, on what account was it destroyed? Because of idolatry and licentiousness and bloodshed that was in it.

C. "But [as to] the latter [building], we know that they devoted themselves to Torah and were meticulous about tithes.

D. "On what account did they go into exile? Because they loved money and hated one another.

E. "This teaches you that hatred of one for another is evil before the Omnipresent, and Scripture deems it equivalent to idolatry, licentiousness, and bloodshed."

T. Men. 13:22

The above two contributions, which supplement the Mishnah, the restatement of concern for public opinion and emphasis on the historical consequences of inappropriate affections, derive directly from the Mishnah's treatment of the same matters. But they do underline in concrete ways the critical place, in the Mishnah's larger system or Judaism, of affections. Deeds and deliberation are important for the religious life, but so, too, are the condition and contents of the heart. Invoking the worst catastrophe imaginable, the destruction of the Temple and the city, the sages declare their view of what matters most of all, that hatred that obliterated from Israel's life the marks of God's love.

The Fathers According to Rabbi Nathan

The exegetes who received the Mishnah, now including the framers of the tractate Abot, amplified but rarely augmented the repertoire of permissible and impermissible emotions. Though in the two chapters that follow we shall confront much repetition and little innovation, we see in the Fathers According to Rabbi Nathan still more clearly the same trait of constancy and stability in doctrines on the affective life. The Fathers According to Rabbi Nathan, a kind of Talmud to tractate Abot, is of indeterminate date. Much found there occurs in essentially the same language as in the Talmuds. Taking up the sayings of Abot, the compilers or authors of the Fathers According to Rabbi Nathan illustrated, exemplified, expanded, but rarely added anything of their own. It suffices to give a few examples of their treatment of some sayings in Abot. These examples are given in the translation of Judah Goldin, and references are to the page of his translation:

1. Another interpretation. BE DELIBERATE IN JUDGMENT: what is that? This teaches that a man should be patient in his speech and not short tempered in his speech, for whoever is short tempered in his speech forgets what he has to say. For thus we find in the case of Moses our master: when he was short tempered in his speech he forgot what he was to tell (Israel). (p. 7)

2. AND RECEIVE ALL MEN WITH A CHEERFUL COUNTE-NANCE: what is that? This teaches that if one gives his fellow all the good gifts in the world with a downcast face, Scripture accounts it to him as though he had given him naught. But if he receives his fellow with a cheerful countenance, even though he gives him naught, Scripture accounts it to him as though he had given him all the good gifts in the world. (p. 73)

3. A GRUDGING EYE: what is that? This teaches that even as a man looks out for his own home, so should he look out for the home of his fellow. And even as no man wishes that his own wife and children be

held in ill repute, so should no man wish that his fellow's wife and his fellow's children be held in ill repute.

Another interpretation. A GRUDGING EYE: what is that? That one should not begrudge another his learning.

There was once a certain man who begrudged his companion his learning. His life was cut short and he passed away. (p. 82)

4. Ben ᶜAzzai says:

If one's mind is serene because of his learning, it is a good sign for him; but if his mind is distressed because of his learning, it is a bad sign for him.

If one's mind is serene because of his impulse, it is a good sign for him; but if his mind is distressed because of his impulse, it is a bad sign for him. (p. 105)

5. He used to say:

. . . If one dies in the midst of joy, it is a good sign for him; if in the midst of sadness, it is a bad sign for him.

If one dies while laughing, it is a good sign for him; if while weeping, it is a bad sign for him. (p. 107)

These virtues of the heart are quite familiar: patience, good cheer, liberality of spirit. The sayings about serenity fit quite well with the established conventions of emotion. These return to the matter of perpetual good cheer, joy, and laughter and counsel against anxiety, distress, melancholy, depression, and sorrow. The main point for our inquiry should not be missed. Those who received tractate Abot guarded the treasure and polished it, but they added little. What is critical for our purposes, therefore, is that the document provides yet another solid example of the constancy and stability of the doctrine of religious affections, as the canon of formative Judaism unfolded through time.

CHAPTER VI

The Virtues of the Heart in the Articulation of the Exegetical Tradition of the Law

The Yerushalmi

The Yerushalmi

The Yerushalmi restates the basic notion that the right demeanor requires restraint and submission to the will of others. Although the Yerushalmi contributes rules for virtue, the authorship as a whole adds nothing new to the matter and changes nothing that had been received. It is tradition in a strict sense: intact and unimpaired in every way. Since it is generally maintained that the Yerushalmi reached closure some two hundred years after the Mishnah, my claim concerning the stability of the doctrine of right attitude and correct feeling finds confirmation in what is now before us.

The first of the two Talmuds devoted to the exegesis and amplification of the Mishnah, the Talmud of the Land of Israel (also known as the Yerushalmi or the Palestinian Talmud) reached closure, people generally assume, in ca. 400. The document is made up of two components: first, tractates of the Mishnah, cited paragraph by paragraph, then, in a mixture of Aramaic and Hebrew, detailed discussions applying to thirty-nine of the Mishnah's sixty-two tractates. Each Mishnah tractate dictates the organization of the Yerushalmi's discussion, which follows the Mishnah's exposition of its topics.

The program of exegesis is simple. The framers of the Yerushalmi systematically bring into relationship with the Mishnah paragraph under discussion the Tosefta's corresponding passage. They ordinarily begin discussion by asking about the scriptural warrant for the rule given in a Mishnah paragraph or by citing the Tosefta's relevant statement and asking about *its* scriptural warrant. They proceed to an exposition of the law at hand and may end their program with a secondary expansion on problems of the law – its theory, on the one side, its concrete application, on the other. In my probe of the Yerushalmi's units of discourse and the

74

proportions of those units devoted to various matters, I found that approximately 90 percent of the units focus on the Mishnah and follow its program, with or without the Tosefta's complement. Only 10 percent served a purpose other than systematic exegesis of the Mishnah.

Apart from articulation of a considerable program of Mishnah exegesis, the framers of the Yerushalmi utilized two other types of material. They provided exegesis of scriptural passages not only in relation to Mishnah rules but also out of their own interest in various verses of Scripture. They further included a repertoire of sages' tales. We may therefore say that, in the mind of the authors of the Yerushalmi (as of the writers of the Bavli later on), the Torah came in three media: first, in the oral form represented by the Mishnah; second, in the written form taken by Scripture; and, third, in the flesh, in the lives and deeds of great sages themselves, who served as living exemplars of teachings of the Torah. All three forms of the Torah supplied guidance on right action. Still more important, all three came under the same rigorous and reasoned scrutiny with respect to both the sources of validation (commonly in Scripture) and the consistency with rules relevant to a given case. But among the three modes of the Torah contained in both Talmuds, the Yerushalmi's predominant interest centered on the Mishnah's articulation and amplification.

By its nature Mishnah exegesis presented to the Yerushalmi's authors only limited occasions for discourse on the character and importance of affections. That is hardly surprising, since, as we know, the topical program of the Mishnah offered only episodic and discrete opportunities for reflection on matters bound up with the heart. If there is no Mishnah tractate on, for example, the love of God or the affective aspect of the impulse to do evil, on hope or despair, or on mourning or rejoicing, the writers of the Yerushalmi and, later, the Bavli would also find only slight occasion to construct sustained and systematic analyses of those topics.

What is important, however, in the growth of the exegetical tradition is simple. Legal topics not covered extensively, or at all, in the Mishnah do find their way onto the agenda of the authors of the Yerushalmi (and of the Bavli afterward). To name four examples, we find extensive discussion on the preparation of a *mezuzah* and other scribal topics, on aspects of the priestly life, on the rules and rites of mourning, and on the laws governing the conduct of the sage and the disciple. None of these topics has a significant impact on the program of the Mishnah, but out of the two Talmuds we could construct for them better than a chapter, possibly even an entire tractate. This fact is shown by the existence of later tractates on rejoicing (meaning "mourning"), the scribal life, and on proper conduct, among the minor tractates attached, in due course, to the Talmud of Babylonia.

When we ask about matters of the heart, we find little that was not adumbrated in the Mishnah. Emotions, as we now see, occasionally surface in accounts of legal discourse. They play no part whatsoever in the making of legal decisions. Where the Mishnah or the Tosefta introduces the theme of an affection, its definition and role, the Yerushalmi takes cognizance of the topic. Where the theme has not already found its place in the program of the law, the authors of the Yerushalmi will not invent or introduce it.

Before proceeding, let me give one example in the Yerushalmi of the part the emotions play in the description of the analysis of laws. The part is minor and yields only a homily. Still, we see that, had the framers of legal traditions wished, they could have given us an account of the affective framework of reasoned inquiry into law. Overall, in the Yerushalmi, they rarely did so.

E.   R. Bibi was in session and repeating the tradition of this story. Said to him R. Isaac bar Kahana, "Up to a quarter-*log* is insusceptible to uncleanness, and a greater volume than that is unclean?" He kicked him. R. Zeriqan said to him, "Because he asked you a question, do you then kick him?"

F.   He said to him, "It was because I did not have my wits about me."

G.   This accords with that which R. Hanin said, " 'Your life shall hang in doubt before you; night and day you shall be in dread, and have no assurance of your life' (Deut. 28:66).

H.   "This refers to someone who purchases wheat for a whole year in advance.

I.   " 'And night and day you shall be in dread' – this refers to one who buys bread from the wholesaler.

J.   " 'And have no assurance of your life' – this refers to one who buys bread from the corner baker."

Y. Shab. 8:1.V

Bibi kicked Isaac bar Kahana, an expression of the attitude or emotion, we are told, of inadequacy, a feeling forthwith repudiated (F). Then the homily that follows (G–J) tells us that people in command of Torah learning enjoy security and certainty and therefore do not confront inadequacy or insufficiency. They will not be dependent on the retailer or even the wholesaler; they will know the certainty that comes only with mastery of the law. In other words, a mark of ignorance is the demeanor of temper, and a sign of learning is restraint. That lesson, here introduced rather casually into the story of a legal discussion, would not have surprised the framers of the tractate Abot. It is commonplace. But it is not a recurrent theme in narrative surrounding exchanges of legal formulas.

Still, the limited place of emotions in legal exegesis is not significant. Quite the contrary, the topic would have proved entirely out of place in the system at hand. Philosophers and jurisprudents, the Yerushalmi's exegetes of the Mishnah and of the Tosefta cannot be expected to have left a legacy of poetry (though there is some in both Talmuds) or of art or of deep thought on affections. But these thinkers did have a rich capacity to extend and broaden the law. They did so not only by exploring the implications of the received system, the Mishnah's. They also reshaped and expanded the system, dropping whole divisions and so elaborating others as to impart to them an importance they by definition had lacked in the original system. Thus, as I said, they exhibited the imagination and wit to develop new topics for legal inquiry based on matters of importance in their own time, extant but neglected in times past. So far as I can see, their fresh perspective and new insight produced little we can call surprising or profound in that dimension of the inner life that is under study here.

Supplementing the Mishnah's Rules

Authors represented in the pages of the Yerushalmi admit that emotions play a role in public discourse. At issue is where emotions enter into the structure of the law, and how (when they do) they make their impact. The latter is a quite separate question. To summarize the result in advance, where the Mishnah's system admits emotions and sorts them out, disposing of one kind and nurturing another, the Yerushalmi's exegetes pursue the same facts in basically the same way. What the Mishnah's system does not admit into the repertoire of standard and conventional, socially recognized and even sanctioned feelings, neither does the Yerushalmi's reworking of that system. That is what I meant in emphasizing the absence, in the Yerushalmi, of a substantial expansion of thought on the program established by the Mishnah's authors.

The yearning for peace and mutual regard, recommended in tractate Abot, comes to expression in a concrete legal context. Specifically, it is given as the reason for requiring that all residents of a courtyard participate in some way in the preparation of the meal of commingling. That is a symbolic meal shared by all the residents so as to merge the distinct private domains of a courtyard into a single, shared domain for the purpose of permitting, on the Sabbath day, acts of carrying an object from one house to another and from all houses to the courtyard. The following reveals that the requirement for such a shared meal, in symbolic terms, on the Sabbath derives from the sages' desire to foster good will within Israel:

A.   Said R. Joshua [b. Levi], "On what account do they prepare a meal of commingling for a courtyard? It is for the sake of peace."

B.   There was the case of a woman who was on bad terms with her neighbor. She sent her meal of commingling with her son. The other took him and hugged and kissed him. He went and told his mother this. She said, "Is this how she loved me, and I did not know about it!" They thus became friends once again.

C.   That is in line with the following verse of Scripture: "Her ways are ways of pleasantness, and all her paths are peace" (Prov. 3:17).

Y. Er. 3:2.III

The passage is explicit. It is the only instance in the Yerushalmi, so far as I can see, in which laws are made or explained on the basis of feelings or emotions.

This is not to suggest that the authors do not consider the intrusion of anger, love, or temper into legal or normative issues. On the contrary, they articulate the effects of anger very well. Anger is regarded as the opposite of deliberation. An act done out of anger stands in contrast to an act done intentionally. What a Gentile does in anger is not regarded as effective action (Y. A.Z. 4:11.IIIE): "What a Gentile does in anger does not impart the status of libation wine to wine." That is, if a Gentile touches wine, he is assumed to make use of a speck of the wine for a libation, and if he does so, his act prohibits the use of all of the remaining wine by the Israelite. But if he touches the wine in a moment of wrath, he is not assumed to have done something deliberate and effective. Over-all, however, the emotion of anger appears mainly in the context of narratives; for example, "the king heard and got mad, the rabbi feared and fled" (Y. Ber. 7:2.III). There are many instances of rabbis' oaths taken in emotional fervor; for example, "May I bury my sons if. . . ." (Y. Hor. 3:2.XIIIV). Rabbis' anger required explanation:

B.   R. Huna was sitting in a certain synagogue. The cantor went and tried to impose upon one person to go up [before the ark to lead the prayer]. He would not accept the call to go. [R. Eleazar got angry].

C.   Afterward the person went to R. Eleazar and said, "Please master, do not be angry at me. I did not go up because I was agitated."

D.   He [Eleazar] said to him, "I was not angry at you. I was angry at the person who tried to impose upon you [to lead the prayer]."

Y. Ber. 5:3.III (Zahavy)

That an affection plays a role in this transaction underlines the simple fact that sages recognized and took account of feelings. These assumed their appropriate place in the exegesis of the law and in its application.

But we can find in the exegetical work of the Yerushalmi only trivial and routine instances in which exegetes gave thought to how the law was affected by emotional considerations.

Two such instances, already entirely familiar, introduced social conventions into the emotional life. One dealt with joy, with stress on rejoicing during festivals:

A. [Illustrating M. M.Q. 2:5E:] The fish trappers of Tiberias, the groat makers of Acre, and the grist millers of Sepphoris undertook not to perform acts of labor on the intermediate days of a festival.

B. There is no difficulty understanding the decision of the grist millers of Sepphoris and the groat makers of Acre. But as to the fish trappers of Tiberias, will they not diminish the joy of the festival [by reducing the availability of fish]?

C. One may nonetheless catch fish with a hook or with nets.

D. Even so, do they not diminish the pleasure of the festival?

E. R. Ammi ridiculed them for diminishing the joy of the festival [by their self-indulgence].

Y. M.Q. 2:5.III

The principle is familiar; only the application's fresh. The other instance deals with mourning, which, as we already know, was an area of considerable legal attention in the Mishnah itself. The law undertook to instruct mourners when they might and might not mourn. That is, they specified when they might exhibit the signs of mourning in *public*, for the emotion by itself, the sages recognized, was intensely personal, "only in the heart." In the following stories, we find a small repertoire of the numerous aspects of the public regulation of mourning that the Yerushalmi lays out:

C. R. Yose, son of R. Halafta, was praising R. Meir before the townfolk of Sepphoris: "He was a great man, a holy man, a modest man. Once he saw a mourner on the Sabbath and he greeted him."

D. They said to him, "Is this how you praise him?"

E. He said to them, "What's the matter?"

F. They said to him, "He saw a mourner on the Sabbath and greeted him?!"

G. He said to them, "Do you want to know how far he would go? This incident teaches us that there may be no mourning on the Sabbath in accord with what is written:

H. " 'The blessing of the Lord makes rich' (Prov. 10:22); this refers to the blessing of the Sabbath. 'And toil adds nothing to it' (ibid.); this refers to mourning, as it says, 'The king is grieving for his son' (2 Sam. 19:2).' "

Y. Ber. 2:6 (Zahavy)

A.   R. Isaac, son of R. Hiyya, at Toba suffered an untimely bereavement. R. Mana and R. Yudan went up (to console him), and they had some good wine, and they drank until they became silly. The next day when they wished to visit him [Isaac] again, he said to them, "Rabbis, is this how a person acts towards his associate? The only thing missing yesterday was dancing, [and we would have had festivity rather than mourning]."

Y. Ber. 3:1.V

In these two stories we see how demeanor and conduct on the occasion of mourning became a topic of social concern, just as in the Mishnah. Therefore, the matter was considered in detail, through restatement or development, following what had been written before. One is not to mourn on the Sabbath, so, as Meir insists, all details of mourning are set aside. Proper conduct on the social occasion of mourning requires appropriate restraint.

What is important in the following story is how their theory of people's feelings affected the sages' judgment of the law. This is a fine instance in which emotions play a role in the determination of a rule. But this rule does not specifically concern emotions, and it does not make feelings an important element of the expression of piety.

A.   " 'They kindle [unclean oil in the status of heave offering] in a house in which there is a wedding feast, but not in a house of mourning' " – the words of R. Judah.

B.   "R. Yose says, '[They do so] in a house of mourning, but not at a wedding feast.'

C.   "R. Meir prohibits in either case.

D.   "R. Simeon permits in either case" [M. Ter. 11:10E–H].

E.   What is R. Judah's reasoning [above, A]?

F.   [Y. claims that the issue is the likelihood that the nonpriests will dirty themselves with the consecrated oil, for example, by adjusting or moving the lamp. This would constitute an improper waste of the heave offering]. In a house in which there is a wedding feast, since the people are cleanly dressed, they will not busy themselves [adjusting or moving] it [i.e., the lamp. Since the people will do their best not to dirty themselves with the oil, Judah allows the kindling of heave offering at a wedding feast.]

G.   [But] in a house of mourning, since people wear dirty clothing, they might busy themselves [adjusting or moving the lamp. Since the mourners are likely to spill and thereby waste some of the oil, Judah does not allow the use of oil in the status of heave offering in a house of mourning.]

H.   What is the reasoning of R. Yose [above, B]?

I.   In a house of mourning, since the people are low-spirited, they will not busy themselves with it [i.e., the lamp. Therefore, Yose allows oil in the status of heave offering to be kindled in a lamp in a house of mourning.]

J.   [But] in a house in which there is a wedding feast, since the people are overly active, they are likely to play with [the lamp. Therefore Yose does not allow oil in the status of heave offering to be kindled in a lamp at a wedding feast.]

K.   What is the reasoning of R. Meir [above, C]?

L.   In a house of mourning, since people wear dirty clothing, they might busy themselves [adjusting or moving the lamp. Since the mourners therefore are likely to spill and waste some of the oil, Meir does not allow the use of consecrated oil in a house of mourning. This is just like the view of Judah, G.]

M.   In a house in which there is a wedding feast, since the people are overly active, they are likely to play with [the lamp. Just as at L, they therefore might spill and waste some of the oil. Meir thus does not allow a lamp filled with consecrated oil to be kindled at a wedding feast (= Yose, J).]

N.   What is the reasoning of R. Simeon [above, D]?

O.   In a house of mourning, since the people are low-spirited, they will not busy themselves with [the lamp. For this reason Simeon allows consecrated oil to be kindled in the house of mourning, just like Yose, I.]

P.   [And] in a house in which there is a wedding feast, since the people are cleanly dressed, they will not busy themselves [adjusting or moving] it [i.e., the lamp. Since the people will not dirty themselves with the oil, Simeon allows the use of consecrated oil at a wedding feast as well (= Judah, F).]

Y. Ter. 11:10.IX (trans. Alan J. Avery-Peck)

In this analysis, we see that peoples' feelings constitute facts of life. The law disposes of these facts, sorting them out and determining, on the basis of how rabbis think people feel, what should be done. As Avery-Peck stresses, at issue is the disposition of oil in a certain status. People's attitudes or feelings about the oil play no role whatsoever. Only the consequences of these same emotions for their likely conduct are of importance. Still more striking is the assumption that there are descriptive rules governing people's feelings as much as their emotions. The socially recognized affections follow a single and uniform path. That is why the law can take account of feelings as much as of intentions or expectations. People almost routinely respond in a single way, with a shared and common feeling, and the rest follows. Thus, there are rules of affections, and as a result rules can accommodate affections too.

When we review stories such as these, we again recognize that the sages invoked the law to deal not with private emotions but with their communal aspect. People had to suppress mourning on the Sabbath. Appropriate conduct in the presence of the mourner required restraint. The comforters, too, had to conduct themselves appropriately, an imposition on action as well as feeling. The assessment of the emotions of the mourners and the of celebrants of a wedding dictated diverse opinions on actions having to do with produce of a given status. In all, feelings constituted facts that did not change, and the law dealt with these enduring facts. No one pretended that feelings were only facts or mattered only when other aspects of correct conduct intruded. But when feelings had little bearing on wrong or right action, the law rarely said anything about regulating or even recognizing them.

When we turn from joy and sorrow to the affection of love, we of course take up the counterpart of love, which in the rabbinic language is the "impulse to do evil." The Mishnah's formulation, we recall, set the love of God up as the opposite to the impulse to do evil. One has to love God in order to transform the impulse to do evil, as much as the one to do good, into a medium for divine service. The love of God frames the highest kind of love, the sort that characterized Abraham, as against David, and Aqiba:

A. Abraham made the impulse to do evil into good.

B. What is the scriptural basis for that statement?

C. "And thou didst find his heart faithful before thee, [and didst make with him the covenant to give to his descendants the land of the Canaanite, the Hittite, the Amorite, the Perizzite, the Jebusite, and the Girgashite]" (Neh. 9:8).

D. Said R. Aha, "He made an agreement with it: '[And thou didst find his heart faithful before thee] and didst make with him the covenant [to give to his descendants the land of the Canaanite, the Hittite, the Amorite, the Perizzite, the Jebusite, and the Girgashite]' (Neh. 9:8)."

E. But David was unable to overcome it, so he had to kill it in his heart.

F. What is the scriptural basis for that statement?

G. "[For I am poor and needy,] and my heart is stricken within me" (Ps. 109:22).

A.   R. Aqiba was on trial before Tonosteropos the Wicked. The time for reciting the Shema came. He began to recite it and smiled.

B.   [The wicked one] said to him, "Old man, old man! You are either a wizard, or you have contempt for pain [that you smile]."

C.   He said to him, "May the soul of that man [me] perish. I am no wizard, nor do I have contempt for pain.

D.   "But for my whole life I have been reciting this verse: 'And you shall love the Lord your God with all your heart, with all your soul, and with all your might' (Deut. 5:6).

E.   "I loved God with all my heart, and I loved him with all my might.

F.   "But 'with all my soul' until now was not demanded of me.

G.   "And now that the time has come for me to love him with all my soul, as the time for reciting the Shema has arrived, I smile that the occasion has come to carry out the verse at that very moment at which I recite the Scripture."

Y. Sot. 5:5.III–IV

What is important is the joining of two themes: serving God even with the evil impulse (III) and serving God with the entire soul (IV). The point expressed in the Mishnah here is given concrete illustration in the persons of Abraham and Aqiba.

What presents the occasion to love God through the impulse to do evil is the existence of prohibitions. What we cannot have we want, and this becomes explicit:

A.   "At each booth they say to him, 'Lo, here is food, here is water' " [M. Yoma 6:4F]:

B.   [This was] to keep up his strength.

C.   Why so?

D.   For the evil impulse craves only what is forbidden.

E.   This is illustrated in the following: R. Mana went up to visit R. Haggai [on the Day of Atonement], who was feeling weak. [Haggai] said to him, "I am thirsty."

F.   He said to him, "Go drink something."

G.   He left him and went away. After a while he came back to him.

H.   He said to him, "What happened to your thirst?"

I.   He said to him, "When you let me [drink], it went away."

Y. Yoma 6:4.III

K.   R. Huna, and it is taught in the name of R. Eleazar b. Jacob: " 'And the Lord will take away from you all illness' (Deut. 7:15) – this refers to ambition.

L.   " 'He will put an iron yoke on your neck' (Deut. 28:48) – this refers to greed."

M.   Said R. Abun, " 'And the Lord will take away from you all sickness' (Deut. 7:15) – this refers to the evil impulse. For in the beginning it is sweet but at the end it is bitter."

Y. Shab. 14:1.VI

The evil impulse provokes a person to want what is forbidden. If the prohibition is removed, the impulse to violate the law also passes. Thus, the prohibition provokes the evil impulse but also provides the occasion for overcoming it through the affection of love, applied to God in particular. None of this would have surprised the authors of the Mishnah. Once more, therefore, we observe in the Yerushalmi an amplification and extension of familiar concepts.

One new aspect of love, an aspect the sages regarded with little respect, is romantic love. The sages would not identify romantic love with a virtue or take account of its requirements. Nonetheless, the language used for love of God also applied to the love of the man for the woman in the following story:

LL.   In the days of R. Eleazar, a man so loved a woman that he was in danger of dying [from unconsummated desire]. They came and asked R. Eleazar, "What is the law governing her 'passing before him' so that he may live?"

MM.   He answered them, "Let him die but [let matters not be done] in such a way."

NN.   "What is the law as to his merely hearing her voice, so that he may live?"

OO.   "Let him die, but [let matters not be done] in such a way."

PP.   Now what was the character of this girl [who was to be kept away from the man pining for her]?

QQ.   R. Jacob bar Idi and R. Isaac bar Nahman – one maintained that she was a married woman, and the other maintained that she was unmarried.

RR.   Now so far as the opinion of the one who maintained that she was a married woman is concerned, there are no problems. But as to the one who maintained that she was unmarried [why should she not have married the man]?

SS.   Now, lo, Bar Koha Nigra so loved a woman in the days of R. Eleazar, that he was in danger of dying [from unconsummated desire]. [Read: R. Eleazar permitted him to marry her.]

TT.   In the former case [LL–OO, we deal] with a married woman, in the latter [SS] with an unmarried woman.

UU.   Now even if you maintain that both cases deal with an unmarried woman, interpret the case to apply to one who formed a desire for the woman while she was still married [in which case even after the divorce he may not marry her].

VV.   There are some who would explain [the rabbis' prohibiting the man to marry the unmarried woman] because she was a woman of high station, and she would not have accepted the judgment of [the rabbi to marry the love-stricken suitor], so whatever [the suitor] might do would be done subject to the prohibition of the rabbi. On that account he did not permit [the marriage].

Y. A.Z. 2:2.III

The story is important in showing that "love" bore several meanings, not all of them important to the framers of the Yerushalmi. What distinguished one kind from another was the object of love. Love of God, that is, service, the highest virtue, contrasted with love of self or of a woman.

It remains to take up the Yerushalmi's elaboration of a passage of the Tosefta that is important for our larger inquiry. We recall (T. Men. 13:22) that hatred without cause destroyed the second Temple (T. Men. 13:22). The passage undergoes the following amplification:

G.   R. Zeirah, R. Jacob bar Aha, and R. Abonah were in session. They said, "[Hatred without cause] is worse, for the first Temple was rebuilt, while the second Temple was not rebuilt."

H.   Said R. Zeira, "The people in the time of the first Temple repented, while those in the time of the second Temple did not repent."

I.   Said R. Eleazar, "In the case of the people in the time of the first Temple, their sin was revealed [for all to see], but the fullness of time [of their suffering] also was revealed. For those in the time of the second Temple their sin was not revealed, and the fullness of time [of their suffering] also was not revealed."

J.   They asked R. Eliezer, "Are the latter generations more suitable people than the former ones?"

K.   He said to them, "Your witness as to the condition of the chosen house will prove the matter. Our fathers have removed the roof: 'He has taken away the covering of Judah' (Isa. 22:8).

L.   "We for our part we smashed the walls. 'Remember, O Lord, against the Edomites the day of Jerusalem, how they said, "Raze it, raze it! Down to its foundations!" ' (Ps. 137:7)."

M.   They said, "Any generation in the time of which the Temple is not rebuilt – Scripture regards it as if that generation itself had destroyed it."

Y. Yoma 1:1.XVII

The Yerushalmi's heirs to the Tosefta here simply reinforce and repeat what had already been said.

The Dimension of Scripture

When we ask how the authors of the Yerushalmi utilize passages of Scripture to provide the setting for comments on the affective life, we must expect no surprising answers, for the same people dealt with the same values, principles, and issues. Whether they expressed their basic convictions through the analysis of a philosophical–legal system or through the exegesis of Scripture, what they said proved uniform and consistent throughout. What is surprising, however, is that the consistency is revealed in the sages' discussion of materials that themselves invite fresh and unconventional response. It is one thing to treat in a conventional way received materials, interpreted essentially within that framework of topic and logic that had generated the materials to begin with. When they came to Scripture, the writers dealt with a text rich in the affective life not only of humanity but of God.

Indeed, in a reading of Scripture as a uniform and cogent statement of God's inner life, God's feelings as much as his attitudes and rules, sages may well have included such affective issues as indignation, wrath, and jealousy, not to mention disappointment, despair, and, above all, renewal and hope, for Scripture presents a nuanced and profound account of a feeling and caring God. Hence, the fixed categories of mourning and rejoicing – on the occasion of death, during a public festival – as much as the conventional classifications of love and hate, humility, modesty, arrogance, and ambition, restraint and acceptance or envy and recrimination simply should not by themselves serve for the diverse and remarkably rich biblical record of divine pathos and human response, human rebellion and divine love. But they do. Emotions not catalogued and sorted out in the Mishnah and in the exegetical expansion of its legal system scarcely make an appearance when the Yerushalmi's exegetes of the Mishnah text turn their attention to the biblical record.

The authors and editors of the Yerushalmi gathered not only exegeses of paragraphs of the Mishnah but also passages resting on extensive citation of Scripture, that is, in their mythic language, the oral Torah. To biblical heroes, not surprisingly, they imputed those same virtues that they ascribed to God. Indeed, the distinctive traits of the true Israelite and the typical characteristics of God correspond. As to the latter:

Q.   R. Yudan bar Hanan in the name of R. Berekiah: "Said the Holy One, blessed be he, to Israel, 'My children, if you see the merit of the patriarchs declining, and the merit of the matriarchs growing feeble, go and cleave unto the trait of steadfast love.' "

R.   What is the scriptural basis for this statement?

S.   "For the mountains may depart and the hills be removed, [but my steadfast love shall not depart from you, and my covenant of peace shall not be removed, says the Lord, who has compassion on you]" (Isa. 54:10).

T.   "For the mountains may depart" – this refers to the merit of the patriarchs.

U.   "And the hills be removed" – this refers to the merit of the matriarchs.

V.   Henceforth: "But my steadfast love shall not depart from you, and my covenant of peace shall not be removed, says the Lord, who has compassion on you."

Y. San. 10:1.VI

The compassion characteristic of God also defines the true Israelite. In what follows, David discovers that the Gibeonites' spirit of vengeance against Saul marks them as alien to Israel:

O.   "And the Lord said, 'There is blood guilt on account of Saul and on his house, because he put the Gibeonites to death' " (2 Sam. 21:1).

P.   "On account of Saul" – because you did not properly bury him.

Q.   "And on account of the blood guilt on his house, because he put the Gibeonites to death."

R.   So David sent and called them and said to them, "What is between you and the house of Saul?"

S.   They said to him, "It is because he killed seven of us, two hewers of wood, two drawers of water, a scribe, a teacher, and a beadle."

T.   He said to them, "And what do you now want?"

U.   They said to him, "Let seven of his sons be given to us, so that we may hang them up before the Lord at Gibeon on the mountain of the Lord" (2 Sam. 21:6).

V.   He said to them, "Now what pleasure do you have if you kill them? Take silver and gold for yourselves."

W.   They said to him, "We don't want anything to do with silver and gold from Saul and his house."

X.   He said, "Perhaps some of them are ashamed before the others to accept such a ransom."

Y.   So he took each one of them and tried to win him over by himself, but none of them went along with him. This is in line with the following verse of Scripture: "It is not a matter of silver and gold between us and

Saul or his house" (1 Sam. 21:4). "Between *me* [individually]... " is written.

Z.   At that moment David said, "The Holy One, blessed be he, gave to Israel three good qualities: modesty, kindness, and caring.

AA.   "Modesty, as it is said, 'And Moses said to the people, "Do not fear; for God has come to prove you, and that the fear of him may be before your eyes, that you may not sin" ' (Exod. 20:20).

BB.   "Kindness, as it is written, '. . . so that he will show you mercy, and have compassion on you, and multiply you, as he swore to your fathers' (Deut. 13:17).

CC.   "Caring, as it is said, 'Know therefore that the Lord your God is God, the faithful God who keeps covenant and steadfast love....' (Deut. 7:9).

DD.   "Now these, by contrast, do not exhibit any one of these traits."

EE.   So he set them afar from the Israelites: "Now the Gibeonites were not of the people of Israel" (2 Sam. 21:2).

Y. San. 6:7

In the foregoing story we see that what marks the Israelite is the affective trait corresponding to God's loving kindness.

Another virtue assigned to the paradigmatic hero David is restraint in the face of provocation:

A.   Now there is not a generation in which there are no scoffers. What did the arrogant of that generation do? They went under David's windows and cried out, "When will the Temple be built? When shall we go up to the house of our Lord?"

B.   And he would say, "Even though they are trying to make me mad, may a curse come on me if I am not happy in my heart: 'I was glad when they said to me, let us go to the house of the Lord!' (Ps. 122:1)."

Y. Sheq. 2:5.VI

God exhibits the same virtue. Though the biblical record leaves no doubt that God may become angry and even lose his temper, the rabbinic reading of the same record imputes to God the trait of restraint that ordinary humans must exhibit:

E.   R. Samuel bar Nahman in the name of R. Jonathan: " 'Long in an act of patience' [in the singular] is not written here (at Joel 2:13), but rather 'Long in acts of patience' [in the plural], thus indicating that he is patient with the righteous, and he also is patient with the wicked."

F.   R. Aha, R. Tanhum b. R. Hiyya in the name of R. Yohanan: " 'Long in an act of patience' is not written here, but rather 'Long in acts of patience.' [It means] he is patient before he begins to collect [imposing punishment on the sinner], and even when he has begun to collect [the penalty for doing evil], he is patient when he collects."

G.   Said R. Haninah, "He who has said that the All Merciful is long-suffering – may his innards be long-suffering.

H.   "But may his life be extended so he may collect what is coming to him."

I.   Said R. Levi, "What is the meaning of 'slow to anger'? It means, 'Distant from wrath.'

J.   "It may be compared to a king who had two tough legions. The king said, 'If they dwell here with me in the metropolis, if the city folk anger me, they will put them down [with force]. But lo, I shall send them a long way away, so that if the city folk anger me, while I am yet summoning the legions, the people will appease me, and I shall accept their plea.'

K.   "Likewise the Holy One, blessed be he, said, 'Anger and wrath are angels of destruction. Lo, I shall send them a long way away, so that if Israel angers me, while I am summoning them to me, Israel will repent, and I shall accept their repentance.' "

L.   That is in line with the following verse of Scripture:

M.   "They come from a distant land, from the end of the heavens, the Lord and the weapons of his indignation, to destroy the whole earth" (Isa. 13:5).

N.   Said R. Isaac, "And not only so, but he locks the gate before them.

O.   "That is in line with what is written: 'The Lord has opened his armory and brought out the weapons of his wrath' (Jer. 50:25).

P.   "While he is yet opening the armory, while he is yet occupied, his mercy draws near."

Y. Ta. 2:1.XI

We see over and over that what the sages demand of human beings they impute to God.

Even though God is praised for restraint, the trait of divine wrath attracted the attention of Scripture's exegetes in the pages of the Yerushalmi:

D.   It was told: R. Zeira, R. Abba bar Kahana, and R. Levi were sitting in study. Now, R. Zeira was berating the homilists, referring to them as fabulists.

E.   Said R. Abba bar Kahana to him: "Why do you berate them? Pose them a problem [of scriptural interpretation] and they shall answer you!"

F.   [R. Zeira] replied: "What is the meaning of that which is written in Scripture as follows: 'Surely the wrath of man shall praise thee; the remainder of wrath shalt thou restrain' (Ps. 76:10)?"

G.   [R. Abba bar Kahana] anwered: "The phrase 'Surely the wrath of man shall praise thee' refers to this world; 'while the remainder of wrath shalt thou restrain' refers to the world to come. [Praise of God in this life forestalls his anger in the next]."

H.   [R. Zeira] retorted: "Or perhaps we might say that the phrase 'Surely the wrath of man shall praise thee' refers to the world to come, while 'the remainder of wrath shalt thou restrain' refers to this world [in which case, the point of Scripture is that God restrains his anger in this world for the sake of our praise in the next: cf. commentaries]!" [Abba bar Kahana, in Zeira's view, has offered no criterion by which we can distinguish between the homily at G and the implausible counter-homily at H.]

I.   Said R. Levi [by way of resolution], "When Your wrath shall be aroused upon the wicked [in this world], then shall the righteous perceive what You are doing on their behalf and then shall they praise Your Name [in both this world and the world to come]!"

J.   R. Zeira concluded: "However you might twist and turn this verse, we learn nothing from [your arbitrary explanations]!"

K.   [Whereupon, R. Zeira said to R. Jeremiah,] "Jeremiah, my son, go and sharpen your query regarding the pruning shear, for it is better than nothing at all!"

Y. Ter. 3:10.II (trans. Avery-Peck)

If we now review the affective traits that attracted the attention of the Yerushalmi's exegetes of Scripture, what do we find? God exhibits the trait of steadfast love and compassion. Israel is marked by the virtues of modesty, kindness, and caring. The proof texts make use of the same terms – compassion and steadfast love – that apply to God. Israelite heroes in the biblical record, like God, show restraint and conquer the impulse to wreak vengeance. They overcome and tame emotions (e.g., anger and wrath). They do not express these emotions but erect barriers against them. So does God. Biblical references to God's wrath naturally prove the opposite, namely, God's long suffering. Now the point is a very simple one. If we look back at the virtues recommended in tractate Abot, we find the same social virtues: restraint, good will, eagerness to please others and to accommodate their wishes, and avoidance of fits of temper, wrath, and other traits of the heart generally rejected as antisocial. Thus, we observe once more that the repertoire of approved affections remains constant.

Torah in the Flesh

The third of the three media by which the Torah reaches Israel, the authors
of the Talmuds profess, comprises the deeds and deliberations of sages.
Sages, as much as the written and the oral media of the Torah, convey
the norms of heaven. Their deeds undergo sustained analysis, as much
as do stories of Scripture and the rules of the Mishnah. Accordingly,
when we want to know where and how expressions of deep feeling make
a difference in concrete action, we turn to stories about what the sages
felt and how they expressed their emotions, as much as to the analysis
of Mishnaic principles, and of the amplification of biblical stories.

In setting forth the repertoire of conventional feelings, we have to keep
in mind an important distinction – that between reports of the emotional
basis of action, on the one side, and recommendations of norms for
affective virtue, on the other. The former tells us how storytellers thought
things were; the latter, how they wanted them to be. Examples of the
former sort of story – the introduction of routine allusions to strong
feeling – involve the patriarch's relationships with sages. The patriarch is
represented as vengeful, easy to anger on the basis of the slightest criticism, and subject to cajoling and calculated fawning:

A.   Yose Meoni interpreted the following verse in the synagogue in
Tiberias: " 'Hear this, O priests!' (Hos. 5:1): Why do you not labor in
the Torah? Have not the twenty-four priestly gifts been given to you?

B.   "They said to him, 'Nothing at all has been given to us.'

C.   " 'And give heed, O House of Israel!' (Hos. 5:1).

D.   " 'Why do you not give the priests the twenty-four gifts concerning which you have been commanded at Sinai?'

E.   "They said to him, 'The king takes them all.'

F.   " 'Hearken, O house of the king! For the judgment pertains to
you' (Hos. 5:1).

G.   "To you have I said, 'And this shall be the priests' due from the
people, from those offering a sacrifice . . . : they shall give to the priest
the shoulder, the two cheeks, and the stomach' (Deut. 18:3).

H.   "I am going to take my seat with them in court and to make a
decision concerning them and blot them [the kings] out of the world."

I.   R. Yudan the Patriarch heard [about this attack on the rulers] and
was angry.

J.   [Yose] feared and fled.

K.   R. Yohanan and R. Simeon b. Laqish went up to make peace with
[the patriarch].

L.   They said to him, "Rabbi, he is a great man."

M.   He said to them, "Is it possible that everything which I ask of him, he will give to me?"

N.   They said to him, "Yes." [So Yose was called back.]

O.   [The patriarch] said to [Yose], "What is the meaning of that which is written: 'For their mother has played the harlot' (Hos. 2:5)?

P.   "Is it possible that our matriarch, Sarah, was a whore?"

Q.   He said to him, "As is the daughter, so is her mother.

R.   "As is the mother, so is the daughter.

S.   "As is the generation, so is the patriarch.

T.   "As is the patriarch, so is the generation.

U.   "As is the altar, so are its priests."

V.   (Kahana said likewise, "As is the garden, so is the gardener.")

W.   He said to them, "Is it not enough for him that he dishonors me one time not in my presence, but also in my presence he does so these three times [Q–T]!"

X.   He said to him, "What is the meaning of that which is written, 'Behold, everyone who uses proverbs will use this proverb about you, "Like mother, like daughter" ' (Ezek. 16:44)?

Y.   "Now was our matriarch, Leah, a whore?

Z.   "As it is written, 'And Dinah went out' (Gen. 34:1) [like a whore, thus reflecting on her mother]."

AA.   He said to him, "It is in accord with that which is written, 'And Leah went out to meet him' (Gen. 30:16).

BB.   "They compared one going out to the other [and Leah went out to meet her husband, and Dinah learned from this that it was all right to go out, so she went out to meet the daughters of the land, but got raped]." [This was an acceptable reply to Yudan.]

Y. San 2:6.V

The point of the story is served, on the surface quite tangentially, by reference to the outrage of the patriarch, contrasted to the calm and courageous response of the sage. The sage controls his emotions, whether anger or fear, and so prevails. The butt of the story in this case, the exilarch, does not control his emotions and also does not gain from his expression of those emotions. Both stories present the same contrast. What is underlined throughout are the familiar virtues, of restraint and self-control, repeatedly recommended in tractate Abot as the proper traits of the sage.

Sages, too, could express envy and outrage at a slight. But they had rules by which to suppress envy and assuage anger. They could appeal to a common law that would apply to all, to reason not bound to the exigencies of power and of politics:

A.   R. Yohanan was leaning on R. Jacob bar Iddi, and R. Eleazar [a Babylonian] saw him and avoided him. [Yohanan] said, "Lo, now there are two things that that Babylonian has done to me! One is that he didn't even bother to greet me, and the other is that he didn't cite a tradition of mine in my name."

B.   [Jacob] said to him, "That is the custom over there, that the lesser party does not greet the more important authority. For they carry out the following verse of Scripture: 'The young men saw me and withdrew, and the aged rose and stood' " (Job 29:8).

C.   As they were going along, they saw a certain schoolhouse.

D.   [Jacob] said to him, "Here is where R. Meir used to go into session and expound the law. And he stated traditions in the name of R. Ishmael, but he did not state traditions in the name of R. Aqiba."

E.   [Yohanan] said to him, "Everybody knows that R. Meir was the disciple of R. Aqiba [so he did not have to cite him]."

F.   [Jacob] said to him, "Everybody knows that R. Eleazar is the disciple of R. Yohanan."

G.   As they were going along, [they passed by a procession in which an idol was carried, and Jacob asked Yohanan,] "What is the law as to passing a procession in which an idol is being carried?"

H.   He said to him, "And do you pay respect to the idol? Go before it and blind its eyes."

I.   [Jacob] said to him, "Well did R. Eleazar do to you, for he did not pass by you [since that would have required an inappropriate gesture]."

J.   [Yohanan] said to him, "Jacob bar Iddi, you know very well how to make peace [between quarreling people]."

K.   R. Yohanan wanted traditions to be stated in his name, for David too prayed for mercy [for the same purpose], saying, "Let me dwell in thy tent for ever! Oh, to be safe under the shelter of thy wings!" (Ps. 61:4).

Y. M.Q. 3:7.XIX

This story, does not, strictly speaking, deal with emotions, but it rests on two blatant ones: resentment and hurt. Jacob's success in explaining matters is exemplary. The disciple assists the sage in overcoming quite natural emotions. These emotions are set aside in favor of approved feelings, those defined by the knowledge of the Torah, such as restraint, avoidance of contention, and attaining good relationships among people. The negative, natural emotions of resentment and hurt are overcome by the positive, supernatural ones of restraint and giving way to others.

The norms for an appropriate affective life demanded, above all, humility and the subjugation of pride:

J.   When R. Samuel bar R. Isaac died, cedars of the land of Israel were uprooted.

K.   They said that [this was to take note of the fact that] he would take a branch [of a cedar] and [dance, so] praising a bride [at her wedding, and thereby giving happiness to the bride].

L.   The rabbis would ridicule them [for lowering himself by doing so]. Said to them R. Zeira, "Leave him be. Does the old man not know what he is doing?"

M.   When he died, a flame came forth from heaven and intervened between his bier and the congregation. For three hours there were voices and thunderings in the world: "Come and see what a sprig of cedar has done for this old man!"

Y. A.Z. 3:1.II

Humility and submissiveness, the recommended virtues, in concrete ways express those affections of restraint and submission to the will of others that we noted in the earlier stories. In the present case the sage surrendered the dignity generally owing to a person of his status. He danced before the bride at a wedding. The point cannot be missed, since L makes it explicit. Thus, the reward for one who surrenders the status owing to him in the name of humility in exchange for the happiness of a young girl derives from heaven itself.

In the story that follows, the same kind of humility in the face of domestic considerations is not only imputed to Meir but also explained by him as an act of imitating God:

A.   R. Zabedeh, son-in-law of R. Levi, would tell the following story.

B.   R. Meir would teach a lesson in the synagogue of Mammata every Sabbath night. There was a woman who would come regularly to hear him. One time the lesson lasted a longer time than usual.

C.   She went home and found that the light had gone out. Her husband said to her, "Where have you been?"

D.   She replied to him, "I was listening to the lesson."

E.   He said to her, "May God do such-and-so and even more, if this woman enters my house before she goes and spits in the face of that sage who gave the lesson."

F.   R. Meir perceived with the help of the Holy Spirit [what had happened], and he pretended to have a pain in his eye.

G.   He said, "Any woman who knows how to recite a charm over an eye – let her come and heal mine."

H.   The woman's neighbors said to her, "Lo, your time to go back home has come. Pretend to be a charmer and go and spit in R. Meir's eye."

I.   She came to him. He said to her, "Do you know how to heal a sore eye through making a charm?"

J.   She became frightened and said to him, "No."

K.   He said to her, "Do they not spit into it seven times, and it is good for it?"

L.   After she had spit in his eye, he said to her, "Go and tell your husband that you did it one time."

M.   She said to him, "And lo, I spit seven times?"

N.   R. Meir's disciples said to him, "Rabbi, in such a way do they disgracefully treat the Torah [which is yours]? If you had told us about the incident with the husband, would we not have brought him and flogged him at the stock, until he was reconciled with his wife?"

O.   He said to them, "And should the honor owing to Meir be tantamount to the honor owing to Meir's creator?

P.   "Now if the Holy Name, which is written in a state of sanctification, the Scripture has said is to be blotted out with water so as to bring peace between a man and his wife, should not the honor owing to Meir be dealt with in the same way?"

Y. Sot. 1:4.II

As we see, the persistent theme of humility and self-abnegation comes to expression in diverse contexts.

We should not suppose that, among the sages themselves, these virtues play no role. Quite the contrary, in what follows a sage speculates that the reason he had lived as long as he had was that he had surrendered the honor owing to him, handing it over to someone else:

M.   After [Rabbi] died, his son [Gamaliel] wanted to appoint [Haninah] sage, but Haninah did not accept the appointment. He said to him, "I shall accept appointment only after you have appointed R. Epes, the Southerner, before me."

N.   Now there was a certain elder there, who said, "If Haninah is appointed before me, then I shall be second, and if R. Epes, the Southerner, is appointed before me, then I shall be second."

O.   So R. Hanina agreed to be appointed third in line.

P.   Said R. Hanina, "I have had the merit of living a long life. I do not know whether it was because of that incident, or because, when I would come up from Tiberias to Sepphoris, I would take the long way about to go and greet R. Simeon b. Halputa in Ein Tinah."

Y. Ta. 4:2.VIII

The opposite of humility is the pursuit of glory for oneself. Stories make it clear that sages must avoid the emotions that produce such behavior:

GG.   One of the members of the household of R. Pazzi did the members of the patriarchate seek to [engage in] marriage [into the family of the patriarchate], but he did not wish [to enter into marriage]. He said, "They should not so degrade me [by such a marriage proposal]."

HH.   When he lay dying, he said, "Clear out the house [of objects that will receive] corpse uncleanness [when I die], and prepare a throne for Jehoshaphat, king of Judah."

II.   They said, "Let this one come, who ran after glory, in the aftermath of that one, who fled from glory."

Y. A.Z. 3:1.II

The preceding story presents no surprises, for it simply says, in a negative way, what the composite of stories about sages' deeds expresses in positive and concrete terms. But it is not sufficient to deal with inappropriate and appropriate feelings. The sages' tales recorded how to avoid these inappropriate feelings. They pointed specifically to what causes them, which is jealousy or envy of others:

D.   The tale is told that R. Aqiba made for his wife a golden tiara, and the wife of Rabban Gamaliel was jealous of her.

E.   He said to her, "If you had done what she did, I would have been glad to make one for you. She sold her braids of hair and gave him the proceeds, so that he might labor in the light [of Torah]."

Y. Shab. 6:1.VIII

The point is that honor and glory come in response to one's concrete achievements, not merely in response to what one demands or requests. The reason, in the present case, that one woman enjoys a piece of jewelry the other does not have is that the former earned it. Hence, there is no reason to feel jealousy or envy. If one wants what the other has, let concrete achievement – in this context, in the study of the Torah and in virtue – prove that that person merits the sign of honor. Yet virtue, including knowledge of the Torah, means that one does not aspire to honor at all. One who pursues glory cannot have it. Accordingly, once again we find ourselves within the same rather limited set of virtues: restraint, concern for the feelings of others, good will toward others, humility, and the like.

Unchanging Virtue

The upshot of our survey requires little spelling out. We observe two simple facts. First, we discern slight evidence of growth, development, and change. Second, a singular, limited program of approved and disapproved affections defined the range of emotions sages expected people to feel. The Mishnah's law took up two paired opposites: arrogance and humility, hate and love. The Yerushalmi's exegetes of the Mishnah developed rules concerning those emotions. So far as I can see, these exegetes did not contribute to the repertoire a single emotion not formerly recognized and evaluated. Scripture presented a broad and nuanced portrait of human and divine feelings, representing God and the individual as sharing these feelings. The exegetes of Scripture in the Yerushalmi persisted in granting recognition to only a few of these emotions and, more striking still, treated unacceptable affections as though they were something other than what Scripture portrays them to be. Accordingly, in this as in other ways, the scriptural record contributes mere examples to the sages' philosophical program. And it goes without saying that the stories about the sages stress the same affective virtues as the stories about God. Thus, in all, the unfolding canon of Judaism demanded that Israel tame its heart and discipline its feelings, not only keeping all affections under control but also reshaping the heart to conform to a single affective model, one of modest proportions. In the sequence of documents, the model persisted, fully exposed at the outset, intact and unimpaired in the fullness of the Yerushalmi's portrait of it.

CHAPTER VII

The Conclusion of the Exegetical Tradition of the Law

The Bavli

The Bavli

The Bavli outlines the outer boundaries of the theological foundations of virtue. In God's image, after God's likeness, when the human heart conforms to the heart of God, then humanity attains virtue. The moral consubstantiality of God's heart and humanity's forms the final stage in the unfolding of the uniform doctrine under discussion here. Though much of the definition of the virtue of attitude and emotion, demeanor and intentionality would not have surprised the great philosophers of the nations of the world, the conception that, in moderation, congeniality, and humility, humanity is like God would not have been self-evident. Still, even at this point we do not claim that the sages had transcended the limits of their philosophical setting. Much that they said, in both the Land of Israel and Babylonia, drew on a common heritage of values, the beliefs of thinkers. Therefore, only the context of their statements (which awaits discussion in Chapter IX) will indicate the distinctive and therefore definitive context in which commonplaces became uncommon truths for Israel.

The Bavli (also known as the Babylonian Talmud or the Talmud of Babylonia) reached closure some time after about A.D. 600, before the Moslem conquest of Babylonia, in ca. 640, among the other Western satrapies of Iran. The date of closure, ca. 600, simply tells us that the Bavli marks the end of the formation of the canon of Judaism in late antiquity. The next major works would not begin to make their appearance until several centuries later and would reflect the remarkable changes wrought by Islamic rule.

The Bavli not only comes at the chronological end but also marks the conclusion of the prior canon, for its redactors utilized both of the then-available modes of organizing materials. One of these was to draw to-

98

gether units of discourse into exegetical exercises on the Mishnah's and Tosefta's statements, paragraph by paragraph, or into thematic and analytical exercises of principles of law connected to those statements. The legal–exegetical work of the Tosefta and of the Yerushalmi had rested on the principles of organization and exposition supplied by the Mishnah and served, to begin with, as Mishnah commentaries.

The other mode of redaction derived from the same exegetical procedures, that is, the explanation of words or phrases and the exposition of thematic principles provoked by the themes of words or phrases. But this method of organization focused not on tractates of the Mishnah but on books of the Hebrew scriptures. Sequences of verses, for example, running parallel to sequences of Mishnah sentences serve as the basis for the organization of sizable compositions comprising numerous units of discourse in sequence. Though the framers of the Yerushalmi, in my sample of three tractates (Sukkah, Sotah, Sanhedrin), rarely utilized passages of Scripture for the aggregation of sizable composites of units of discourse, those of the Bavli did so quite commonly. My very rough estimate is that less than 10 percent of the Yerushalmi's and more than 40 percent of the Bavli's units of discourse find their order and proportion in passages of Scripture rather than in passages of the Mishnah.

Joining the two components of the "one whole Torah of Moses, our rabbi," the Mishnah and Scripture, the oral and the written Torahs, in redactional terms signified a much more substantial achievement. In substantive terms the framers of the Bavli drew together into their vast composition an enormous sample of materials ordinarily kept apart. That is, they put legal and scriptural–theological exegeses and expositions in one place. Why was this new? To state matters simply, available collections of exegeses of Scripture tended to intersect with other such collections (e.g., Genesis Rabbah, Leviticus Rabbah, Pesiqta deR. Kahana), just as collections of exegeses of the Mishnah did (e.g., the Tosefta and the Yerushalmi). But both sorts of compositions intersect fully and richly with the Bavli. That document, as I said, draws nearly as lavishly on Scripture and its themes as it does on the Mishnah and its topics.

The Bavli's points of innovation emerge in particular in its repertoire of comments on Scripture and on associated theological issues. We briefly survey the familiar ground of the place of emotions in the exposition of the law, compensating with a more generous sample of the equivalent materials in the Bavli's units of discourse devoted to scriptural and theological matters. We shall see that the third sort of Torah, that deriving from the deeds of living sages, makes a contributions as well.

In what follows, any passages that I have not translated are taken from the Soncino translation of the Talmud, which I cite as "Soncino" with a page reference.

Supplementing the Mishnah's Rules

A brief survey of how the framers of the Bavli explained passages of the Mishnah and Tosefta in which emotions play a role yields exactly those main lines of explication followed by the entire corpus of materials. Essentially, the legal materials of the Bavli augmented what had already been said. They rarely added anything new. Emotions that were relevant to a given rule came under explanation or, mainly, further instantiation. Emotions that did not appear earlier did not now come to the surface. In the former category is an explanation of why the high priest weeps when he begins his vigil on the eve of the Day of Atonement:

He turned aside and wept and they turned aside and wept. He turned aside and wept because they suspected him of being a Sadducee, and they turned aside and wept, for R. Joshua B. Levi said: Whosoever suspects good folks will suffer [for it] on his own body. Why was all this [solemn adjuration] necessary? Lest he arrange the incense outside and thus bring it in, in the manner of the Sadduces:

B. Yoma 19b (Soncino, pp. 83–4)

The point is that the high priest was guarded lest he be suspected of adhering to improper rites. Neither the authors of the Mishnah nor the commentators of the Tosefta invoked this historical explanation, but as we have seen, they gave no better one.

An example of the latter – the recurrence of familiar and conventional emotions – shows us the representation of conventional emotions, (e.g., anger and indignation) in the context of legal analysis:

A.   [As to the dispute about what blessing to be said for boiled vegetables] May one propose that there is a disagreement among Tannaite authorities on the same matter?

B.   For there were two disciples in session before Bar Qappara. They brought him cabbage, Damascene plums, and poultry.

C.   Bar Qappara gave the honor to one of the disciples to say the blessing. He went and said the blessing appropriate to poultry.

D.   His fellow ridiculed him.

E.   Bar Qappara grew angry, explaining, "It is not against who said the blessing that I am angry, but against the one who made fun. If your fellow is like someone who has never in his life had a taste of meat [and so regards it as preferable and chooses that for the blessing], what right have you to ridicule him?"

F.   Then he retracted and said, "I am not angry at the one who made fun but at the one who said the blessing."

G.   And he said, "If there is no knowledge here, is there no claim to the dignity of age [since you did not pay me the courtesy of *asking* me what to do]?"

H.   A Tannaite authority [stated]: And neither one of them lived out the year.

B. Ber. 39a

In another instance (B. Nid. 23a) one authority tries, by asking ridiculous questions, to make another authority laugh. He does not succeed.

When, therefore, we wish to follow the unfolding of the conventions of the virtuous heart within the Bavli, we do not look for data in the legal type of discourse that dominates the document. The authors of discourse on the law devoted their attention to abstract and philosophical or analytical inquiry. Only occasionally did they think it important to make reference to the context in which the inquiry was made. The literary requirements of this form of discourse, not the traits of heart and intellect of its framers, account for the lack of evidence on the virtues of the heart.

The Dimension of Scripture

By contrast, the authors of the Bavli responded with considerable detail on the affective life to the challenge of scriptural exegesis and theological discourse. This discourse was nearly always conducted in the same context of study of the scriptural record. As we noted earlier, the character of the written Torah was such as to provoke deep throught on the question at hand. The characters of Scripture, both the heroes and God alike, emerge in a narrative rich in detail about how people felt, on the one side, and the meaning and effects of feelings, on the other. The Bavli's framers drew units of discourse that systematically recorded emotion and its consequence, value, and meaning. Still more commonly, our survey shows, they episodically noted the occurrence of the same theme. But through all, we note remarkably conventional categories. The emotions are familiar, the things said about them standard and entirely ordinary. Thus, the setting of exegesis and exposition of Scripture provides yet another opportunity for those writing about the affections to say what they had said everywhere else.

The repertoire of conventional emotions provides a cogent account of how people were admonished, by the sages, to feel. The most salient of these qualities were accommodation, congeniality, and humility. The virtues of the heart, if broadly characteristic of the community, would yield a serene and pleasant collective life. True, individuals then would have to tame their inclinations toward self-expression, particularly as self-expression impinged on the community. For example, individuals would not be free to lose their temper but would have to suppress their private feelings for the sake of the public good. Individuals would want to subordinate their wishes to the will of the community. Self-abnegation, humility, and restraint would produce that socially well-constructed personality repeatedly praised in the documents we have examined.

The same traits, translated into the common life, yield as their counterpart a politics of passivity and restraint. Personal emotions involving acceptance yield a public persona characteristic of a subordinated community, able to endure insult and humiliation without making vigorous and, for the weak, dangerous response. The virtues of the heart therefore prove remarkably congruent, as we have seen, with the political context of the Israelite community to which sages recommended the virtues of the weak and humble. But, of course, that observation derives from our perspective, not from that of sages. They found the same virtues in Scripture, on the one side, and in the encounter with the compassionate and suffering God, on the other.

We shall survey at some length passages from the Bavli, because they convey in rich detail the main point of the system of virtue as a whole. We find ourselves reviewing in abundant detail those very principles of attitude and right demeanor, namely, self-denial, restraint, and moderation, that we found stated in abstract terms in tractate Abot. In many ways, therefore, the large sample of texts that follows states in concrete terms precisely the point at which, in the aftermath of the Mishnah, the system as a whole began. All that the Bavli contributes is the fleshing out of the notion of humanity's imitation of God's heart.

In all things, God's example, as Scripture portrays it, is invoked. The basic principle of the affective life, the stress on the communal virtues of mutual acceptance and restraint of the individual by the demands of public opinion, guided God's choice of Israel's leaders:

A.   Said R. Isaac, "People do not appoint a leader over the community unless they have consulted the community.

B.   "For it is said, 'See, the Lord has called by name Bezalel, son of Uri' (Exod. 5:30).

C.   "Said the Holy One, blessed be he, to Moses, 'Moses, is Bezalel acceptable to you?'

D.   "He said to him, 'Lord of the Universe, if he is acceptable to you, how much more so to me!'

E.   "He said to him, 'Nonetheless, go and report the matter to them.'

F.   "He went and reported the matter to Israel, 'Is Bezalel acceptable to you?'

G.   "They said to him, 'If to the Holy One, blessed be he, and to you, he is acceptable, how much the more so to us!' "

B. Ber. 55a

What is important in this transaction is the mutual agreement. God consults Israel. Israel accepts God's choice.

The principal expression of restraint is forbearance, and the primary mode of imposition on others takes the form of aggressive hatred. As to the former, one should follow the model of Moses in seeking to resolve disputes:

A.   "And Moses rose up and went to Dathan and Abiram" (Num. 16:25):

B.   Said R. Simeon b. Laqish, "On the basis of this verse we learn that one should not hold onto a quarrel [but should be eager to end it, in the model of Moses, who modestly went out to the other side to seek a resolution]."

C.   For Rab said, "Whoever holds onto a quarrel [and does not seek to end it] violates a negative commandment, for it is said, 'And let him not be as Korah and as his company' (Num. 17:5)."

D.   R. Ashi said, "He is worthy of being smitten with saraat.

E.   "Here it is written, 'As the Lord said to him by the hand of Moses' (Num. 17:5), and elsewhere it is written, 'And the Lord said to him, "Put your hand into your bosom" [and when he took it out, behold, his hand was leprous as snow' (Exod. 4:6)."

B. San. 110a

In contrast to the example of Moses' restraint and conciliatory spirit, we confront the paired affections temper and hatred. Those who lose their temper are "exposed to all the torments of Gehenna" (B. Ned. 22a). The hot-tempered have no life (B. Pes. 113b).

The now-familiar claim that the second Temple was destroyed because of causeless hatred recurs:

Why was the first Sanctuary destroyed? Because of three [evil] things which prevailed there: idolatry, immorality, bloodshed. . . . But why was the second Sanctuary destroyed seeing that in its time they were occupying themselves with Torah [observance of] precepts, and the practice of charity? Because therein prevailed hatred without cause. That teaches you that groundless hatred is considered as of even gravity with the three sins of idolatry, immorality, and bloodshed together. And [during the time of] the first Sanctuary did not groundless hatred prevail? Surely it is written: "They are thrust down to the sword with my people; smite therefore upon my thigh," and R. Eleazar said: This refers to people who eat and drink together and then thrust each other through with the daggers of their tongue! That [passage] speaks of the princes in Israel, for it is written, "Cry and wail, son of man; for it is upon my people" (Ezek. 21:17), etc. [The text reads] "Cry and wail, son of man." One might have assumed [it is upon] all [Israel], therefore it goes on. "Upon all the princes of Israel."

B. Yoma 9b (Soncino, pp. 39–40)

It was taught, R. Nehemiah said: As a punishment for causeless hate strife multiplies in a man's house, his wife miscarries, and his sons and daughters die young.

B. Shab. 32b (Soncino, p. 149)

These sayings show that the affective sin of hatred applies to both the national and the individual life, with the same destructive consequence.

Hatred comes from arrogance, which permits the nation and the individual to place private feelings over public good. The life of the nation depends on communal harmony. The life of the home requires domestic tranquility. Both collapse before unrestrained self-expression, which derives from arrogance. Those who do not abnegate their will before the requirements of the public good mark themselves as arrogant. To be sure, there is a distinction between impudence (hutzbah) and arrogance, which we find in the following:

A.   Said R. Nahman, "Hutzbah [impudence], even against heaven, serves some good. To begin with, it is written, 'You shall not go with them' (Num. 22:12), and then it is said, 'Rise up and go with them' (Num. 22:20)."

B.   Said R. Sheshet, "Hutzbah is dominion without a crown. For it is written, 'And I am this day weak, though anointed king, and these men, the sons of Zeruiah, be too hard for me' (2 Sam. 3:39) [Freedman, p. 717, n. 1: Thus their boldness and impudence outweighed sovereignty]."

B. San. 105a

Arrogance stands forth as the single cause of public catastrophe and private calamity alike. A repertoire of sayings and stories that make the point follows:

D.   R. Eleazar said, "Whoever is arrogant – his dust will not be stirred up [in the resurrection of the dead].

E.   "For it is said, 'Awake and sing, you that dwell in the dust' (Isa. 26:19).

F.   "It is stated not 'you who lie in the dust' but 'you who dwell in the dust,' meaning, one who has become a neighbor to the dust [by constant humility] even in his lifetime."

G.   And R. Eleazar said, "For whoever is arrogant the Presence of God laments,

H.   "as it is said, 'But the haughty he knows from afar' (Ps. 138:6)."

A.   R. Avira expounded, and some say it was R. Eleazar, "Come and take note of the fact that not like the trait of the Holy One, blessed be he, is the trait of flesh and blood.

B.   "The trait of flesh and blood is that those who are high take note of those who are high, but the one who is high does not take note of the one who is low.

C.   "But the trait of the Holy One, blessed be he, is not that way. He is high, but he takes note of the low,

D.   "as it is said, 'For though the Lord is high, yet he takes note of the low' (Ps. 138:6)."

A.   Said R. Hisda, and some say it was Mar Uqba, "Concerning whoever is arrogant said the Holy One, blessed be he, 'he and I cannot live in the same world,'

B.   "as it is said, 'Whoever slanders his neighbor in secret – him will I destroy; him who has a haughty look and a proud heart I will not endure' (Ps. 101:5).

C.   "Do not read, 'him [I cannot endure]' but 'with [I cannot endure].' "

D.   There are those who apply the foregoing teaching to those who slander, as it is said, "Whoever slanders his neighbor in secret – him will I destroy" (Ps. 101:5).

A.   Said R. Alexandri, "Whoever is arrogant – even the slightest breeze shakes him,

B.   "as it is said, 'But the wicked are like the troubled sea' (Isa. 57:20).

C.   "Now if the sea, which is so vast [lit.: which has so many quarter-logs (of water)] – the slightest breeze shakes it, a man, who is not so vast – all the more so [that the slightest breeze would shake him]."

A.   Said Hezekiah, "The prayer of a person is heard only if he makes his heart as soft as flesh,

B.   "as it is said, 'And it shall come to pass, that from one new moon to the next, all flesh shall come to worship' (Isa. 66:23)."

C. Said R. Zira, "In regard to flesh, it is written, 'And it is healed' (Lev. 13:18). In regard to man, it is not written, 'And he is healed.' "

A. Said R. Yohanan, "The letters for the word Adam stand for dust, blood, and gall.
B. "The letters for the word for flesh stand for shame, stench, and worm."
C. Some say, "Sheol," for [Cohen:] its initial letter corresponds [Cohen, p. 20, n. 12: "The initial of the word for 'stench' is *samek*, whereas the second letter in *basar* is similar in form to that of 'Sheol.' "]

A. Said R. Ashi, "Whoever is arrogant in the end will be diminished,
B. "as it is said, 'For a rising and for a scab' (Lev. 14:56), and rising refers only to elevation, as it is said 'Upon all the high mountains and upon all the hills that are lifted up' (Isa. 2:14).
C. "Scab means only 'attachment,' as it is said, 'Attach me, I ask you, to one of the priests' offices, so that I may eat a piece of bread' (1 Sam. 2:36)."

A. Said R. Joshua b. Levi, "Come and take note of how great are the humble in the sight of the Holy One, blessed be he.
B. "For when the sanctuary stood, a person would bring a burnt offering, gaining thereby the reward for bringing a burnt offering, or a meal offering, and gaining the reward for a meal offering.
C. "But a person who is genuinely humble does Scripture treat as if he had made offering of *all* the sacrifices,
D. "as it is said, 'The sacrifices [plural] of God are a broken spirit' (Ps. 51:19).
E. "And not only so, but his prayer is not rejected, as it is said, 'A broken and contrite heart, O God, you will not despise' (Ps. 51:19)."
F. And R. Joshua b. Levi said, "Whoever properly sets his ways in this world will have the merit of witnessing the salvation of the Holy One, blessed be he,
G. "as it is said, 'To him who orders his way I will show the salvation of God' (Ps. 50:23).
H. "Do not read 'orders' but 'properly sets' [his] way." [Cohen, p. 21, n. 6: "He calculates the loss incurred in fulfilling a precept against the reward it will bring him."]

B. Sot. 5a–b

N. Said Rab, "For four reasons is the property of householders confiscated for taxes:

O. "because of those who hold back the wages of a hired hand,

P. "because of those who oppress a hired hand,

Q. "because of those who remove the yoke from their shoulders and put it on their fellow,

R. "and because of arrogance.

S. "But arrogance outweighs all the others.

T. "And with reference to humble people, it is written, 'But the humble shall inherit the earth and delight themselves in the abundance of peace' (Ps. 37:11)."

B. Suk. 29b

We note that God's virtues define what is asked of humanity, and God is humble and favors humility. Not surprisingly, other examples of the paradigms of Israel's life, Moses and David, provide further expression of the same viewpoint:

A. "A prayer of David: Keep my soul, for I am pious" (Ps. 86:1–2).

B. Levi and R. Isaac.

C. One of them said, "This is what David said before the Holy One, blessed be he, 'Lord of the world, am I not pious? For all kings, east and west, sleep to the third hour, but as for me: "At midnight, I rise to give thanks to you' (Ps. 119:62)."

D. The other said, "This is what David said before the Holy One, blessed be he, 'Lord of the world, am I not pious? For all kings, east and west, sit in all their glory with their retinues, but as for me, my hands are sloppy with menstrual blood and the blood of the fetus and placenta, which I examine so as to declare a woman clean for sexual relations with her husband.

E. "And not only so, but, further, in whatever I do, I take counsel with Mephibosheth, my master, and I say to him, 'Rabbi Mephibosheth, did I do right in the judgment I gave? Did I do right in acquitting? Did I do right in awarding an advantage? Did I do right in declaring something clean? Did I do right in declaring something unclean?' and in no way have I been ashamed [to depend on his judgment]."

F. Said R. Joshua, son of R. Idi, "What verse of Scripture supports that view of David? 'And I recite your testimonies before kings and am not ashamed' (Ps. 119:46)."

B. Ber. 4a

Arrogance within Israel's national life accounts for the arrogance of those perceived as Israel's oppressors:

A.   Said Ulla, "Jerusalem will be redeemed only through righteous-ness, as it is written, 'Zion shall be redeemed with judgment and her converts with righteousness' (Isa. 1:27)."

B.   Said R. Pappa, "If the arrogant end [in Israel], the Magi will end [in Iran]; if the judges end [in Israel], the rulers of thousands will come to an end [in Iran].

C.   "If the arrogant end [in Israel], the magi will end [in Iran], as it is written, 'And I will purely purge away your haughty ones and take away all your sin' (Isa. 1:25).

D.   "If judges end [in Israel], the rulers of thousands will come to an end [in Iran], as it is written, 'The Lord has taken away your judgments, he has cast out your enemy' (Zeph. 3:15)."

B. San. 98a

The affective life of Israel, given these definitions, will come to ap-propriate expression at this time not in rejoicing but in mourning, just as, in the age to come when matters are reversed, Israel will properly rejoice and mourn no more. The occasion for mourning in the encom-passing system will be both national and private. Israel weeps for the destroyed Temple, just as the individual mourns for the loss of a loved one:

A.   "She weeps, yes, she weeps in the night" (Lam. 1:2):

B.   Why these two acts of weeping?

C.   Said Rabbah said R. Yohanan, "One is for the first Temple and the other is for the second Temple."

D.   "At night":

E.   On account of things done in the night, as it is said, "And all the congregation lifted up their voice and cried, and the people wept that night [at the spies' false report]" (Num. 14:1).

F.   Said Rabbah said R. Yohanan, "That was the ninth of Ab. Said the Holy One, blessed be he, to Israel, 'You have wept tears for nothing. I now shall set up for you weeping for generations to come.' "

G.   Another interpretation of "At night":

H.   Whoever cries at night will find that his voice is heard.

I.   Another interpretation of "At night":

J.   Whoever cries at night finds that the stars and planets will cry with him.

K.   Another interpretation of "At night":

L.   Whoever cries at night finds that whoever hears his voice will cry along with him.

M.   That was the case of a woman in the neighborhood of Rabban Gameliel, whose child died. She was weeping by night on account of the child. Rabban Gamaliel heard her voice and cried with her, until his eyelashes fell out. The next day, his disciples recognized what had happened and removed the woman from his neighborhood.

B. San. 104b

Rejoicing is the appropriate emotion when the wicked fall, both in this age and in the age to come:

A. "Therefore man was created alone" [M. San. 4:5]:

B. "And there went out a song throughout the host" (1 Kings. 22:36) [at Ahab's death at Ramoth in Gilead].

C. Said R. Aha b. Hanina, " 'When the wicked perish, there is song' (Prov. 11:10).

D. "When Ahab b. Omri perished, there was a song."

E. But does the Holy One, blessed be he, rejoice at the downfall of the wicked?

F. Is it not written, "That they should praise as they went out before the army and say, 'Give thanks to the Lord, for his mercy endures forever' (2 Chron. 20:21)?"

G. And said R. Jonathan, "On what account are the words in this psalm of praise omitted, 'Because he is good'? Because the Holy One, blessed be he, does not rejoice at the downfall of the wicked."

H. For R. Samuel bar Nahman said R. Jonathan said, "What is the meaning of the verse of Scripture 'And one did not come near the other all night' (Exod. 14:20)?

I. "At that time, the ministering angels want to recite a song [of rejoicing] before the Holy One, blessed be he.

J. "Said to them the Holy One, blessed be he, 'The works of my hands are perishing in the sea, and do you want to sing a song before me?' "

K. Said R. Yose bar Hanina, "He does not rejoice, but others do rejoice. Note that it is written, '[And it shall come to pass, as the Lord rejoiced over you to do good, so the Lord] will *cause* rejoicing over you by destroying you' (Deut. 28:63) – and not 'so will the Lord [himself] rejoice.' "

B. San. 39b

The compassion of God even for Israel's enemies shows the sages' highest ideal. Israel may rejoice at their victory. God, "the man of war" of Exod. 15:2, mourns the slain enemy. More striking, God expresses love in this world by inflicting suffering. Those who suffer may know that God loves them in particular:

A.   Said Raba, and some say, R. Hisda, "If a person sees that sufferings afflict him, let him examine his deeds.

B.   "For it is said, 'Let us search and try our ways and return to the Lord' (Lam. 3:40).

C.   "If he examined his ways and found no cause [for his suffering], let him blame the matter on his wasting [time better spent in studying] the Torah.

D.   "For it is said, 'Happy is the man whom you chastise, O Lord, and teach out of your Torah' (Ps. 94:12).

E.   "If he blamed it on something and found [after correcting the fault] that that had not, in fact, been the cause at all, he may be sure that he suffers the afflications that come from God's love.

F.   "For it is said, 'For the one whom the Lord loves he corrects' (Prov. 3:12)."

G.   Said Raba said R. Sehorah said R. Huna, "Whomever the Holy One, blessed be he, prefers, he crushes with suffering.

H.   "For it is said, 'The Lord was pleased with him, hence he crushed him with disease' (Isa. 53:10).

I.   "Is it possible that even if the victim did not accept the suffering with love, the same is so?

J.   "Scripture states, 'To see if his victim would offer itself in restitution' (Isa. 53:10).

K.   "Just as the offering must be offered with the knowledge and consent [of the sacrifier], so sufferings must be accepted with knowledge and consent.

L.   "If one accepted them in that way, what is his reward?

M.   " 'He will see his seed, prolong his days' (Isa. 53:10).

N.   "Not only so, but his learning will remain with him, as it is said, 'The purpose of the Lord will prosper in his hand' (Isa. 53:10)."

A.   R. Jacob bar Idi and R. Aha bar Hanina differed. One of them said, "What are sufferings brought on by God's love? They are any form of suffering that does not involve one's having to give up studying Torah.

B.   "For it is said, 'Happy is the man whom you chasten, O Lord, and yet teach out of your Torah' (Ps. 94:12)."

C.   The other said, "What are sufferings brought on by God's love? They are any form of suffering that does not involve having to give up praying.

D.   "For it is said, 'Blessed be God, who has not turned away my prayer nor his mercy from me' (Ps. 66:20)."

E.   Said to them R. Abba, son of R. Hiyya bar Abba, "This is what R. Hiyya bar Abba said R. Yohanan said, 'Both constitute forms of suffering brought on by God's love.'

F.   "For it is said, 'For him whom the Lord loves he corrects' (Prov. 3:12).

G.   "What is the sense of the Scripture's statement 'And you teach him out of your Torah'? Do not read it as 'You teach him,' but 'You teach us.'

H.   "This matter you teach us out of your law, namely, the argument [concerning the meaning of the suffering brought on by God's love] a fortiori resting on the traits of the tooth and the eye:

I.   "Now if, on account of an injury done to the slave's tooth or eye, which are only one of a person's limbs, a slave goes forth to freedom, sufferings, which drain away the whole of a person's body, how much the more so [should a person find true freedom on their account]."

J.   This furthermore accords with what R. Simeon b. Laqish said.

K.   For R. Simeon b. Laqish said, "A 'covenant' is stated in respect to salt, and a covenant is mentioned with respect to suffering.

L.   "With respect to a covenant with salt: 'Neither shall you allow the salt of the covenant of your God to be lacking' (Lev. 2:13).

M.   "With respect to a covenant with suffering: 'These are the words of the covenant' (Deut. 28:69) [followed by discourse on Israel's suffering].

N.   "Just as the covenant noted with salt indicates that salt sweetens meat, so the covenant noted with suffering indicates that suffering wipes away all of a person's sins."

B. Ber. 5a

The prescriptions against anger and in favor of submission contrast with the scriptural testimonies to God's power to express wrath. God's anger, unlike humanity's, is just and always for a cause. Just as human suffering may be inflicted by God out of love, so God's anger serves to express what sages grasp and understand. That is why the Bavli presents ample explanation for the presence, in Scripture and in perceived reality, of an emotion that, in mortals, sages wish to limit. The following are instances in which sages invoke the notion that God becomes angry:

A.   Said R. Yohanan, "When the Holy One, blessed be he, comes to a synagogue and does not find ten present, he forthwith becomes angry.

B.   "For it is said, 'Why when I came was there no one there? When I called, there was no answer?' (Isa. 50:2)."

B. Ber. 6b

N.   Now if Balaam did not even know what his beast was thinking, was he likely to know what the Most High is thinking?

O.   But this teaches that he knew exactly how to reckon the very moment that the Holy One, blessed be he, would be angry.

P.   That is in line with what the prophet said to Israel, "O my people, remember now what Balak, king of Moab, devised, and what Balaam, son of Beor, answered him . . . that you may know the righteous acts of the Lord" (Mic. 6:5).

Q.   Said R. Eleazar, "The Holy One, blessed be he, said to Israel, 'Know that I did any number of acts of righteousness with you, for I did not get angry in the time of the wicked Balaam. For had I gotten angry, not one of [the enemies of] Israel would have survived, not a remnant.'

R.   "That is in line with what Balaam said to Balak, 'How shall I curse whom God has not cursed, and how shall I execrate whom the Lord has not execrated?' (Num. 23:8).

S.   "This teaches that for that entire time [God] did not get mad."

T.   And how long is God's anger?

U.   It is a moment.

V.   And how long is a moment?

W.   Said R. Abin, and some say, R. Abina, "A moment lasts as long as it takes to say 'a moment.' "

X.   And how do we know that a moment is how long God is angry?

Y.   For it is said, "For his anger is but for a moment, his favor is for a lifetime" (Ps. 30:6).

Z.   If you like, you may derive the lesson from the following: "Hide yourself for a little while until the anger be past" (Isa. 26:20).

AA.   And when is God angry?

BB.   Said Abayye, "It is during the first three hours of the day, when the comb of the cock is white, and it stands on one foot."

CC.   But it stands on one foot every hour.

DD.   To be sure, it stands on its foot every hour, but in all the others it has red streaks, and in the moment at hand there are no red streaks [in the comb of the cock].

A.   It has been taught on Tannaite authority in the name of R. Meir, "When the sun comes up, and all kings, east and west, put their crowns on their heads and bow down to the sun, forthwith the Holy One, blessed be he, grows angry."

B. Ber. 7a

So, too, we find reference to God's love and God's hatred:

Three the Holy One, blessed be He, loves: he who does not display temper, he who does not become intoxicated, and he who does not insist on his [full] rights [in the sense that he does not retaliate].

Three the Holy One, blessed be He, hates: he who speaks one thing with his mouth and another thing in his heart; and he who possesses evidence concerning his neighbor and does not testify for him; and he who sees something indecent in his neighbor and testifies against him alone [being the only person who has seen it].

B. Pes. 113b (Soncino, p. 583)

If God loves and hates, God's principal traits of the heart derive from the power to love. What marks God above all is the power to be long-suffering, hence compassionate. Just as we noted in connection with Pharaoh's dying army, so in the following, God shows humanity how to suffer:

A.   "And Moses made haste and bowed his head toward the earth and worshipped" (Exod. 34:8):

B.   What did Moses see?

C.   R. Hanina b. Gamula said, "He saw [God's attribute of] being long-suffering [Exod. 34:7]."

D.   Rabbis say, "He saw [the attribute of] truth [Exod. 34:7]."

E.   It has been taught on Tannaite authority in accord with him who has said, "He saw God's attribute of being long-suffering." For it has been taught of Tannaite authority:

F.   When Moses went up on high, he found the Holy One, blessed be he, sitting and writing "long-suffering."

G.   He said before him, "Lord of the world, long-suffering [only] for the righteous?"

H.   He said to him, "Also for the wicked."

I.   [Moses] said to him, "Let the wicked perish."

J.   He said to him, "Now you will see what you want."

K.   When the Israelites sinned, he said to him, "Did I not say to you, 'Long suffering for the righteous?' "

L.   [P. 111B] He said to him, "Lord of the world, did I not say to you, 'Also for the wicked?' "

M.   That is in line with what is written, 'And now I beseech you, let the power of my Lord be great, according as you have spoken, saying' (Num. 14:17). [Freedman, p. 764, n. 7: What called forth Moses' worship of God when Israel sinned through the Golden Calf was his vision of the Almighty as long-suffering.]

B. San. 111a

God's power to love finds its counterpart in the individual's capacity to love God. The commandment to love God is expounded in the pages of the Bavli. It is not surprising that we find a reiteration of ideas first set forth in the Mishnah and then repeated in the Talmud. What the Bavli contributes is predictable: the expansion and articulation of established conceptions. Thus, we find in the following:

J. R. Eliezer says, "[Scripture states,] 'And you shall love the Lord your God with all your heart, with all your soul, with all your might' (Deut. 6:5). If it is said, 'With all your soul' (Deut. 6:5), why is it also said, 'With all your might'? And if it is said, 'With all your might,' why is it also said, 'With all your soul'?

K. "But if there is someone who places greater value on his body than on his possessions, for such a one it is said, 'With all your soul.'

L. "And if there is someone who places greater value on his possessions than on his life, for such a one it is said, 'With all your might.' "

B. San. 74a

The love of God complements the fear of God. We already know that sages asked which of the two affections takes precedence. Not only do the materials in the Bavli provide an answer to that question – the familiar one that Abraham, who loved God, set a better example than Job, who feared God. They also explain the meaning of that preference:

A. It has been taught on Tannaite authority:

B. R. Meir says, "The words 'feared God' are used with reference to Job, and the words 'feared God' are used with reference to Abraham.

C. "Just as 'God-fearing,' stated with respect to Abraham, means that he did so out of love, so 'God-fearing' stated with reference to Job means that he feared God out of love."

D. And how do we know that Abraham himself did so out of love?

E. As it is written, 'The seed of Abraham, who loved me' (Isa. 41:8).

F. What is the difference between one who acts out of love and one who acts out of fear?

G. The difference is in line with that which has been taught on Tannaite authority:

H. R. Simeon b. Eleazar says, "Greater is [the achievement of one] who acts out of love than of one who acts out of fear.

I. "For the [merit attained] through fear suspends [punishment] for thousands of generations.

J. "Here it is written, 'Unto thousands of them that love me and keep my commandments' (Exod. 20:6), while elsewhere it is written, 'And keep his commandments to a thousand generations' (Deut. 7:9)."

K. But as to the latter, it also is written, "With those who love him and keep his commandments to a thousand generations.' "

L. In the former, [the word "thousand"] is joined [to "those who love me,"] and in the latter, [the word "thousand"] is attached [to "keep his commandments"]. [Cohen, p. 151, n. "Seven": "So in the former the motive is love, in the latter fear of punishment."]

M.   Two disciples were in session before Raba. One of them said to him, "In my dream, the following verse of Scripture was recited to me: 'O how great is your goodness, you have laid up for those who fear you' (Ps. 31:20)."

N.   The other said to him, "In my dream, the following verse of Scripture was recited to me: 'But let all those who put their trust in you rejoice, let them shout for joy, because you defend them, let them also who love your name be joyful in you' (Ps. 6:12)."

O.   He said to them, "Both of you are completely righteous masters. One [does the right thing] out of love, the other out of fear. [Both are correct.]"

B. Sot. 31a

The familiar story of Aqiba's martyrdom here is given more general expression.

The commandment to love God is joined, at Lev. 19:17–18, to the commandment not to hate one's fellow but to love one's neighbor as oneself. What form is this love to take? It is the love that comes to expression in concern that the other not sin. Given the prevailing emphasis on the social virtues of restraint and concern for public opinion, it is hardly surprising that the love of one fellow takes the form of interfering in the affairs of the other. The counterpart of restraint is loving rebuke of the other, the latter being expected to understand and accept the rebuke:

A.   Our rabbis have taught on Tannaite authority: "You shall not hate your brother in your heart" (Lev. 19:17).

B.   Is it possible to suppose that all one should not do is not smite, slap, or curse him [and that is what is at issue only]?

C.   Scripture says, '... in your heart,' thus speaking of the sort of hatred that is in the heart [as much as hatred expressed through physical means].

D.   How do we know [from Scripture] that one who sees in his fellow an unworthy trait is liable to remonstrate with him?

E.   It is said, 'You shall surely rebuke your fellow' (Lev. 19:17).

F.   [If] one has rebuked him, and he has not accepted rebuke, how do we know [from Scripture] that one should go and rebuke him again?

G.   Scripture says, 'You shall surely rebuke...' under all circumstances. [The emphatic word "surely" implies that one must do so under all circumstances.]

H.   Is it possible to suppose that one should do so even if one's face fell [in embarrassment]?

I.   Scripture states, 'You shall not bear sin on his account' (Lev. 19:17).

B. Ar. 16b

R. Amram son of R. Simeon b. Abba said in R. Simeon b. Abba's name in R. Hanina's name: Jerusalem was destroyed only because they did not rebuke each other: for it is said, "Her princes are become like harts that find no pasture" (Lam. 1:6) just as the hart, the head of one is at the side of the other's tail, so Israel of that generation hid their faces in the earth, and did not rebuke each other.

B. Shab. 119b (Soncino, p. 590)

One important and fresh topic in the affective life concerns faith or hope. One must develop trust in God, reliance on God's power to provide. An attitude of confidence yields a feeling of trust, an inner hopefulness:

D.   R. Eliezer the Great says, "Whoever has a piece of bread in his wallet and says, 'What shall I eat tomorrow' is only one of those of little faith."

E.   That is in line with what R. Eleazar said, "What is the meaning of that which is written, 'For who has despised the day of small things' (Zech. 4:10)?

F.   "Who caused the table of the righteous to be despoiled in the age to come?

G.   "It was the smallness [of spirit] that characterized them, for they did not believe in the Holy One, blessed be he."

B. Sot. 48b

Naturally, a private virtue finds its counterpart in the history of the nation. "Jerusalem was destroyed because..." in the present context is completed with a reason:

Raba said: Jerusalem was destroyed only because men of faith [i.e., men completely truthful and trustworthy] ceased therein: for it is said, "Run ye to and fro in the streets of Jerusalem, and see now, and know, and seek in the broad places thereof, if ye can find a man, if there be any that doeth justly, that seeketh faithfulness; and I will pardon her" (Jer. 5:1).

B. Shab. 119b (Soncino, p. 591)

We need not continue to review the long stretch of sayings and stories. What I find blatant is their repetitive character, almost to the point of tedium. In consequence, my claim that we deal with a single, cogent doctrine is justified. We find the same thing again and again: a single doctrine worked out in rich detail according to the context: historical or eschatological or moral, individual or social, theological o'r political. One category joins all other categories: Israel's humility, like God's. When the sages who stand behind the Bavli sum it all up, they say simply, "God demands the heart." But the *kind* of heart God wants – that requires considerable amplification, as these passages of review and amplification have shown us.

Torah in the Flesh

Like the earlier Talmud, the one produced in the Land of Israel, the framers of the Talmud of Babylonia gathered aggregates of materials – three, four, five, or more units of discourse, joined to create a sizable composite – of yet a third type. This was a set of materials organized around the names and deeds of sages. These writings focused neither on exegesis of the Mishnah and the law nor on amplification and reading of Scripture or the Mishnah but on what the sages said and did about important topics in Scripture and the Mishnah. How the sages exemplified the teachings of the Torah was at issue. The lessons came in the medium of tales about, and citations of, the sage as an authority coequal to Scripture and the Mishnah. Hence, the third medium by which the Torah came to Israel, the medium of the living sage, demands its own hearing. What we find is that values standard in the system took concrete form in sayings taught with no proof text other than the authority of a given sage. Values exemplified by a sage, validated by the sage's deed or sayings alone, expressed views we have already heard in other media.

A repertoire of these standard teachings invoked the traits of the heart and recommended affections we have come to expect: humility, self-abnegation, resignation, good will, and restraint:

A.   They sent from there, "Who is someone who will inherit the world to come?

B.   "It is one who is meek and humble, who bends when he comes and bends when he goes out, who always is studying the Torah, but does not take pride in himself on that account."

C.   Rabbis gazed at R. Ulla bar Abba.

B. San. 88b

Our Rabbis have taught: A man should always be gentle as the reed and never unyielding as the cedar.

B. Ta. 20a (Soncino, p. 100)

Our Rabbis taught: A man should always be gentle like Hillel, and not impatient like Shammai.

> B. Shab. 31a (Soncino, p. 138)

Shammai's impatience sought to drive us from the world, but Hillel's gentleness brought us under the wings of the *Shechinah*.

> B. Shab. 31a (Soncino, p. 141)

Bar Kappara lectured: A bad tempered man gains nothing but [the ill effect of] his temper, but a good man is fed with the fruit of his deeds. And he who lacks Bible, Mishnah and worldly pursuits, vows not to benefit from him, as it is said, "Nor sitteth in the seat of the scoffers" (Ps. 1:1) his seat is the seat of scoffers.

> B. Qid. 40b–41a (Soncino, p. 203)

Improper affections, as much as sins, account for suffering from various ailments:

Our Rabbis taught: There are four signs: dropsy is a sign of sin; jaundice is a sign of causeless hatred; poverty is a sign of conceit (Qid. 49b); croup is a sign of slander.

> B. Shab. 33a (Soncino, p. 154)

Sages in particular were warned that if they violated the bounds of appropriate affections, they would lose the one gift that distinguished them, namely, their learning:

Rab Judah said in Rab's name: Whoever is boastful, if he is a sage, his wisdom departs from him; if he is a prophet, his prophecy departs from him.

Resh Lakish said: As to every man who becomes angry, if he is a sage, his wisdom departs from him; if he is a prophet, his prophecy departs from him. If he is a sage, his wisdom departs from him.

R. Mani b. Pattish said: Whoever becomes angry, even if greatness has been decreed for him by Heaven, is cast down.

> B. Pes. 66b (Soncino, pp. 337–8)

Once more we observe a circumscribed and uniform program for the emotional life, promising in context exactly those things sages valued, in exchange for the restraint, patience, and good will the system exacted as its principal affective virtues.

A sizable passage containing prayers composed by sages for their individual use contains important facts on the affective life. What people are represented as beseeching from God reveals which emotions are favored, for God provided the model, and God's affective life in this system shapes that of the individual. Hence, when we review the substance of these prayers, we see the critical role affections play in defining the character and configuration of the virtuous person:

A.   When R. Eleazar finished saying his prayer, this is what he said: "May it be pleasing before you, O Lord our God, to bring to dwell within our lot love, brotherhood, peace, and friendship, and make our territories rich in disciples, and make our destiny succeed with a future and a hope, and place our portion in the Garden of Eden, and provide us with a good colleague and good impulse in your world. And may we get up in the morning and find the yearning of our heart to fear your name. And may the serenity of our souls come before you for good."

B.   When R. Yohanan had finished saying his prayer, this is what he said: "May it be pleasing before you, O Lord our God, to look upon our shame and see our suffering, and clothe yourself in mercy, cover yourself in your strength, and cloak yourself in your loyalty, and gird yourself in your compassion, and may the attribute of goodness come before you and that of your gentleness."

C.   When R. Zira had finished saying his prayer, this is what he said: "May it be pleasing before you, O Lord our God, that we not sin or be ashamed or disgrace ourselves more than did our fathers."

E.   When Rab had finished saying his prayer, this is what he said: "May it be pleasing before you, O Lord our God, to give us long life, peaceful life, good life, blessed life, abundant life, secure life, a life of fear of sin, a life not marred by shame or humiliation, a life of wealth and honor, a life of love of Torah and fear of heaven, a life in which you fill all the desires of our hearts for good."

F.   When Rabbi had finished saying his prayer, this is what he said: "May it be pleasing before you, O Lord our God and God of our fathers, that you save us from those who are arrogant and from arrogance, from a bad man and a bad encounter, from the evil impulse and a bad associate, from a bad neighbor and from the destructive Satan, from a bad judgment and from a difficult litigant, whether a member of the covenant or not."

G.   [He said that prayer] even though there were guards standing over Rabbi.

M.   When Raba finished saying his prayer, this is what he said: "My God, before I was created, I was unworthy, and now that I have been created, it is as if I had not been created. I am dust in my life, all the more so in my death. Lo, I am before you as a utensil filled with shame and humilitation. May it be pleasing before you, O Lord my God, that I not sin again, and as to the sins that I have committed before you, wipe them out in your great mercies. But this should not be done through suffering or painful ailments."

O.   When Mar, son of Rabina, finished saying his prayer, this is what he said: "My God, guard my tongue from gossiping and my lips from deceit. To those who curse me may my soul be silent, and may my soul be as dust to everyone. Open my heart to your Torah, and let my soul pursue your religious duties. Keep me from a bad encounter, a bad impulse, a bad woman, and from all sorts of bad events that may come into the world. Quickly nullify the counsel of all who plan to do me ill and frustrate their plans. May what my mouth says and what my heart reflects be pleasing before you, O Lord, my rock and redeemer."

Q.   When R. Yohanan would finish [the study of] the book of Job, this is what he said: "The destiny of a person is to die, and the destiny of a beast is to be slaughtered, so all are destined to death. Happy is the one who grows in knowledge of Torah, whose labor is in Torah, who thereby brings pleasure to his Creator, who grows in good repute, and who dies in good repute in this world. Concerning such a one Solomon said, 'A good name is better than precious oil, and the day of death than the day of one's birth' (Qoh. 7:1)."

R.   A pearl in the mouth of Abayye: "A person should always be subtle [in finding ways to] fear [heaven]. 'A soft answer turns away anger' (Prov. 15:1). One should increase peace with his brethren and relatives and everyone, even with a gentile in the marketplace, so that he may be beloved above and pleasing below and accepted by people."

B. Ber. 16b–17a

This sequence of private prayers underlines the earlier thesis. The sages' prescription for the correct affective life of virtue involved those same traits of restraint, perpetual patience, and good will recommended in the earliest redacted documents of the canon. Sages prayed for love, a good impulse, good will, divine compassion, and divine gentleness. They promised to exhibit the same traits. They asked to be spared shame and disgrace and humiliation. They asked to be saved from arrogance, a bad associate, a bad impulse. The emphasis on the sage's inconsequence ("unworthy," "dust in my life," "a utensil filled with shame") was the liturgical counterpart to the appropriate affections, namely, modesty, restraint, and self-abnegation. Such an attitude would lead the virtuous person to accept the status of "dust to everyone." So the sages' prayers, as much as their teachings, outlined a cogent repertoire of virtues of the emotional life. Such a set of affections, we need hardly note, accorded well with the status of a defeated nation and the politics of a tolerated caste.

Compositions about the sages' deeds and the emotions associated with them portray men full of uncertainty, humble before God, and aware of their limitations. A common motif in stories about sages, the death scene, invariably introduces the theme of the sage's awareness that he has not really feared God or loved his neighbor. So with the deaths of Yohanan ben Zakkai and Eliezer:

D.   And when R. Yohanan b. Zakkai fell ill, his disciples came in to pay a call on him. When he saw them, he began to cry. His disciples said to him, "Light of Israel! Pillar at the right hand! Mighty hammer! On what account are you crying?"

E.   He said to them, "If I were going to be brought before a mortal king, who is here today and tomorrow gone to the grave, who, should he be angry with me, will not be angry forever, and, if he should imprison me, will not imprison me forever, and, if he should put me to death, whose sentence of death is not for eternity, and whom I can appease with the right words or bribe with money, even so, I should weep.

F.   "But now that I am being brought before the King of kings of kings, the Holy One, blessed be he, who endures forever and ever, who, should he be angry with me, will be angry forever, and, if he should imprison me, will imprison me forever, and, if he should put me to death, whose sentence of death is for eternity, and whom I cannot appease with the right words or bribe with money,

G.   "and not only so, but before me are two paths, one to the Garden of Eden and the other to Gehenna, and I do not know by which path I shall be brought,

H.   "and should I not weep?"

I.   They said to him, "Our master, bless us."

J.   He said to them, "May it be God's will that the fear of heaven be upon you as much as the fear of mortal man."

K.   His disciples said, "Just so much?"

L.   He said to them, "Would that it were that much. You should know that, when a person commits a transgression, he says, 'I hope no man sees me.' "

B. Ber. 28b

A.   Said Rabbah bar bar Hanah, "When R. Eliezer fell ill, his disciples came in to call on him.

B.   "He said to them, 'There is great anger in the world [to account for my sickness].'

C.   "They began to cry, but R. Aqiba began to laugh. They said to him, 'Why are you laughing?'

D.   "He said to them, 'Why are you crying?'

E.   "They said to him, 'Is it possible that, when a scroll of the Torah [such as Eliezer] is afflicted with disease, we should not cry?'

F.   "He said to them, 'For that reason I am laughing. So long as I
observed that, as to my master, his wine did not turn to vinegar, his flax
was not smitten, his oil did not putrefy, and his honey did not become
rancid,

G.   " 'I thought to myself, "Perhaps, God forbid, my master has
received his reward in this world." But now that I see my master in
distress, I rejoice [knowing that he will receive his full reward in the
world to come.]'

H.   "[Eliezer] said to him, 'Aqiba, have I left out anything at all from
the whole of the Torah?'

I.   "He said to him, '[Indeed so, for] you have taught us, our master,
"For there is not a just man upon earth, who does good and does not
sin" (Qoh. 7:20).' "

B. San. 101a

The emotional aspect of the story is paramount: weeping because of
uncertainty, the blessing that the disciples cultivate fear of heaven at least
as much as their fear of humanity.

The same motif – weeping over the human condition or Israel's circumstance – introduces yet another theme: recognition of the alienation
between Israel and God.

R. Huna, when he came to this verse, "Yir'eh, Yera'eh," (Exod. 23:17)
wept. He said: The slave whom his Master longs to see should become
estranged from him! For it is written: "When ye come to appear before
Me, who hath required this at your hand, to trample My courts?" (Isa.
1:12).

R. Huna, when he came to the [following] verse, wept: "And thou
shalt sacrifice peace-offerings, and shalt eat there" (Deut. 27:7). The slave
at whose table his Master longs to eat should become estranged from
him! For it is written: " 'To what purpose is the abundance of your
sacrifices unto Me?' saith the Lord" (Isa. 1:11).

R. Eleazar, when he came to the [following] verse, wept: "And his
brethren could not answer him, for they were affrighted at his presence"
(Gen. 47:3). Now if the rebuke of flesh and blood be such, how much
more so the rebuke of the Holy One, blessed be He!

R. Eleazar, when he came to the [following] verse, wept: "And Samuel
said to Saul: Why hast thou disquieted me, to bring me up?" (1 Sam.
28:15). Now if Samuel, the righteous, was afraid of the Judgment, how
much more so should we be!

R. Ami, when he came to the [following] verse, wept: "Let him put
his mouth in the dust, perhaps there may be hope" (Lam. 3:29). He said:
All this, and [only] perhaps!

R. Ami, when he came to the [following] verse, wept: "Seek right-eousness, seek humility, perhaps ye shall be hid in the day of the Lord's anger" (Zeph. 2:3). He said: All this, and [only] perhaps!

R. Assi, when he came to the [following] verse, wept: "Hate the evil, and love the good, and establish justice in the gate, perhaps the Lord, the God of hosts, will be gracious" (Amos 5:15). All this, and [only] perhaps!

R. Yohanan, when he came to the [following] verse, wept: "And thou didst incite Me against him, to destroy him without cause" (Job 11:3). A slave whose Master, when they incite him, yields, is there any help for him?

R. Yohanan, when he came to the [following] verse, wept: "Behold, He putteth no trust in His holy ones" (Job. 15:15). If He does not put His trust in His holy ones, in whom will He put His trust?

B. Hag. 5a (Soncino, pp. 16–18)

These stories impute to sages a sense of alienation from God, a fear of God's rebuke and judgment, an absence of trust between God and Israel. In these ways the historical circumstances of a defeated people were translated into the inner affective life of individuals. The vanquished people found themselves alienated and estranged. The individual, in that situation, expressed the appropriate response to God's displeasure. One *should* feel guilt, uncertainty, and rejection. These feelings form the dark underside of the virtues of restraint, self-abnegation, and humility. Feel-ing guilty before God, and ashamed before the common and rejected, the sage will cultivate the complementary qualities of humility and re-straint. There is no call for the sage, standing for Israel, to be arrogant or to act pridefully. The sage here embodies the feelings the nation as a whole is meant to have. But he also stands for the outcome of appropriate affections. The emotions imputed to God accorded with those cultivated in the sages themselves. Just as Israel was to attain humility and express contrition, God responded to the same affections:

R. Hama b. Hanina ordained a fast but no rain fell. People said to him: When R. Joshua b. Levi ordained a fast rain *did* fall. He replied: I am I, and he is the son of Levi. Go and ask him that he may come [and pray for us] and let us concentrate on our prayer, perhaps the whole community will be contrite in heart and rain will fall. They prayed and no rain fell. He then asked them: Are you content that rain should fall on our account? They replied: Yes. He then exclaimed: heaven, heaven, cover thy face. But it did not cover [its face]. He then added: How brazen is the face of heaven! It then became covered and rain fell.

Levi ordained a fast but no rain fell. He thereupon exclaimed: Master

of the Universe, Thou didst go up and take Thy seat on high and hast
no mercy upon Thy children. Rain fell but he became lame. R. Eleazar
said: Let a man never address himself in a reproachful manner towards
God, seeing that one great man did so and he became lame, and he is
Levi. But was this actually the cause [of his lameness]? Was it not rather
because he demonstrated to Rabbi a particular form of prostration? Both
were the cause of his lameness.

> B. Ta. 25a (Soncino, p. 131)

As the story indicates, God does not favor arrogance and punishes it,
even while responding to humiliation. In the following, God weeps for,
among other things, a domineering authority:

> Our Rabbis taught: Over three the Holy One, blessed be He, weeps
> every day: over him who is able to occupy himself with [the study of]
> the Torah and does not; and over him who is unable to occupy himself
> with [the study of] the Torah and does; and over a leader who domineers
> over the community.

> B. Hag. 5b (Soncino, p. 24)

God shares the condition of Israel, therefore also mourns for it, as much
as the sages embody Israel's condition and the requisite sorrow:

> "But if ye will not hear it, My soul shall weep in secret for the pride"
> (Jer. 13:17). R. Samuel b. Inia said in the name of Rab: The Holy One,
> blessed be He, has a place and its name is "Secret."
> What is the meaning of [the expression] *for the pride?*
> R. Samuel b. Isaac said: For the glory that has been taken from and
> given to the nations of the world.
> R. Samuel b. Nahmani said: For the glory of the Kingdom of Heaven.
> But is there any weeping in the presence of the Holy One, blessed be
> He? For behold R. Papa said: There is no grief in the presence of the
> Holy One, blessed be He, for it is said: "Honor and majesty are before
> Him; strength and beauty are in His sanctuary!" (Ps. 96:6).
> There is no contradiction; the one case [refers to] the inner chambers,
> the other case [refers to] the outer chambers.
> But behold it is written: "And in that day did the Lord, the God of
> Hosts, call to weeping and to lamentation, and to baldness, and to girding
> with sackcloth!" (Isa. 22:12).
> The destruction of the Temple is different, for even the angels of peace
> wept [over it]; for it is said: "Behold for their altar they cried without;
> the angels of peace wept bitterly" (Isa. 33:7).
> "And mine eye shall drop tears and tears, and run down with tears,

because the Lord's flock is carried away captive" (Jer. 13:17). R. Eleazar said: Wherefore these three [expressions of] *tears?* One for the first Temple, and one for the second Temple, and one for Israel, who have become exiled from their place.

B. Hag. 5b (Soncino, p. 23)

God also celebrates achievement in Torah study. What is involved in the following is the question of how God responded when, in the earthly academy, a sage got the better of heaven in an argument:

R. Nathan met Elijah and asked him: What did the Holy One, Blessed be He, do in that hour?

He laughed [with joy], he replied, saying, "My sons have defeated Me, My sons have defeated Me."

B. B.M. 59b (Soncino, p. 353)

What God wants above all, as the following indicates, is the heart, meaning humility:

B. Said Raba, "Is there any recognition of the achievement of raising questions? In the time of R. Judah, all of their repetition of Mishnah teachings concerned the civil laws [of Baba Qamma, Baba Mesia, and Baba Batra], while for our part, we repeat the Mishnah traditions even dealing with tractate Uqsin [a rather peripheral topic].

C. "When for his part R. Judah came to the law, 'A woman who pickles vegetables in a pot' [M. Toh. 2:1], or some say, 'Olives which were pickled with their leaves are insusceptible to uncleanness' [M. Uqs. 2:1], he would say, 'I see here all the points of reflection of Rab and Samuel.'

D. "But we repeat the tractate of Uqsin at thirteen sessions [having much more to say about it].

E. "When R. Judah merely removed his shoes [in preparation for a fast], it would rain. When we cry out [in supplication], no one pays any attention to us.

F. "But the Holy One, blessed be he, demands the heart, as it is written, 'But the Lord looks on the heart' (1 Sam. 16:7)."

B. San. 106b

Divine Pathos, Human Alienation

If the Bavli does stand at the end of the canon of Judaism, at what points do we find an exercise of completion? In my view the materials that we have just examined, with their emphasis God's feelings, bring to a natural conclusion that single line of thought begun in the Mishnah, inclusive of tractate Abot. To begin with, in Abot, the human being is to exhibit the traits of restraint, humility, and conciliation. At the end, in the Bavli, God's situation explains why. God shares the human condition of feeling. God's heart and the human heart are alike. What lies at the center of divine pathos is the alienation of God from the world, matching the separation of humanity from God. Transcending wrath, regret, and despair, feelings imputed to God on the occasion of the Flood, the affection of alienation responds to the supernatural and cosmic calamity caused (in the sages' language) or symbolized (in ours) by the destruction of the Temple.

What God really wants is the heart. God responds to how human beings feel as much as to what they do. Because the sages were humble, however limited their learning, their prayers were answered. Because the sages were arrogant, taking pride in their achievements, they did not. Why? God demands the heart: attitude, affection, and consequent right action, all together. Thus, the Bavli moves beyond anything we have seen in its placing at the center of the life of Israel, in this world and in the world to come, in history, and in eternity, the affairs of the heart. And yet, in light of the verse "You will love the Lord your God with all your heart, with all your soul, and with all your might," who could find surprising this last, climactic claim? God always commanded love. God now wants the heart.

CHAPTER VIII

The Other Torah

Affections in the Exegetical Tradition of Scripture

Compilations of Exegeses of Scripture (*Midrashim*)

Though the exegesis of passages of Scripture began long before the closure of the Hebrew scriptures themselves, within the circle of sages the work of composing compilations of exegeses of scriptures presented an innovation. Such compilations were not made before the third century. Scripture itself, the written medium of the Torah, of course, had long formed the center of study. But gathering together into sustained and cogent compositions the results of that study and so creating a genre of writings constituted a response to a particular context.

That context, set in the third and fourth centuries, was the appearance and authority of the Mishnah, issued, we recall, in 200. Once the law code proved authoritative, sponsored by the patriarchate of the Land of Israel and, shortly thereafter it would seem, by the exilarchate of the Jews of Babylonia, the sages had to explain its status. Attributing the origin of the document to God's revelation at Sinai, as the rabbinic Torah myth ultimately did, was the final step in the naturalization of the new code into the Torah as a whole. But then the work of exegesis of the Mishnah required a systematic inquiry into the relationships between the rules of the Mishnah and the corresponding rules or statements of Scripture. That would set the Mishnah into the Torah of Sinai. This very particular mode of exegesis, the discovery in Scripture of proof texts for the Mishnah's statements, yielded a sizable corpus of results.

One substantial component of the earliest compilations of exegeses of Scripture, those that dealt with Exodus, Leviticus, Numbers, and Deuteronomy, contained only the names of late first and second authorities, those that also appear in the Mishnah. These compilations present line-by-line comments on scriptural passages. The Mekhilta of R. Ishmael to Exodus, Sifra to Leviticus, Sifré to Numbers, and another Sifré to Deuteronomy probably reached closure at some point in the later third or fourth century, though that is only a guess.

Systematic exegesis of the Mishnah *not* in relationship to Scripture produced modes of inquiry of the same classification, but now applied to Scripture itself. Specifically, the ways in which the Mishnah exegetes of the third and fourth centuries read the Mishnah's statements – word for word, line for line, by whole paragraphs, through larger conceptual exercises – influenced their mode of reading of Scripture. What resulted was a set of line-for-line and clause-for-clause exegeses, first of Genesis in Genesis Rabbah, then of Leviticus in Leviticus Rabbah. The first of these writings fall into exactly those classifications of hermeneutics that pertain to the Mishnah. Viewed taxonomically, therefore, the third- and fourth-century sages' exegesis of the Mishnah, as laid out in the Talmud of the Land of Israel, provided the model for the same sages' exegeses of Scripture. Thus, in the way sages read the Torah in the one medium, the oral, they proceeded to read it in the other, the written. Line-by-line exegesis of Scripture dominates Sifra, the two Sifrés, and Genesis Rabbah.

A different mode of utilizing verses of Scripture aimed at a more discursive inquiry into autonomous principles of theology and law. This approach is paramount in Leviticus Rabbah. Here scriptures serve as illustrations of broader principles, ordinarily to be discovered by locating the commonalities of propositions expressed only by example and never as abstract philosophical propositions. A still more abstract and discursive mode of discourse dominates Pesiqta deR. Kahana and some of the later compilations of scriptural exegeses.

Assigning dates of closure to these several compilations is exceedingly parlous. We have little evidence on which to conclude that a given document reached closure at some finite point. Unless we take as fact the assignment of sayings to named authorities, and we surely cannot assume that nothing is ever pseudoepigraphic, we can only guess which document comes first and which later on. For the present purpose that difficulty would be a considerable obstacle were it not for one simple fact, which we shall shortly discuss in detail. It is that, as a group, compilations of scriptural exegeses make scant reference to the issue under discussion in this book. Only on rare occasions do the compilers of scriptural exegeses take an interest in the theme of emotions. We find casual allusion to happiness and sorrow but little sustained attention to these categories. There is nothing like the profound and discursive work in the Bavli in the corpus of scriptural interpretation, so far as I can see. Still less common is deep concern for the way people are supposed to feel. Since the pertinent materials are so episodic and infrequent, the matter of when a document reached closure and to what time and even place it gives distinctive testimony therefore makes slight difference.

As we shall see, the entire exegetical corpus reinforces the impression that religious affections define a given, a datum of life subjected to only occasional inquiry, and that not sustained. Emotion is to be subject to social rules. The upshot for our larger study is simple. Affections are a topic for law, not for speculation on history or theology such as fills the exegetical compositions. We here confirm our original discovery that, in the unfolding of the rabbinic corpus of writings in late antiquity, religious affections constitute one of the enduring, unchanging themes, subject to fixed rules. What we are supposed to feel, and when, form part of the unchanging background of legal regulation, the fixed stars against which, as we shall see in Chapter IX, movement is measured in other matters (e.g., of teleology and symbolism).

Once more we shall rapidly review a sizable corpus of sayings and stories that document familiar things. Though the reader may find this loving and repetitious recapitulation of sources tedious, the exercise is a critical component of the larger argument of this book. It is that from beginning to end we find a linear and uniform exposition of a single category of virtue – humility, moderation, self-restraint, and self-abnegation, an attitude of conciliation and an eagerness to please – alongside the opposite traits of attitude, expression, and emotion – avoidance of arrogance, self-aggrandizment, and disregard for the feelings of others and the rights of the community at large – the old familiar themes. How better to demonstrate the recurrence of the same ideas than to reveal their existence, time and again, in both exegetical and legal documents. That is why I provide a sizable selection of what I claim to be representative and definitive doctrine, whether it be law, scriptural exegesis, or hagiography about sages.

Let me now specify the compilations of biblical exegeses that constitute our sample in this chapter. In dating these compilations, I rely on M. D. Heer, *Encyclopaedia Judaica* 11:1507–14. For the first part of the sample, I turn to the compilations universally regarded as the earliest. This first set of compilations of biblical exegeses *(midrashim)* bears attributions only to authorities who flourished in the first and second centuries (Tannaim). Among them we shall draw our sample from Mekhilta deR. Ishmael, part of Sifra, and Sifré on Numbers. We turn then to the second set of compilations, those assigned to authorities who lived in the third through the sixth centuries (Amoraim), surveying Genesis Rabbah, Leviticus Rabbah, and the like.

Following Heer's judgment *(Encyclopaedia Judaica* 14:1518–19), we assign Sifra to the end of the fourth century at the earliest. For the present purpose, a survey of two large *parashiyyot*, Negaim and Mesora, which I translated in my *History of the Mishnaic Law of Purities*, Vol. 7: *Negaim. Sifra* (Leiden, 1975), suffices. In these protracted passages, I should estimate nearly a fourth of the entire document, I find no reference to the virtuous life at all.

In his article, "Midrash" (*Encyclopaedia Judaica* 11:1507–14) Heer treats as documents of late antiquity, beyond those attributed to late first and second-century authorities (Tannaim), the following: Genesis Rabbah, Leviticus Rabbah, Lamentations Rabbah, Esther Rabbah I, Pesiqta deR. Kahana, Songs Rabbah, and Ruth Rabbah. We shall review them all.

A Probe of the Earlier Compilations of Scriptural Exegeses

Allusions to the topic of emotions are few and far between in the Mekhilta attributed to R. Ishmael, and those that exist touch on familiar themes. The first of two noteworthy items is that God and Israel, including the individual Israelite, follow the same affective rules, so God shares Israel's emotional life and condition:

> *Even the Selfsame Day It Came to Pass, that All the Hosts of the Lord Went Out from the Land of Egypt.* The hosts of the Lord are the ministering angels. And so you find that whenever Israel is enslaved, the Shekinah [God's presence], as it were, is enslaved with them, as it is said: "And they saw the God of Israel; and there was under His feet" etc. But after they were redeemed what does it say? "And the like of the very heaven for clearness" (Exod. 24:10). And it also says, "In all their affliction he was afflicted" (Isa. 63:10). So far I know only that he shares in the affliction in the community. How about the affliction of the individual? Scripture says: "He shall call upon me, and I will answer him; I will be with him in trouble" (Ps. 91:15). It also says: "And Joseph's master took him," etc. (Gen. 39:20). And what does it say then? "But the Lord was with Joseph" (Gen. 39:21).
>
> Mekhilta Pisha 14 (Lauterbach) 2:113–14.

The second noteworthy item is the distinction to be drawn when a single emotion is directed to diverse ends. We have already noted that love and hatred by themselves do not constitute desirable or inappropriate feelings. It is the object or purpose that matters. Here, too, the affection of joy may or may not find approval:

> There were four who did their harnessing with joy. Abraham harnessed with joy, as it is said: "And Abraham rose early in the morning, and saddled his ass" (Gen. 22:3). Balaam harnessed with joy, as it said: "And Balaam rose up in the morning, and saddled his ass" (Num. 22:21). Joseph

harnessed with joy, as it is said: "And Joseph made ready his chariot" (Gen. 46:29). Pharaoh harnessed with joy, as it is said: "And he made ready his chariot." Let the work of saddling that our father Abraham did in order to go and do the will of his Creator come and stand out against the work of saddling that Balaam, the wicked, did in order to go and curse Israel. Let the work of making ready the chariot done by Joseph in order to go to meet his father come and stand out against the work of making ready the chariot done by Pharaoh in order to go and pursue the Israelites.

Mekhilta Beshallah 2 (Lauterbach) 1:190,

Isa. 161–70 (= B. San. 105b)

As I said, nothing in the sample of the Sifra is relevant to our inquiry. When we come to Sifré on Numbers a modest repertoire of pertinent items makes an appearance. Most noteworthy, but entirely commonplace, is the statement that God treats Israel with special love:

"Command the children of Israel that they put out of the camp every leper, etc., that they defile not their campus in the midst whereof I dwell" (Num. 5:1). What manner of love has God bestowed upon Israel that even when they are defiled the Shekina rests among them; cf. also Lev. 16:16. "Who dwelt with them in the midst of their impurity."

Sifré Num. 1 (Levertoff, p. 1)

What love has God bestowed upon Israel, that when He calls them by a pet name, He calls them "priests," as it is said (Isa. 61:6): "And ye shall be called the priests of the Lord."

What love has God bestowed upon the "priests," that when he calls them by a pet name, He calls them "ministering angels," as it is said (Mal. 2:7): "For the lips of the priest keep knowledge and they seek teaching at his mouth, for he is the angel of the Lord of Hosts."

Sifré Num. 119 (Levertoff, p. 128)

Along the same lines, it was important for one who became a proselyte to do so out of love:

[Moses said to Jethro]: "If thou art not willing to accept the rich pastural grounds of Jericho, I order thee (to do so), for otherwise Israel will say: 'Jethro did not become a proselyte out of love, for he thought that his gift would be great, but now that he sees that his gift is not so great, he has left them and returned to his own land!' "

Sifré, Num. 80 (Levertoff, p. 57)

This modest sample presents no surprises. I do not see a single new theme or idea, but only a ringing of changes on conventional motifs.

A Survey of the Later Compilations

I find nothing noteworthy in Genesis Rabbah. Leviticus Rabbah presents an important statement on the control of temper, a theme, we recall, well expounded in tractate Abot:

A.   Forthwith: "And he was angry with Eleazar and Ithamar, the sons of Aaron [who were left]" (Lev. 10:16).

B.   And because he lost his temper, the knowledge of the correct law left him.

C.   Said R. Huna, "In three contexts Moses lost his temper, with the result that knowledge of the law left him.

D.   "These are they: in the matters of the Sabbath, metal utensils, and the bereaved prior to the burial of the deceased.

E.   "How do we know the case of the Sabbath?

F.   " 'Some of them left some of [the manna] until the morning, [and it got wormy and rotted,] and Moses lost his temper with them' (Exod. 16:20).

G.   "Since he had lost his temper, he forgot to tell them the laws of the Sabbath.

H.   "What in fact did he say to them? 'Eat it today [for today is a sabbath to the Lord. Today you will not find it in the field]' (Exod. 16:25). [So he forgot to tell them that they should gather an extra portion on the day preceding the Sabbath.]

I.   "[How do we know Moses was angry and forgot to mention] the matter of metal utensils?

J.   " 'And Moses was angry with the officers of the army, [the commanders of thousands and the commanders of hundreds, who had come from service in the war]' (Num. 31:14).

K.   "Since he lost his temper, knowledge of the right law left him. He therefore forgot to inform them of the laws governing metal utensils. And since he had forgotten to inform them, Eleazar, the priest, did so in his stead: 'And Eleazar the priest said to the men of war [who had gone to battle, "This is the statute of the law which the Lord has commanded Moses: only the gold, silver, bronze, iron, tin, and lead, everything that can stand the fire, you shall pass through the fire and it shall be clean"]' (Num. 31:21–2).

L. "[Eleazar] said to them, 'It was to Moses, my lord, that [God] gave the commandment, and not to me that he gave it.'

M. "[How do we know Moses was angry and forgot to mention] the matter of the bereaved who has not yet buried his deceased?

N. " 'And he was angry with Eleazar and Ithamar, the sons of Aaron [who were left and who had not yet buried their deceased brothers, Nadab and Abihu].'

O. "Since he lost his temper, he forgot to tell them that a priest who has not yet buried his deceased is forbidden to eat Holy Things."

Lev. R. XIII:I.3

Another familiar affection to be suppressed is arrogance or boastfulness. To the sages, merrymaking is one sign of arrogance, for it indicates that a person is ignoring the true conditions of life.

1. A. R. Levi opened [discourse by citing the following verse:] " 'I say to the boastful (HWLLYM) [Do not boast, and to the wicked, Do not life up your horn]' (Ps. 75:4).

B. "The word 'to the boastful' refers to those who create confusion. They are people whose hearts are filled with evil intrigues (HWLHWLYWT)."

C. R. Levi called them "woe makers" because they bring woe into the world.

2. A. "And to the wicked, Do not lift up your horn" (Ps. 75:4).

B. Said the Holy One, blessed be he, to the wicked, "The righteous men do not make merry in my world, but you seek to make merry in my world.

C. "The first man did not make merry in my world, but you seek to make merry in my world."

3. A. Abraham did not make merry in my world, and yet you make merry in my world.

B. To Abraham was born a son when he was one hundred years old, and yet in the end, the Holy One, blessed be he, said to him, "Take your son [your only son, whom you have loved, and offer him . . . for a burnt offering]" (Gen. 22:2).

4. A. The Israelites did not make merry in my world:

B. "Israel rejoiced in his maker" is not written here, but rather " . . . will rejoice" (Ps. 149:2).

C. They are going to rejoice in the works of the Holy One, blessed be he, in the age to come.

5.   A.   It is as if to say that the Holy One, blessed be he, did not make merry in his world, and yet you are making merry in my [God's] world.

B.   "The Lord has rejoiced in his works" is not written here, but rather, "The Lord will rejoice in his works" (Ps. 104:31).

C.   The Holy One, blessed be he, is destined to rejoice in the works of the righteous in the age to come.

6.   A.   Elisheba, daughter of Amminadab, did not make merry in my world, and yet you are making merry in my world.

B.   Elisheba saw five crowns in a single day: her levirate husband as king; her brother as patriarch; her husband as high priest; her two sons as prefects of the priesthood; and Phineas, her grandson, as the priest anointed for war.

C.   When her sons went in to make an offering, they came out burned, and her rejoicing turned to mourning.

D.   That is in line with the following verse of Scripture: "After the death of the two sons of Aaron" (Lev. 16:2)

Lev. R. XX:II

What strikes the exegete is the contrast between the rejoicing of Aaron and his family at their consecration to the priesthood and the mourning that overtakes them on the day of their celebration. This then leads to the observation that the boastful or the ones who rejoice soon come to mourning. This point is made concerning Adam (No. 2). Then we have the case of Abraham, whose rejoicing was turned to mourning at Sarah's death, and, finally, the wife of Aaron and mother of Nadab and Abihu.

A.   Abba b. R. Kahana opened [his discourse by citing the following verse of Scripture:] "I said of laughter, It is mad [and of pleasure, What use is it?]" (Qoh. 2:2).

B.   If joy is only mixed, then what use is rejoicing?

C.   There was the case of one of the great lords of Kabul, who married off his son. On the fourth day [of the week of rejoicing], he invited guests to his house.

D.   After they had eaten and drunk and made merry, he said to his son, "Go up and bring us a jug of wine from the upper room."

E.   When he got up there, a snake bit him and he died.

F.   He waited for him to come down, but he did not come down. He said, "Shall I not go up and see what's going on with my son?"

G.   He went up and found that a snake had bitten him and he had died, and he was sprawled out between the jugs.

H.   He waited until the guests had finished their meal.

I.   He said to them, "My lords, is it not to say a blessing for my son as a groom that you have come? Say a blessing for him as mourners. Is it not to bring my son into the marriage canopy that you have come? Rather, bring him to his grave."

J. R. Zakkai from Kabul gave a eulogy for him, "I said of laughter, It is mad" (Qoh. 2:2)."

Lev. R. XX:III

The point here is the same as that above.

Yet another condemnation of arrogance is made in the context of Aaron's sons' not finding suitable mates:

1. A.   R. Levi said, "They were snooty. Many unmarried women were sitting gloomy [sad] and waiting for them. But what did they have to say about themselves? 'Our father's brother is king, our mother's brother is patriarch, our father is the high priest, we two are deputy high priests! What woman is worthy of us?' "

2. A.   [And the fact that they were power hungry may] further [be shown in] the following:

B.   "And he said to Moses, 'Come up to the Lord, you and Aaron, Nadab and Abihu, and seventy of the elders of Israel' " (Exod. 24:1).

C.   This teaches that Moses and Aaron went first, then Nadab and Abihu went after them, while all Israel followed after them. So the two brothers said, "In a little while these two old men will die, and you and I are going to lord it over this community."

D.   R. Yudan in the name of R. Aibu said: "They said this out loud to one another."

E.   R. Phineas said, "They merely thought it in their hearts."

F.   Said R. Berekhiah, "The Holy One, blessed be he, said to them, 'Do not take pride today concerning what will be tomorrow' (Prov. 27:1). Many foals have died and had their hides turned into saddles for their mothers' backs."

Lev. R. XX:X

The contrasting affection is gentleness and humility. The several compilations before us present tales of humble action, although most of these deal with deed rather than emotion itself, as in the following:

A.   Rab made a banquet for his disciples. He brought before them soft tongues and hard tongues. They began to select the soft ones and to leave the hard ones. He said to them, "My disciples, note what you are doing when you select the soft ones and leave the hard ones.

B.   "So should your tongues be, soft for one another."

Lev. R. XXX:I

Lamentations Rabbah, on the Book of Lamentations, obviously provides numerous references to sorrow, weeping, and mourning, but none
of these passages isolates a given emotion and presents a message particular
to it. Affections form part of a scarcely differentiated background, a
setting for the important public and historical themes of the composition.
Pesiqta de R. Kahana hardly differs. What it presents is familiar, for
example, God's love for Israel:

R. Yudan said: Come and see how much the Holy One loves Israel,
for in a single verse He mentions them five times: "And I have given the
Levites – they are given to Aaron and to his sons from among the children
of Israel, to do the service of the children of Israel in the Tent of Meeting,
and to make atonement for the children of Israel, that there be no plague
among the children of Israel, through the children of Israel coming nigh
unto the Sanctuary" (Num. 8:19). [Rabbi Yudan's comment was in keeping with] the *Baraita* wherein R. Simeon ben Yohai told the parable of
a king who entrusted his son to a tutor. The king, after giving the tutor
specific instructions, kept inquiring: "Has my son eaten? Has my son
had something to drink? Did my son go to school? Has my son returned
from school?" So, too, [R. Yudan concluded,] the Holy One covets
occasions to keep mentioning the children of Israel.

Pesiqta de R. Kahana 2 (Barude and Kapstein, p. 32)

Several references to Israel's and God's shared rejoicing include the
following:

"And the Levite, because he hath no portion nor inheritance with thee,
and the stranger . . . shall come" (Deut. 14:29). According to R. Luliani
of Daroma who cited R. Judah bar R. Simon, the Holy One said: You
have four persons in your household, and I, too, have four persons in
My household. The four persons in your household are your son, your
daughter, your manservant and your maidservant. The four persons in
My household are the Levite, the stranger, the fatherless, and the widow.
Scripture refers to all the persons, yours and mine, in a single verse: "And
thou shalt rejoice in thy feast, thou, and thy son, and thy daughter, and
thy manservant, and thy maidservant, and the Levite, and the stranger,
and the widow, that are within thy gates" (Deut. 16:14). By these words
the Holy One meant: I told you that you were to bring joy to the persons
in My household and to those in yours on the festal days I gave you. If
you do so, I, for My part, will bring joy to yours and to Mine. To these

as well as to those I shall bring joy in the Temple in Jerusalem: "Even then will I bring to My holy mountain, and make them joyful in My house of prayer" (Isa. 56:7).

Pesiqta de R. Kahana 10 (Braude and Kapstein, p. 198)

"You Will Love the Lord Your God with All Your Heart, with All Your Soul, and with All Your Might" in the Rabbinic Compilations of Scriptural Exegeses

The uniformity of the treatment of emotions is best revealed by a survey of a critical verse of Scripture, Deut. 6:5. As we follow the exegesis of this important statement on religious affections, we see very little development, which reinforces the observations we have already made about the compilations of scriptural exegesis. A survey of references to Deut. 6:5 in the rabbinic corpus redacted before ca. A.D. 600 follows:

Mishnah

A.   One must say a blessing for evil as for good [Deut. 6:5 as proof text].

B.   "With all your heart" means with both inclinations, the good and the evil.

C.   "And with all your soul" – even if he takes your soul.

D.   "And with all your might" – with all your money.

E.   "With all your might" – for each measure that he metes out for you, thank him much.

M. Ber. 9:5

Tosefta

A.   R. Meir says, "Lo, Scripture says, 'You will love the Lord your God with all your heart' – with both your impulses, the one to do good and the one to do evil.

B.   " 'And with all your soul' – even if he takes your soul.

C.   "And so Scripture says, 'For your sake we are slain all the day long' (Ps. 44:22)."

D.   Another matter: "With all your soul" – with each soul that he created in you, as it is said, "Let my soul live, that I may praise you" (Ps. 119:175).

E.   "And Scripture says, "All my bones shall say, 'Lord, who is like you' " (Ps. 35:10).

T. Ber. 6:7

Talmud of the Land of Israel

[Aqiba:] "For my whole life I have been troubled about this verse, 'With all your soul,' meaning even though he takes your soul. I wondered when I shall have the privilege of carrying out this commandment. Now that it has come to hand, should I not carry it out?"

Y. Ber. 9:5 (= Y. Sot. 5:5; also B. Ber. 61b)

[It is possible to derive the ten commandments from the recitation of the Shema.] "You will love the Lord your God" yields "You will not take the name of the Lord, your God, in vain" (Exod. 20:7). One who loves the king will not falsely take an oath in his name.

Y. Ber. 1:5

The Talmud of Babylonia

A.   It has been taught on Tannaite authority:
B.   R. Eliezer says, "If it says, 'with all your soul,' why is 'with all your might' said, and if 'with all your might,' why 'with all your soul'? It is to indicate to you that if there is someone whose body is more valued by him than his money, for such a one it is said, 'with all your soul,' and if there is one whose money is more valued to him than his body, for such it is said, 'with all your might.' "

B. Pes. 52a (= Yoma 82a = San. 74a = Ber. 61b)

Mekhilta of R. Ishmael

It was fitting that the heaven, which had no heart but to which a heart was ascribed, should come and cause manna, like dew, to come down for the Israelites, who possessed a heart and received the Torah and served God with all their heart and with all their soul, as it is said, "And you shall love the Lord your God with all your heart and with all your soul" (Deut. 6:5).

Mekhilta Shirata 6:141

The fixed exegetical principle attached to this verse focuses on the heart, soul, and might, asking how one loves God with all three. That inquiry derives from the Mishnah's treatment of the verse. The Tosefta's authorities add only the attribution to Meir. The Talmud of the Yerushalmi contributes the detail that serving God with all one's soul means serving him through martyrdom. The Talmud of Babylonia completes the explanation for loving God with soul and might, meaning wealth. Exegeses that do not fall into the simple pattern inaugurated by the Mishnah scarcely change the picture of a fixed exegetical tradition, yielding new details but no fresh point of view.

Affections as Law

Two points are noteworthy here. First, what the sources that deal with law tell us about emotions, the compilations of scriptural exegeses repeat. That fact is striking because Scripture itself provides innumerable opportunities for fresh comment and innovative reflection on the affective life. Nonetheless, these opportunities provoked no new thought and, indeed, provided few occasions for expression of any ideas at all. And that leads us to the second point. The sheer paucity of relevant materials is a genuine surprise. We may say quite flatly that, when the framers of the canon as a whole (if we may imagine such a nonexistent group) had something to say about the affective life, as a matter of convention they chose legal, not exegetical or theological, contexts in which to say it. True, statements about emotions were attached to the exegeses of verses, but they rarely contributed to the interpretation of the base verse. Equally true, sayings were recorded about God's feelings. But in the aggregate, these facts were too slight in substance and too minimal in volume to have had much impact. The conventions governing topics covered in diverse documents dictated a simple rule. Sages made statements about emotions in the context of normative rules, laws. They rarely found Scripture commentary a suitable context for laying down their opinions on how people should feel.

What does that simple fact prove? So far as the sages were concerned, feelings were a component of the discipline of the holy life. Since there were rules for the heart as much as for the hearth, kosher feelings as much as kosher food, so to speak, the sages quite naturally discussed those rules in the setting in which, in general, the disciplines of the holy way of life were expounded Hence, rules for mourning and rejoicing, remorse and public regret, laws governing how people ordinarily should feel, decisions based on how people did feel ("if he was happy . . . ") took their rightful place alongside the many other rules.

No equivalent motive evidently provoked the sages to introduce the same topic in their reading of Scripture. There their repertoire of theological, moral, and historical issues to be discerned in scriptural passages encompassed a quite different set of concerns, those encompassing values to be imputed to (or, from *their* perspective, discovered in) scriptural models and heroes, human and divine. For example, a common motif of the exegetical literature requires the exegete to discover Torah study sayings and examples throughout the biblical narrative. We recall how David showed his humility by his devotion to the study of the Torah. A catalogue of Torah exegeses of Scripture would fill this entire book, not a brief chapter, such as the one that closes here.

When we realize that *kosher* emotions compare to *kosher* foods, we penetrate the heart of matters. The sages do not prohibit *wanting* to eat pork, they prohibit eating it. Indeed, some of them maintain that one should not claim to refrain from eating pork merely out of distaste. Rather, one should want it but refrain because God wants otherwise. Hence, refraining becomes an act of will: positive and expressive, a statement of attitude, an act of virtue. Here, too, the sages recognize the natural traits of humanity: anger, rebellion, arrogance, selfishness. They demand, in God's name and in God's likeness, the opposite: patience, forgiveness, restraint. They know the natural bent of the heart of humanity, since, after all, with terrible words God had remarked with resignation that the impulse of humanity is only to do evil. The sages understand how things really are and insist that humanity can change them. But how? By making action inaction: virtue, restraint, commitment, submission. Things are opposite to what they seem when courage demonstrates self-restraint.

The life of the virtuous heart expresses humanity's submission to God. In conciliation, one shows the true state of one's will and demeanor: to be like God, one acts like God among other human beings. That conviction forms the foundation of the system as a whole. To be sure, it is stated mainly at the end of the sequence of doctrines, in the Bavli. The original theory of virtue finds its true, solid foundation in theology: The heart of the human being must be shaped according to the model of the heart of God. The one dimension, after all, in which humanity and divinity come together is the virtue of the heart. God's will is humanity's measure; humanity's virtue on earth incarnates God in heaven.

CHAPTER IX

Constant Affections, Inconstant Heart

Emotion as Tradition

In the early, middle, and late phases of formative Judaism, a single doctrine and program dictated how Israel should tame its heart. In the unfolding canon of Judaism, emotions formed part of an iron tradition. That is, a repertoire of rules and relationships handed down from the past, always intact and unimpaired, governed the issue. As successive documents came to closure, each one added improvements while leaving the structure basically the same. Like a cathedral that takes a thousand years to build but, throughout the construction and not only at the end, always looks uniform and antique, so the view of the affective life over centuries remained not only cogent but essentially uniform.

In many categories of thought we cannot reasonably define what Judaism or our sages thought all at once and all together. Why not? Because the components of the canonical literature of Judaism, read in sequence of closure, yield ample evidence of change, development, growth, and, above all, response to circumstance and context. But here the same sources, read sequentially, do not. Whereas the formative centuries in the history of Judaism overall mark a period of remarkable growth and change in various substantial ideas, in the matter of emotions they do not. The single fact emerging from the survey in Chapters III through VIII – a fact that a much larger selection of examples would only have validated – is that the sages' doctrine of affections remained constant in an age of change. Before we ask why that fact demands explanation, however, let us rapidly review the main points established in our survey of the main canonical compositions, from the Mishnah through the Bavli and the more important compilations of biblical exegeses.

Although the Mishnah casually refers to emotions (e.g., tears of joy, tears of sorrow), it does so only in a public and communal context. The underlying principle affecting all emotions in the Mishnah is that feelings must be kept under control, never fully expressed witl.out consideration of the appropriate context. Emotions must always lay down judgments. We see in most cases in which emotions play a systemic, not merely a tangential, role that the basic principle is the same. We can, and must, so frame our feelings that they accord with the appropriate rule.

Tractate Abot presents the most comprehensive account of religious affections. The reason is that, in that document above all, how we feel defines virtue. The issue is central, the doctrine fully exposed. A simple catalogue of permissible feelings comprises humility, generosity, self-abnegation, love, a spirit of conciliation, and eagerness to please. A list of impermissible emotions consists of envy, ambition, jealousy, arrogance, holding to one's opinion, self-centeredness, a grudging spirit, vengefulness, and the like. People should aim at eliciting from others acceptance and good will and should avoid confrontation, rejection, and humiliation of another. This they must do through conciliation and giving up their own claims and rights. Both catalogues form a harmonious and uniform whole, aiming at the cultivation of the humble and malleable person, one who accepts everything and resents nothing.

True, these virtues, in this tractate as in the system as a whole, derive from knowledge of what God wants. But God favors those who please others. The virtues appreciated by human beings prove identical to the ones to which God responds as well. And what single virtue of the heart encompasses the rest? Restraint, the source of self-abnegation and humility, serves as the antidote for ambition, vengefulness, and, above all, arrogance. It is restraint of our own interest that enables us to deal generously with others, humility that generates a liberal spirit toward others.

The authors or compilers of the Tosefta succeeded in adding only a few fresh and important developments of established themes. What is striking, first, is the stress on the communal stake in an individual's emotional life. Second is the Tosefta's authors' explicit effort to invoke an exact correspondence between public and private feelings. In both realms emotions are to be tamed, kept in hand and within accepted proportions. Public sanctions for inappropriate, or disproportionate, emotions entail negative emotions, such as shame. It need hardly be added that feeling shame for displaying improper feelings once again underlies the social, judgmental character of feelings. Shame is public, guilt private. People are responsible for the way they feel, as much as for the way, in word or deed, they express feeling. Hence, an appropriate penalty derives from the same aspect of social life, that is, the affections. I cannot imagine a more stunning tribute to the power of feeling than the allegation in the Tosefta that the Temple was destroyed because of vain hatred. That sort of hatred, self-serving and arrogant, stands against the love that characterizes God's relationship to Israel. Accordingly, it was improper affections that destroyed the relationship embodied in the ancient Temple cult.

Our survey of the Yerushalmi confirmed the result that predominated throughout our inquiry. Emotions not taken up earlier now did not come under discussion. Principles introduced earlier enjoyed restatement and extensive exemplification. Some principles of proper feelings even generated secondary developments. But the system was essentially complete in the earliest statement of its main points, and everything that followed for four hundred years simply reinforced and restated what had already emerged. In general, where the Mishnah introduced issues of the affective life, the Yerushalmi's authors and compilers took up those issues. But they never said much about them, and they rarely introduced them on their own. What then did the compilers of the Yerushalmi contribute? They taught that temper marks the ignorant person, restraint and serenity, the learned one. They instructed us to respect public opinion and cultivate social harmony.

The Bavli carried forward with little change the now-traditional program of emotions, listing the same ones catalogued earlier and no new ones. The authors said about those feelings what had been said earlier. A leader must be someone acceptable to the community. God then accepts him too. People should be ready to give up quarrels and forgive. The correspondence of social and personal virtues reaches explicit statement: The community must forbear; the individual must forgive. Communal tolerance for causeless hatred destroyed the Temple; individual vendettas yield miscarriages. The two coincide. In both cases people nurture feelings that reflect arrogance. Arrogance is what permits the individual to express emotions without discipline, and arrogance is what leads the community to undertake what it cannot accomplish.

The strikingly fresh medium for conveying traditional doctrines in the Bavli takes the form of prayers composed by sages. Here the values of the system came to eloquent expression. Sages prayed that their souls might be as dust for everyone to tread upon. They asked for humility, congenial colleagues, good will, good impulses. They ask God to take cognizance of their humiliation, to spare them from disgrace. The familiar affective virtues and sins, for example, self-abnegation as against arrogance, made their appearance in liturgical form as well. Another noteworthy type of material, also not new, in which the pages of the Bavli prove rich, portrayed the deaths of sages. One dominant motif is uncertainty in the face of death, a sign of humility and self-abnegation.

The basic motif – theological as much as affective – encompassing all the materials of the Bavli is simple. Israel is estranged from God and therefore should exhibit the traits of humility and uncertainty, acceptance and conciliation. When God recognizes in Israel's heart, as much as in the nation's deeds and deliberation, the proper feelings, God will respond by ending that estrangement that marks the present age. Hence, the single word encompassing the entire affective doctrine of the canon of Judaism is "alienation." No contemporary who has survived the Holocaust can miss the psychological depth of the system, which joins the human condition to the fate of the nation and the world, and links the whole to the broken heart of God.

We therefore find ourselves where we started, in those verses which say that, if one wants something, one should aspire to its opposite. Things are never what they seem. To be rich, accept what you have. To be powerful, conciliate your enemy. To be endowed with public recognition, express humility. So, too, the doctrine of the emotional life expressed in law, scriptural interpretation, and tales of sages alike is uniform and simple. Emotions well up uncontrolled and spontaneous. Anger, vengeance, pride, arrogance – these people feel by nature. Feelings as much as affirmations and actions must become what by nature they are not. One must pursue humility, for example, by doing nothing to aggrandize oneself. The life of the emotions, in conformity with the life of reflection and of concrete deed, consists in the transformation of what things *seem* into what they *ought* to be. No contemporary psychology or philosophy can miss the point. Here we have an example of the view that emotions constitute constructs, and feelings lay down judgments. Thus, the heart contributes, together with the mind, to the human being's power to form reasoned viewpoints. Such an opinion surely coheres with the context and circumstance of those who held it – the sages, who were intellectuals to their core.

This theory of the emotional life, whichs presists through the unfolding of the canonical documents of Judaism, fits into a larger way of viewing the world. How shall we describe this mode of thought? It seems to me we may call it an *as if* way of seeing things. That is to say, it is *as if* a common object or symbol actually represented an uncommon one. Nothing says what it means. Everything important speaks metonymically, elliptically, parabolically, symbolically. All statements carry deeper meaning, which is inherent in other statements altogether. So, too, each emotion bears a negative and a positive charge, as each matches and balances the other: humility, arrogance, love, hate. If a negative emotion is natural to the heart, the individual has the power to sanctify that negative, sinful feeling and turn it into a positive, holy emotion. Ambition must be tamed and transformed into humility; hatred and vengeance must be changed to love and acceptance.

What we see in the materials surveyed is an application of a large-scale, encompassing exercise in analogical thinking – something is like something else, stands for, evokes, or symbolizes that which is quite outside itself. It may be the opposite of something else, in which case it conforms to the opposite of the rules that govern that something else. The reasoning is analogical or it is contrastive, and the fundamental logic is taxonomic. The taxonomy rests on those comparisons and contrasts we should call, as I said, metonymic and parabolic. In that case what lies on the surface misleads. What lies beneath or beyond the surface is the true reality.

How shall we characterize people who see things this way? They are the opposite of those who call a thing as it is. Self-evidently, they have become accustomed to perceiving more – or less – than is apparent. Perhaps that is a natural mode of thought for the Jews of this period (and other times as well), so long used to calling themselves God's first love, yet now seeing others with greater worldly reason claiming that same advantaged relationship. Not in mind only, but still more in the politics of the world, the people that remembered its origins along with the very creation of the world and founding of humanity, that recalled how it alone served, and serves, the one and only God, for hundreds of years had confronted a quite different existence. The radical disjuncture between the way things were and the way Scripture said things were supposed to be, and in actuality would some day become, surely imposed an unbearable tension. It was one thing for the slave born to slavery to endure. It was another for the free person sold into slavery to accept that same condition. The vanquished people, the broken-hearted nation that had lost its city and its Temple, that had, moreover, produced another nation from its midst to take over its Scripture and much else, could not bear too much reality. That defeated people, through its intellectuals, as represented in the sources we have surveyed, then found refuge in a mode of thought that trained the vision to see things other than as the eyes perceived them. Among the diverse ways by which the weak and subordinated accommodate themselves to their circumstance, the one of iron-willed pretense in life, is most likely to yield the mode of thought I am suggesting: Things never are, because they cannot be, what they seem. The uniform tradition on emotions persisted intact because the social realities of Israel's life proved permanent, until, in our own time, they changed.

Constancy and Change

If the reader concurs that, early, middle, and late in the formation of Judaism, emotions are portrayed in essentially one way, the obvious question must now come to center stage: So what? One may fairly ask why we should regard as a fact demanding explanation the simple observation that a single view of human nature, including permissible and forbidden feelings, predominates among a coherent social group of intellectuals. People take for granted, not entirely without reason, that the sages' culture defined itself along traditional lines. A mark of the disciple of a sage was imitation of the master, the sage. A critical doctrine of the Judaism defined by the sages of the rabbinical canon emphasized that people memorized the received books of rules and exegesis and made decisions (as in any tradition of jurisprudence) in line with those already made. A list of those definitive traits of the book culture portrayed by the canon would encompass pages of items characteristic of a traditional, stable, uniform, and therefore constant culture – a tradition. Why, then, should I have expressed an interest in demonstrating, in Chapters III through VIII, so unsurprising a fact as the constancy of the doctrine of emotions in the literary culture fully exposed in the sequence of writings we have surveyed?

The answer requires two simple sentences. First, in general, traditional cultures, and even literary cultures, do change over time, in the present case a span of five hundred years. Second, and more probative for the present case, within the same books of the same canon, read in the same sequence, definitive traits of culture do exhibit massive marks of revision. I shall discuss three: hermeneutics, symbolism, and teleology. We shall now see how the same sources, arranged in the same way, reveal growth and development, not traditional stability, in these areas. Then the constancy of the doctrine of emotions will be all the more striking.

First, I shall summarize results worked out elsewhere. In those results we see three sets of facts that stunningly contradict the constancy of the sages' doctrine of affections. In their implications for the stability of the literary culture of the sages, these facts portray the opposite of a stable and orderly, cogent and temporally coherent doctrine, unfolding in a single, unchallenged path for five hundred years. They point toward a revolution in the formation of Judaism.

This revolution took place in a single century, the fourth, after the Roman Empire had become Christian. As an analogy of the inductive discovery of what happened at that time, we think of Krakatoa's explosion. That volcanic eruption affected the natural course of growth throughout the world for decades. Long before people grasped the full dimensions of the cataclysm near far-off Java, however, they observed in a broad cross section of natural life the confluence of a single pattern – one pointing toward something that had had an impact nearly everywhere on earth. Only then did the effects of Krakatoa become clear. The comparison here is between the three sets of facts under discussion and the rings of giant trees, each in a different climatic region of the world, examined in the aftermath of Krakatoa. A tree in New Guinea, another in Peru, and a third in the Congo, when cut down, all showed a sudden and marked diminution in growth at exactly the same point. Naturalists wondered what had happened at that one time to affect the growth of trees in such widely separated regions of the earth. In a reasonable set of steps, they reached the conclusion that Krakatoa's explosion had darkened the skies and obstructed the rays of the sun, so diminishing growth around the world. Only then did the full impact of the calamity make its mark on human consciousness. And to exhaust the analogy, if in some sheltered region, always open to the sun and sufficiently far from the latitudes affected by Krakatoa's ashes, growth continued undiminished, the rings of trees uniform from year to year, people would naturally ask why.

The point is, if much else changes, as I shall now demonstrate was the case, then why, in the very writings that yield ample evidence of change, does one thing remain constant? First, I review all the changes converging on the later fourth century; then I proffer an explanation of why some things stayed the same, even after that turning point.

Change in the Use of Scripture: Compiling Exegeses

The first change revealed in the unfolding of the sages' canon pertains to the use of Scripture: the making of books from the collection of exegeses of Scripture. Why was that an innovation? Because the Mishnah and the exegetical literature that served the Mishnah were not shaped around the explanation of verses of Scripture. The authorship of the Mishnah and its principal heirs followed their own program, which was a topical one. They arranged ideas by subject matter. But in the third, and especially, in the later fourth centuries, other writings were organized around the explanation of verses of Scripture, not a set of topics. This meant that a mode of organizing ideas other than the topical mode that predominated in the Mishnah, the Tosefta, the Yerushalmi (and later the Bavli) was now making its way into the canon of Judaic doctrine.

Making books out of scriptural exegeses began, probably in the third or earlier part of the fourth century, with the linking of statements in the Mishnah to proof texts in Scripture. The authors of the Mishnah, for their part, had usually considered it unnecessary to validate the rules of the Mishnah by citing texts of Scripture. Their heirs, beginning with the Sifra and the two Sifrés, worked their way through legal passages of Scripture. They meant in part to show how those passages proved the correctness of rules of the Mishnah, which, not uncommonly, was cited verbatim.

Beyond the first task, that of searching for proof texts for the Mishnah's rules and legal propositions, a second one, involving the same compilations of scriptural exegeses, developed. This work was to explain verses of Scripture on their own, not only in relation to the received laws of the Mishnah. The legal passages of the Pentateuch defined the arena for study.

Once the systematic exegesis of scriptures on legal topics had become routine, nonlegal passages came to the fore, first in the book of Genesis. A natural step was to read legal passages for reasons other than exposition of the law. Leviticus Rabbah's writers compiled materials to present Leviticus not as a sequence of detailed rules but as a set of closely argued syllogisms.

These several approaches to Scripture, first in relation to the Mishnah, second in regard to the law of Scripture, and third with respect to Scripture read on its own, reached canonical status in a single way. Compilations of books of scriptural exegeses took shape and joined the canon. A single important change is thus represented in these documents.

As I have said, sages did not start compiling collections of biblical exegeses until, approximately, the end of the third to the end of the fourth century. These collections represented a totally new kind of book in rabbinic Judaism (although other kinds of Judaism had been making them for close to a thousand years). Before this time, so far as we know, no one in rabbinic Judaism, then nearly four hundred years in the making, had ever conceived of compiling or writing that kind of book of biblical exegeses. Gradually, however, such collections, using the names of talmudic heroes and pseudoepigraphically assigning to them a wide variety of opinions, rapidly became a literary and theological convention in Judaism. (Even the thirteenth-century Zohar, a mystical speculation, was given the literary framework of biblical exegeses written in the names of talmudic sages.) What was done in rabbinic Judaism for the first time in the fourth, fifth, and sixth centuries thus set the model for well over a thousand years, up to the eighteenth century: the systematic collection, arrangement, and composition of biblical exegeses into authoritative books. Thus, one acceptable mode of creative expression in the profoundly traditional world of Judaism came to full exposure at this time.

Why, particularly within the circles of talmudic rabbis in the third and fourth centuries, did people begin to compile exegeses of Scripture and make books of them? The problem is *not* why Jews in general began to undertake exegesis of the Hebrew scriptures. Many other kinds of Jews had done so, as we know, certainly throughout the preceding thousand years, back to the sixth century B.C. Since the Hebrew Bible itself is rich in exegetical materials, the books of Chronicles being a systematic commentary and revision of the books of Kings, for example, we cannot ask why at just this time people read and interpreted Scripture. Judaism in all forms had always done that.

Nor was there anything new even in collecting exegeses and framing them for a particular polemical purpose, that is, creating a book from comments on Scripture and in the form of a commentary. The Essene library at Qumran contains compositions of biblical commentary and exegesis. The school of Matthew provides another sort of exercise in systematic composition based on the amplification and application of Israel's ancient scriptures. We recognize, moreover, that both Israelite communities – the Essenes and the Christian Jews around Matthew – produced their collections not merely to preserve opinions, but to make important statements in a stunning way. We also know, surely in the instance of Matthew, that the power of a brilliantly composed exegetical collection and arrangement can make an impact even after two thousand years. That is why, to begin with, people made and preserved such collections and arrangements: to say what they believed God had told them.

But in the formation of the holy literature, the canon, of rabbinic Judaism, so far as we know, no one before the fourth century had produced a collection of biblical exegeses in the form of holy books.

Why the fourth century? Why at all? My answer, as is clear, is that making such collections defined the natural next step in the process precipitated by the appearance of the Mishnah and the task of exegesis of the Mishnah. The Talmud, the great work of exegesis of the Mishnah, set the pattern. The compilers of the exegetical collections then followed that pattern. They composed discourses for Scripture within precisely the same taxonomical framework as the Talmud's discourses for the Mishnah. So the context of the composition of exegetical collections and the Talmud alike was defined by the Mishnah.

Let me explain. The original work of collecting and arranging the exegeses of Scripture followed the patterns set in collecting and arranging exegeses of the Mishnah. Just as the Talmud, which is Mishnah exegesis, treats the Mishnah, so the earliest collections of scriptural exegesis treat Scripture. The Mishnah was the first in Judaism to ignore the antecedent holy literature. Furthermore, it rapidly assumed the chief place in the Jewish government of the Land of Israel as the constitution and bylaws of the Jewish nation in its land. Accordingly, the heirs of the Mishnah demanded a theory of its origin, standing, claim to authority, and ground for compelling obedience, whether in sanctions or in a myth of supernatural origin through revelation.

How was the road to be paved from the Mishnah to Scripture? The answer lay in one age-old and conventional way of reading Scripture, commonly called *midrash* and here called simply *exegesis*. The sages now sought through biblical exegesis to link the Mishnah to Scripture, detail by detail. In this context the making of books from exegeses of Scripture represented a striking change in what by the early fourth century were well-established traditions.

To return to the main point, the same canonical writings of formative

Judaism, read in the same order, reveal stability in one matter and change in another. Once more, the program of appropriate feelings remained constant. The policy in the selection and organization of knowledge, in the making of books, shifted radically. However, what was said in the old kind of book, in the Mishnah and its later exegeses, and what was said in the new kind of book, in collections of exegeses of Scripture, on the topic of emotions remained the same. I need not exaggerate the importance of the new principle for the literary organization of learning and tradition, around the framework of books of Scripture as much as tractates of the Mishnah. I need merely point to the fact that in the unfolding of Judaism in its formative age, in critical matters of aesthetics and the formation of learning, changes did take place. In the affairs of the heart, we see none.

Change in the Definition of the Generative Symbol: Torah

The generative symbol of the literary culture of the sages, the Torah, stands for the system as a whole. "Torah," revelation, defines the classification for what is true. At the beginning of the canonical development, in the Mishnah, the Torah bore as its principal points of reference, first, the scriptures, second, the level of highest authority, as distinct from the lesser authority of the sages, and, third, a range of familiar meanings, such as a scroll of revealed Scripture. At the end, from the Yerushalmi onward, the symbol of the Torah took on yet another meaning, one that, when Judaism had reached its final form at the end of this period, proved distinctive. It was the doctrine that, when Moses received the Torah at Mount Sinai, it came down with him in two media: written and oral. The written Torah was transmitted, as its name says, through writing and is now contained in the canon of Scripture. The oral Torah was transmitted through the process of formulation for ease of memorization and then transmitted in the memories of sages and their disciples, from Moses and Joshua to the most current generation.

That doctrine of the dual Torah, that is of the Torah in two media, came about in response to the problem of explaining the standing and authority of the Mishnah. But the broadening of the symbol of the Torah first took shape around the figure of the sage. That symbolism accounted for the sages' authority. Only later on, in the fourth century, in the pages of the Yerushalmi, did the doctrine of the dual Torah find expression.

Thus, in the unfolding of the documents of the canon of Judaism, the generative symbol of the Torah reveals a striking change. Beginning as a rather generalized account of how sages' teachings are related to God's will, the symbol of the Torah gains concrete form in its application to the dual Torah, written and oral, Scripture and Mishnah. This shift represents a symbolic change of fundamental character.

Let us begin the work of elaborating this statement by surveying the meanings imputed to the symbol of the Torah. In the Judaism that took shape in the formative age, everything was contained in that one thing. When we speak of "Torah" in rabbinical literature of late antiquity, we no longer denote a particular book or its contents. Instead, we connote a broad range of clearly distinct categories of noun and verb, concrete fact and abstract relationship alike. "Torah" stands for a kind of human being. It denotes a social status and social group. It refers to a type of social relationship. It further denotes a legal status and differentiates things and persons, actions and status, points of social differentiation, and legal and normative standing, as well as "revealed truth." In all, the main points of emphasis of the whole of Israel's life as viewed by sages come to full symbolic expression in that single word. If people wanted to explain how they would be saved, they would use the word "Torah." If they wished to sort out their parlous relationships with Gentiles, they would use the word "Torah." "Torah" stood for salvation and accounted for Israel's this-worldly condition and the hope, for both individual and nation alike, of life in the world to come. In formative Judaism, the word "Torah" stood for everything. The Torah symbolized the whole, at once and entire.

Beyond the appearance of the Mishnah, the movement of the Torah from standing for a concrete, material object, a scroll, to symbolizing a broad range of relationships, proceeds in two significant stages. The first is marked off by tractate Abot, the second by the Yerushalmi. As to the former, Abot regards study of the Torah as something a sage does. The substance of the Torah is what a sage says. That is so whether or not the sage's saying is related to scriptural revelation. The content of the sayings attributed to sages endows those sayings with self-validating status. The sages usually do not quote verses of Scripture and explain them, nor do they speak in God's name. Yet, it is clear, sages talk Torah. What follows? It is this: If a sage says something, what he says is Torah. More accurately, what he says falls into the classification of Torah. Accordingly, Abot treats Torah learning as symptomatic, an indicator of the status of the sage, hence, as I said, as merely instrumental. At issue in Abot is not Torah, but the authority of the sage. It is that standing that transforms a saying into a Torah saying or, more appropriately, that places a saying into the classification of Torah. Abot then stands as the first document of incipient rabbinism, that is, the doctrine that the sage embodies the Torah and is a holy man, like Moses "our rabbi," in the likeness and image of God. The beginning is to claim that a saying falls into the category of Torah if a sage says it as Torah. The end is to view the sage himself as Torah incarnate.

In the pages of the Yerushalmi, about 150 years later, evoking the word "Torah" forms the centerpiece of a theory of Israel's history, on the one side, and an account of the teleology of the entire system, on the other. Torah indeed has ceased to be a specific thing or even a category. Stories about studying the Torah yield not a judgment as to status (i.e., praise for the learned man) but promise for supernatural blessing now and salvation in time to come.

To the rabbis the principal salvific deed was to "study Torah," by which they meant memorizing Torah sayings by constant repetition and, as the Yerushalmi itself amply testifies, for some sages profound analytic inquiry into the meanings of those sayings. The innovation now is that this act of "study of Torah" imparts supernatural power of a material nature. For example, by repeating words of Torah, the sage could ward off the angel of death and accomplish other kinds of miracles. Thus, Torah formulas served as incantations. Mastery of Torah transformed the man engaged in Torah learning into a supernatural figure who could do things ordinary folk could not do. The category of "Torah" had already vastly expanded so that, through transformation of the Torah from a concrete thing to a symbol, a Torah scroll could be compared to a man of Torah, namely, a rabbi. Now the principle had been established that salvation would come from keeping God's will in general, as Israelite holy men had insisted for so many centuries, so it was a small step for rabbis to identify their corpus of learning, namely, the Mishnah and associated sayings, with God's will expressed in Scripture, the universally acknowledged medium of revelation.

The history of the symbolization of the Torah proceeds from its removal from the framework of material objects, even from the limitations of its own contents, to its transformation into something quite abstract, quite distinct from the document and its teachings. The Torah stands for this something more, specifically when it comes to be identified with a living person, the sage, and endowed with those traits the sage claimed for himself. The word "Torah," as a abstract symbol serving to distinguish one abstract status from another, regained concrete reality of a new order.

The message of Abot, as I said, was that the Torah served the sage: The Torah indicated who was a sage and who was not. Accordingly, the Abot's apology for the Mishnah was that the Mishnah contained things sages had said. Their sayings formed a chain of tradition extending back to Sinai. Hence, it was equivalent to the Torah. The upshot is that the words of sages enjoyed the status of the Torah. A small step beyond, I think, was to claim that what the sages said was Torah, *as much as what Scripture said was Torah.*

Another small step (and the steps need not have been taken separately or in the order here suggested) led to the position that there were two media in which the Torah reached Israel: One in writing, the other handed down orally, by memory. This final step, fully revealed in the Yerushalmi, brought the conception of Torah to its logical conclusion. Torah came in several media: written, oral, incarnate. Hence, what the sage said had the status of Torah, was Torah, because the sage was Torah incarnate. The abstract symbol now had become concrete once more. We recognize the many, diverse ways in which the Talmud stated that conviction. Every passage in which knowledge of the Torah yields power over this world and the next, that grants the sage the capacity to coerce to his will the natural and supernatural worlds alike, rests on the same viewpoint.

The Yerushalmi's theory of the Torah thus carries us through several stages in the process of the symbolization of the word "Torah." First transformed from something concrete into something abstract and beyond metaphor, the word "Torah" finally emerges once more in a concrete aspect, now as the encompassing and universal mode of stating the whole doctrine, all at once, of Judaism in its formative age.

Why is that fact important to us? Because once more it indicates how, if we read the canonical literature in the order in which we have read it here, the successive documents yield a picture of change and development. The symbol of the Torah changed in manifest and important ways. The doctrine of affections did not.

Change in the Determination of Destiny: Messiah

The third striking change in the literary culture of rabbinical Judaism was the restatement of the goal and purpose of the system. The Mishnah at the outset focused on the sanctification of Israel, in a grid formed by nature and supernature. At the other end of the canon, in the Talmud of Babylonia, the goal of the Judaic system had become the salvation of Israel, in a grid defined by this world and the world to come or, more commonly, by this age and the age of the Messiah. Thus, the teleological statement of the system, originally not defined in eschatological terms at all, in the end appealed to the coming of the Messiah to explain doctrinal prescriptions and their consequences. Whereas the Mishnah and the earlier writings, those that reached closure in the third and early fourth centuries, rarely appealed to the teleology based on a messianic eschatology, from the Talmud of the Land of Israel onward, principal components of the canon promised the coming of the Messiah as the reward for right action. It follows that the canon as a whole reveals a shift in the statement of goals, from a teleology lacking eschatological focus and emphasizing the steady state of santified stasis, to one promising movement from here to eternity.

The Mishnah's framers constructed a complete teleological system, explaining the purpose and goal of their document, without appealing to the figure of the Messiah or claiming that at the end of time the Messiah would come and solve all the problems of the world. They defined the end of their system in other terms entirely. Since they did not so shape their teleology as to point toward the end of time, they also took slight interest in events and in that pattern of events that others called "history." To them the important categories were those of nature and supernature rather than time and the end of time (eschatology) or history and eternity. That is why the Mishnah's framers present us with no elaborate theory of events, a fact fully consonant with their systemic points of emphasis and encompassing concern. Individual events do not matter. Nor do the philosopher-lawyers offer a theory of history. Their conception of Israel's destiny in no way calls on historical categories of either narrative or didactic explanation to describe and account for the future. The small importance attributed to the figure of the Messiah as a historical-eschatological person, therefore, accords with the larger traits of their system as a whole. Let me emphasize: If, as in the Mishnah, what is important in Israel's existence is sanctification, an ongoing process, and not salvation, understood as a final, one-time event, then no one would find reason to tell stories or to narrate history. Few would then develop the obsession about the Messiah that became so characteristic of Judaism in its later, rabbinic mode, as expressed in the Talmud of the Land of Israel and associated writings. The salvific figure becomes an instrument of consecration and so fits into a system quite different from the one originally built around the Messiah.

When, in analyzing the foundation of Judaism, we move from the species, eschatology, upward to the genus, teleology, we find ourselves addressing the motives and goals of the Mishnaic system. The system is so constructed as *not* to point toward a destination at the end of time. But still it does speak of final things. Accordingly, we ask, where, if not in the eschaton, do things end? The answer provided by Abot, the Mishnah's first apologetic, is clear. Death is the destination. In life we prepare for the voyage. We keep the law in order to make the move required of us. What is supposed in Abot to make the system work, what explains why we should act as the Mishnah says, is that other end. The end that I mean is that to which history and national destiny are remote or, rather, irrelevant. Abot constructs a teleology beyond time, providing a goal for every individual. Life is the antechamber, death the destination; what we do is weighed and measured. When we die, we stand on one side of the balance while our life and deeds stand on the other.

The Mishnah's teleology as supplied by Abot presents a curious contrast to the focus of the Mishnah itself. Abot addresses the life of the individual but only incidentally the construct of the nation. The system of the Mishnah, however, designs a whole society, one component after another. Mishnaic discourse speaks of the individual in the context of a national life of collective sanctification. Self-evidently, tensions between individual and community reach ready resolution; that is hardly the point. The main thing is that the Mishnah addresses not the stages of individual life but the constituents of the life of village and Temple, the former shaped, where possible, into the counterpart and mirror image of the latter. For the system of sanctification imagined in the Mishnah, the individual is not a principal building block. The householder and his *ménage* form the smallest whole unit of social construction. Hence, as I said, the teleology contributed by Abot to the Mishnaic system turns out to be no more appropriate than the one that might have, but did not, come out of messianic eschatology. Yet the world beyond historical time to which Abot makes reference provides precisely the right metaphysical setting for the system of order and stasis, of proper and correct classification, that underlay, as foundation and goal, the Mishnah's own detailed statements.

When we come to the Yerushalmi (and later the Bavli), the situation once more changes, but now radically. The figure of the Messiah looms large in both documents. The teleology of the system portrayed in them rests on the premise of the coming of the Messiah. If one does so and so, the Messiah will come, and if not, the Messiah will tarry. Thus, the compilers and authors of the two Talmuds laid enormous emphasis on the sin of Israel and the capacity of Israel through repentance both to overcome sin and to bring the Messiah. "The attribute of justice" delays the Messiah's coming. The Messiah will come this very day, if Israel is deserving. The Messiah will come when there are no more arrogant ("conceited") Israelites, when judges and officers disappear, when the haughty and judges cease to exist, "Today, if you will obey" (Ps. 95:7). What alternatives are excluded? First, no one maintains that the Messiah will come when the Israelites successfully rebel against Iran or Rome. Second, few express eagerness to live through the coming of the Messiah, through the catastrophes, both social and national, that will mark the event. The contrast between this age and the messianic age, moreover, is drawn in some measure in narrowly political terms. Servitude to foreign powers will come to an end. That view is entirely consistent with the opinion, familiar from some of the exegetical collections, that Israel must accept the government of the pagans and that the pagans must not "excessively" oppress Israel.

In the hands of the framers of the late canonical literature of Judaism, the Messiah keeps things basically as they are while at the same time promising dramatic change. The condition of that change is not richly instantiated. It is given in the most general terms. But it is not difficult to define. Israel must keep God's will, expressed in the Torah and the observance of the rites described therein. Israel must demonstrate its acceptance of God's rule. Accordingly, the net effect is to reinforce that larger system of the Judaism of Torah study and the performing of religious duties expressed partially in the Talmuds of the Land of Israel and of Babylonia, with their exegesis of the Mishnah, and partially in the various exegetical compositions organized around the order and program of some of the books of Scripture.

It was first in the Yerushalmi that Judaism drew into its sphere that weighty conception embodied in the Messiah myth. The issue of the Messiah remained subordinated: *If you do this or that*, the Messiah will come. Hence, the Messiah myth supplied the uniform apodosis of diverse protases, the fixed teleology for the variety of ineluctable demands of the system as a whole. But the symbolic expression of the system's teleology underwent remarkable revision, once more surfacing in a late-fourth-century composition. It follows that the Mishnah and its successor documents, Abot and the Tosefta, in particular, presented one picture of the purpose of the system, a teleology without eschatological focus. The two Talmuds, along with some intermediate documents, later set forth a different picture, specifically, an eschatological teleology. The documents do cohere. The Talmuds, beginning with the former of the two, carried forward not only the exegesis of the Mishnah but also the basic values of the Mishnah's system. But they did present substantial changes as well, and that is the main point for our purpose. Once more, we notice that, when we read the documents in the order that we followed in our survey of sayings on emotions, we find that what people said about the affective life remains constant, whereas what they said about the issue of teleology shifts in substantial ways.

To state matters simply, the philosophers of the Mishnah did not make use of the Messiah myth to construct a teleology for their system. They found it possible to present a statement of goals for their projected life of Israel that was entirely divorced from history and eschatology. Since they certainly knew, and even alluded to, long-standing and widely held convictions on eschatological subjects, beginning with those in Scripture, the framers thereby testified that they had made choices different from others before and after them. Their document accurately and ubiquitously expresses these choices, both affirmative and negative. The appearance in the Talmuds of a messianic eschatology fully consonant with the larger characteristic of the rabbinic system – with its stress on the viewpoints and proof texts of Scripture, its interest in what was happening to Israel, and its focus on the national–historical dimension of the life of the group – indicates that the encompassing rabbinic system is essentially independent of the prior, Mishnaic system. True, what had gone before was absorbed and fully assimilated. But the talmudic system, expressed in part in each of the non-Mishnaic segments of the canon and fully spelled out in all of them, is different in the aggregate from the Mishnaic system.

We should not overestimate the magnitude of the shift from the mishnaic to the talmudic system. The change is noteworthy only because of the contrast to the stability of the doctrine of affections. But, in fact, there is a deeper harmony between the Mishnaic and the later talmudic doctrine of teleology and therefore of history, a harmony that, moreover, points toward the explanation of the cogency of the canonical treatment of emotions. In fact, what happened was that the rabbinic system of the Talmuds transformed the Messiah myth in its totality into an essentially ahistorical force. If people wanted to reach the end of time, they had to rise above time, that is, above history, and stand off to the side of great ephemeral movements of political and military character. That is the message of the Messiah myth as it reaches full exposure in the rabbinic system of the two Talmuds. At its foundation it is *precisely* the message of that teleology without eschatology expressed by the Mishnah and its associated documents. Accordingly, we cannot claim that the talmudic system in this regard constitutes a reaction against the Mishnaic one. We must conclude, on the contrary, that in the Talmuds and their associated documents we see the restatement, in classical mythic form, of the ontological convictions that had informed the minds of the second-century philosophers of the Mishnah The new medium contained the old, enduring message: Israel must turn away from time and change, must submit to whatever happens, so as to win for itself the only government worth having, that is, God's rule accomplished through God's anointed agent, the Messiah.

I need not repeat the simple observation that the affective program of the early, middle, and late canon fits tightly in every detail with this doctrine of an ontological teleology in eschatological disguise. Israel is to tame its heart so that it will feel that same humility, within, that Israel's world view and way of living demand in life. Submit, accept, conciliate, stay cool in emotion as much as in attitude, inside and outside – and the Messiah will come.

Who Is Israel and Why?

We now recognize that, in the formation of Judaism, some things changed, others remained constant. What changed? Fundamentals of Judaism: the generative exegetical method, the critical symbol, the teleological doctrine. What remained the same? The equally profound program of virtue: the sages' statement of how people should feel and why they should take charge of their emotions, attitudes, and intentionality. The same books, read in the same order, that reveal the one in flux portray the other in stasis. No one can imagine that Jews in their hearts felt the way sages said they should. The repertoire of permissible and forbidden attitudes hardly can have defined the broad range of actual emotions, whether private or social, of the community of Israel. In fact, we have no evidence about how people really felt. We see only a picture of what sages thought they should, and should not, feel: a literary picture of the heart of God and humanity.

But, as I have stressed, the unchanging repertoire of feelings and other virtues of the heart contrasts strikingly with the shifts and turns of critical components of Judaism as these emerge in the same authoritative writings. Writings that reveal stunning shifts in doctrine, teleology, and herme- neutical method lay forth from beginning to end the one picture of the ideal Israelite: someone who accepts, forgives, conciliates, makes the soul "like dirt beneath other peoples' feet." In a century of total war, such as our own, it may be difficult to appreciate the virtue of submission to the will of others, first one's neighbors in community, second, the world beyond. People with this capacity bear such uncomplimentary sobriquets as milquetoast, wimp, or merely coward. Ours is an age that admires the strong-minded individual, the uncompromising hero, the warrior whether on the battlefield or in the academy.

Why sages counseled a different kind of courage is obvious. Given the situation of Israel, vanquished on the battlefield, broken in the turning of history's wheel, we need hardly wonder why wise men advised con- ciliation and acceptance. Exalting humility made sense, there being little choice. Whether or not these virtues found advocates in other contexts for other reasons, in the circumstance of the vanquished nation, for the people of broken heart, the policy of forbearance proved instrumental, entirely appropriate to both the politics and social conditions of the times.

Why? If Israel had produced a battlefield hero, the nation could not have given him an army. If Jewry had cultivated strong-minded individ- uals, they would have been sentenced to a useless life of ineffective protest. The nation required not strong-minded leadership but consensus. The social virtues of conciliation, moreover, reinforced the bonds that joined a nation lacking frontiers, a people without a politics of its own, for all there was to hold Israel together to sustain its life as a society would have to come forth out of its inner resources. Bonding emerged mainly from within. Thus, consensus, conciliation, self-abnegation, and humility, the search for acceptance within the group were appropriate emotions because they dictated wise policy and shrewd politics.

We cannot imagine that the counsel of sages covered ground not explored by others and private to them. Quite the contrary, much that the sages taught were commonplaces of philosophical virtue in their time and circumstance. But it was their context – the ground of their being, namely, Israel – that made that counsel sharp and controversial, therefore important. Saying to a people such as Israel what Aristotle had said had imparted to the perennial teaching a distinctive and particular wisdom. Virtue for humanity in general became for Israel sound public policy – and that is what is important about the sages' position. Saying what they said, when and where and to whom they said it, made particular the shared sentiments of the ages. What made the sages' views astounding therefore? It was the circumstance, not the text.

Israel could survive only on the sufferance of others. Israel, therefore, not only would nurture policies of subordination and acceptance of diminished status among nations. Israel also would develop, in its own heart, the requisite structure of virtue. The composition of individuals' hearts would then comprise the counterpart virtues. A policy of acceptance of the rule of others dictated conciliation to the will of others. A defeated people meant to endure defeat would have to get along by going along. How would it be possible to persuade each Jew to accept what all Jews had to do in order to endure? By persuading the heart, not only the mind. Then each one privately would feel what everyone publicly had in any case to think.

That, I think, accounts for the persistence of the sages' wise teachings on temper, their sagacious counsel on conciliating others and seeking the approval of the group. Society, in the canonical writings, set the style for the self's deepest sentiments. The approved feelings retained approval for so long because emotions, in the thought of the sages, conformed to rules. Feelings laid down judgments. Affections, therefore, constituted not mindless effusions but deliberate constructions. Whether the facts then conformed to the sages' view (or now with the mind of psychology, philosophy, and anthropology) we do not know. But the sages' view did penetrate deeply into what had to be – whether or not what had to be would ever correspond to what was.

Then why did some things, important and public things, change, while the doctrine of affections remained the same? That final question now demands an answer. To find it, let us seek an analogy. Can we point to the endurance of a single attitude, policy, or institution over a very long period of time in Israel's ongoing history? And can we explain why it persisted, amid time and change, essentially unimpaired? To answer these questions, I shall point to a persistent structure so deep in the consciousness and culture of Israel as to transcend changes of still more consequence than those that swept over Israel in the period from the first through the seventh centuries. It was a structure so enduring that it came to expression among diverse and unrelated groups. Thus far, we have examined only a small matter, how a singular group of writings treated a given topic. But now we turn to a greater issue: how diverse Israelites, working out different and distinct forms of Judaism, constructed several systems in the same way, in a single model. That seems to me a matter of constancy well worth considering and explaining.

I refer specifically to the fact that, from the formation of the Priestly Code, the priests' conception of the Temple and its world view and way of life provided the structural model for a number of groups within Israel. But each of these defined its distinctive world view and way of life, its Judaism, for its own group. We may point to three such groups, all of them turning for definitive structure to the Priestly Code and its generative symbols and myths: the Essenes of Qumran, the Pharisees, and the framers of the earliest strata of the Mishnaic system (who may or may not also have been Pharisees). The literary statements of these three groups make constant reference to issues of the Priestly Code. For example, all three groups stress cultic cleanness and uncleanness, the preservation of food and of meals under conditions prescribed in the Priestly Code of Leviticus and Numbers only for the Temple and the priests.

Let me phrase matters with particular reference to the founders of the earliest phases of the system ultimately revealed in the Mishnah. Elsewhere, in *Judaism: The Evidence of the Mishnah,* I have peeled back the layers of the Mishnaic law. When reaching the earliest of them, I found a system focused on a social group that defined itself around the eating of cultic meals in the state of cleanness prescribed by Leviticus for Temple priests in the eating of their share of the Temple sacrifices. Why, we ask, should the Temple and the ideas of its priests have played so important a role in the mind of the people (whoever they were) represented by the earliest layer of ideas ultimately contained in the Mishnah? What the Mishnah presents is not uncommonly nothing other than what Scripture says. The verses of Scripture that are chosen for representation time and again are those in the Priestly Code. Accordingly, we have to wonder why the priestly themes and repertoire of concerns should have so occupied the imagination and fantasy of the people who formed the group (or groups) represented in the laws before us. It is the continuity from the Priestly Code of the seventh through the fifth centuries B.C. to the beginnings of the Mishnaic code of the first and second centuries A.D. that requires explanation. In the end as much as the beginning, the Mishnah embodies the priestly perspective on the condition of Israel.

If the founders of the Mishnaic code had something distinctive to say, it was in the vocabulary and images of the Priestly Code. The words were their own, but the syntax of the sacred, the metaphysical grammar, belonged to the priesthood from olden times. That is why it is urgent to speculate why the Priestly Code Lev. 1–15, should have exercised so profound and formative an influence on the founders and first framers of Mishnaic law.

That it did so is explained by the fact that the problems it addressed and (for some) solved remained chronic long after the period of its formulation, from the seventh century down to its closure in the time of Ezra and Nehemiah. True, there were many ways to confront and cope with the problems I shall specify. After all, third and fourth Isaiahs flourished in the same time as did the philosophers, storytellers, and lawyers whose ideas ultimately come to a single formation and to closure in the Priestly Code. Jeremiah and the writers and editors of Deuteronomy were contemporaries too. But the Priestly Code states a powerful answer to an urgent question. Since, as I shall now suggest, that question would continue to trouble Israelites for a long time, it is not surprising that the priestly answer to it, so profound and fundamental, should for its part have continued to attract and impress people too.

That is the argument I wish now to lay out. In order to follow it, we have first to locate ourselves in the time of closure of the Priestly Code, that is, in the late sixth and fifth centuries B.C., and to specify the critical tensions of that period. Once we have seen the character of these tensions, we shall realize without much exposition that the same tensions persisted and confronted the thinkers whose reflection led to the conclusions, in resolution of those ongoing points of dissonance, that the Temple's holiness enveloped and surrounded Israel's land and demarcated its people as well.

What marks ancient Israel is its preoccupation with defining itself. In one way or another Israel sought means of declaring itself distinct from its neighbors. The stress on exclusion of neighbors from the group, and of the group from neighbors, runs contrary to the situation of ancient Israel, with unmarked frontiers of culture, the constant giving and receiving among diverse groups, generally characteristic of ancient times. The persistent stress on differentiation yielded a preoccupation with self-definition. But that point of concern contradicts the fact that in the time of the formulation of the Priestly Code, Israel was deeply affected by the changes in social, cultural, and political life and institutions captured by the word "Hellenization." That was the case long before the conquest of Alexander. We may trace the ongoing preoccupation with self-definition to the context that yielded the later scriptural legacy of the Pentateuchal redaction, for it was in that protracted moment of confusion and change that the Priestly Code came to closure, and with it, the Pentateuchal heritage.

The upshot of the codification and closure of the law under Ezra and

Nehemiah was the formulation of a law code that laid heavy emphasis on the exclusivist character of the Israelite God and cult. "Judaism" acquired the character of a cultically centered way of life and world view. Both rite and myth aimed at the continuing self-definition of Israel by separation from, and exclusion of, the rest of the world. Order against chaos meant holiness over uncleanness, life over death. The purpose was to define Israel against the background of the other peoples of the Near and Middle East, with whom Israel had much in common, and, especially, to differentiate Israel from its neighbors (e.g., Samaritans) in the same country. Acute differentiation was required in particular because the social and cultural facts – common traits hardly bespeaking clear-cut points of difference, except of idiom – were precisely to the contrary. The mode of differentiation taken by the Torah literature in general and the priestly sector of that literature in particular was cultic. The meaning, however, was also social. The power of the Torah composed in this time lay in its authors' control of the Temple. The Torah made that Temple the pivot and focus of Israel. The Torah literature, with its jealous God who cares what people do about rather curious matters, and the Temple cult, with its total exclusion of the non-Israelite from participation and (even more so) from cultic comensality, raised high those walls of separation and underlined such distinctiveness as already existed. The life of Israel flowed from the altar; what made Israel Israel was the center, the altar.

So long as Israel remained essentially within its own land and frame of social reference, that is, before the conflagration of the sixth century B.C., the issue of separation from neighbors could be treated casually. When the very core of what made Israel Israel was penetrated by the doubly desolating and disorienting experiences of both losing the land and then coming back, the issue of who Israel is came to the fore. Confusion in economic and social relationships and the fact that the land to which Israelites returned in no way permitted contiguous and isolated Israelite settlement made it certain that the issue of self-definition would emerge. It would remain on the surface and chronic. And it would persist for the rest of Israelite history, from the return to Zion and the formation of the Torah literature even to our own day.

The reason for its persistence is that the social forces that lent urgency to the issue of who Israel is (later, who a Jew is) would remain. It is hardly an exaggeration to say that this confusion about the identity to be assigned to Israel would define the very framework of the social and imaginative ecology of the Jewish people. So long as memory remained, the conflicting claims of exclusivist Torah literature and universalist prophecy, of a people living in utopia, in no particular place, while framing its vision to itself in the deeply locative symbols of cult and center, would make vivid the abiding issue of self-definition.

Now when we ask why the Temple with its cult proved enduringly central in the imagination of the Israelites in the country, we have only to repeat the statements that the priests of the Temple and their imitators in the sects were prepared to make. These explain the critical importance of cult and rite. The altar was the center of life, the conduit of life from heaven to earth and from earth to heaven. All things are to be arrayed in relation to the altar. The movement of the heavens demarcated and celebrated at the cult marked out the divisions of time in relation to the altar. The spatial dimension of the land was likewise demarcated and celebrated in relation to the altar. The natural life of Israel's fields and corrals, the social life of its hierarchical caste system, and the political life (not only in theory by any means) centered on the Temple as the locus of ongoing government – all things in order and in place expressed the single message. The natural order of the world corresponded to, reinforced, and was reinforced by the social order of Israel. Both were fully realized in the cult, the nexus between those opposite and corresponding forces, heaven and earth.

The lines of structure emanated from the altar. And it was these that constituted the wide and impenetrable frontiers separating Israel from the Gentiles – Israel, which was holy, ate holy food, reproduced itself in accord with the laws of holiness, and conducted all of its affairs, both of state and of table and bed, in accord with the demands of holiness. Thus, the cult defined holiness. Holiness meant separateness. Separateness meant life. Why? Because outside the land, the realm of the holy, lay the domain of death. The lands are unclean. The land is holy. In the scriptural vocabulary, one antonym for "holy" is "unclean," and one opposite of "unclean" is "holy." The synonym of "holy" is "life." The principal force and symbol of uncleanness and its highest expression are death.

The case at hand, the persistence of the priestly mentality in a new world, points toward a thesis worth exploring. It has two parts. First, what endures lasts because society sets the terms of persistence. Second, what changes does so because the social group itself has undergone metamorphosis in some way.

Symbol change, such as is represented by a shift in the doctrine of affective behavior, rests on social change. Social change comes to expression in symbol change. Hence, the fact that a single program of emotions served for so long to instruct Israelites how to live the inner life suggests that an underlying social stability endured. Specifically, a single basic mindset, that attitude expressed in the Priestly Code, served for a long time, in diverse forms and among various social groups, to state the norm. We therefore conclude that, for the period in which the Priestly Code set the norm, the social realities remained constant. Change, in contrast to persistence, points toward shifts in the social foundations of symbolic behavior, including doctrine. To understand change, we appeal to that same court to which we addressed our question about constancy, namely, the basic structure and construction of the social group. When, I take as premise, symbols change, attention is shifted to social change beyond. And when society changes, we ask how its symbolic system, expressed in a way of life and in a world view, has shifted. Each must come to testify to the condition of the other. As a matter of hypothsis, therefore, we must speculate about the interplay of society and symbol. The striking shifts in method, symbol of doctrine, and teleology revealed in the unfolding of the canon of Judaism in its formative changes point toward changes in the social world of Israel, as sages, among all Israel, perceived that social world.

Since the several fundamental shifts in symbolic system appear at one point, namely, in the movement from the Mishnah and its nearby exegetical and apologetic literature to the Talmuds and, in particular, to the Yerushalmi, we turn our gaze to the fourth century. We ask what change was so radical as to have redefined Israel's social and political circumstances. Obviously, the answer for the Land of Israel was the same in the fourth century as it was in the second. The change that marked the advent of the Mishnah, a revolution in its age, was the same as the one that had accompanied the appearance of the Yerushalmi (viewed as a process of approximately a century). It was a considerable political turning point.

In both the second and the fourth centuries, the matter reached to full symbolic realization in the name by which the Land of Israel would be known. In the second century the Land of Israel became "Palestine." Israel was defeated, so Rome renamed the land. In the fourth century the Land of Israel became, for Christian Rome that ruled, "the Holy Land." Israel was now vanquished in heaven as much as on earth, so triumphant Christianity now renamed the land. But for Israel, let me say, the land would always be what it had been from the beginning and what it is once more in our day, namely, the Land of Israel, now the state, if not the condition, of Israel. That symbolic order, that rule for unknown ages ahead, stood for all else.

In speculating on the social foundations of symbol change, we have moved far beyond the issue with which we began. But that is appropriate, for if, as I have argued, emotions in the view of the sages who created Judaism remain always the same and if, as I maintain, the reason has to do with the social realities that give meaning to emotion and definition to the possibilities of feeling, there can be no other conclusion. If we begin with private feeling, we end up in society. Affection constitutes a construct of culture. A small step takes us to the position, just now expressed, that affections, no less than convictions, stand for something beyond themselves. So emotions, too, should be interpreted as forms of symbolic behavior. To state the conclusion in a simple way: The heart's deep sentiments serve also as symbols and therefore affectively speak a social vocabulary. How "I" feel stands for everyone, all at once. In the language of theology of Judaism of this age, the *mensch* of the Yiddish language, the fully human person, in Judaism must become the Israel *mensch*. And who is this? It is the Judaic human being in affection, action, attitude, and affirmation. Together, these determine who is Israel, the Jewish nation.

Bibliographical Essay and Source List

Chapter I: Emotions, the Individual, and Society

Averill, James R. "The Acquisition of Emotions During Adulthood." In
C. Z. Malatesta and C. E. Izard, eds., *Emotion in Adult Development* (Beverly Hills, Calif., 1984: Sage).

"A Constructive View of Emotion." In *Emotion: Theory, Research,
and Experience. Vol. 1: Theories of Emotion.* (Orlando, Fla., 1980:
Academic Press).

"The Functions of Grief." In C. Izard, ed., *Emotions in Personality
and Psychopathology* (New York, 1979: Plenum).

"On the Paucity of Positive Emotions." In K. Blankstein, P. Pliner,
and J. Polivy, eds., *Advances in the Study of Communication and
Affect. Vol. 6: Assessment and Modification of Emotional Behavior.*
(New York, 1980: Plenum).

"The Role of Emotion and Psychological Defense in Self-Protective
Behavior." In N. Weinstein, ed., *Taking Care: Understanding and
Encouraging Self-Protective Behavior* (Cambridge University Press,
in press).

"The Social Construction of Emotion: With Special Reference to
Love." In K. Gergen and K. Davis, eds., *The Social Construction
of the Person* (New York, n.d.: Springer).

"Stress as Fact and Artifact: An Inquiry into the Social Origins and
Functions of Some Stress Reactions." C. D. Spielberger and J. Stre-
lau, eds. *Stress and Anxiety* (in press).

Jonathan Edwards, *Religious Affections.* John E. Smith, ed. (New Haven,
Conn., 1959: Yale University Press).

Hochschild, Arlie Russell. *The Managed Heart: Commercialization of
Human Feeling* (Berkeley, 1983: University of California Press).

Lutz, Catherine. "The Domain of Emotion Words on Ifaluk." *American
Ethnologist*, 1982, 9, 113–28.

Niebuhr, Richard R. *Schleiermacher on Christ and Religion: A New Introduction* (New York, 1964: Scribner's).

Solomon, Robert C. "Emotions and Anthropology: The Logic of Emotional World Views." *Inquiry*, 1978, 21:181–99.

"The Logic of Emotion." *Nous*, 1977, 11:41–9.

Love, Emotion, Myth and Metaphor (Garden City, N.J., 1981: Anchor/Doubleday).

The Passions: The Myth and Nature of Human Emotion. (Garden City, N.J., 1977: Anchor/Doubleday).

Chapters III through VIII: The Sources

The canon of holy books comes first. Let me spell out in greater detail the several books we have probed and how they are related to one another. Then I shall explain why we have followed the conventional order in which it is assumed the books made their appearance. Since many sayings are attributed to specific authorities, why not examine the sayings in the order of the authorities to whom they are attributed?

The system of Judaism represented by the views on the Messiah outlined in Chapter IX was given its first literary expression around A.D. 200 and its last around A.D. 600. The first document, the Mishnah, drew together teachings of authorities of the period beginning in the first century, before 70, when the Temple was destroyed and autonomous government ended, and ending with the publication of the code in ca. 200. The last, the Talmud of Babylonia (Bavli), provided the authoritative commentary on thirty-seven of the sixty-two tractates of the Mishnah as well as on substantial portions of the Hebrew scriptures. In joining sustained discourse on the scriptures, called, in the mythic of the present system, the written Torah, the Bavli's framers presented a summa, an encyclopedia, of Judaism to guide Israel, the Jewish people, for many cenuries to come.

Between ca. 200, when autonomous government was well established again, and ca. 600 the continuous movement of sages, holding positions of authority in the Jewish governments recognized by Rome and Iran, as political leaders of the Jewish communities of the Land of Israel (to just after 400) and Babylonia (to ca. 600), respectively, wrote two types of books. One sort extended, amplified, systematized, and harmonized components of the legal system laid forth in the Mishnah. The work of Mishnah exegesis produced four principal documents as well as an apologia for the Mishnah. The apologia was written first, about a generation or so after the Mishnah itself. It was tractate Abot (ca. A.D. 250), a collection of sayings attributed both to authorities whose names also occur in the Mishnah and to some sages who flourished after the conclusion of the Mishnah. The sayings of these later figures, who make no appearance in the Mishnah, appear at the end of the compilation.

The other three principal documents of Mishnah exegesis were the Tosefta, the Talmud of the Land of Israel (the Yerushalmi), and the Bavli. The Tosefta, containing a small proportion of materials contemporaneous with those in the Mishnah and a very sizable proportion secondary to and dependent, even verbatim, on the Mishnah, reached conclusion some time after ca. 300 and before ca. 400. The Yerushalmi closed in ca. 400. The Bavli, as I said, was completed by ca. 600. All these dates, of course, are rough guesses, but the sequence in which the documents made their appearance is not.

The Tosefta addresses the Mishnah; its name means "supplement," and its function was to supplement the rules of the original document. The Yerushalmi mediates between the Tosefta and the Mishnah, commonly citing a paragraph of the Tosefta in juxtaposition with a paragraph of the Mishnah and commenting on both, or so arranging the material that the paragraph of the Tosefta serves, just as it should, to complement a paragraph of the Mishnah. The Bavli, following the Yerushalmi by about two centuries, pursues its own program, which, as I said, was to link the two Torahs and restate them as one.

The stream of exegesis of the Mishnah and exploration of its themes of law and philosophy flowed side by side with a second. This other stream coursed up out of the deep wells of the written Scripture. But it surfaced only long after the work of Mishnah exegesis was well underway and followed the course of that exegesis, now extended to Scripture. The exegesis of the Hebrew scriptures, a convention of all systems of Judaism from before the conclusion of Scripture itself, obviously occupied sages from the very origins of their group. No one began anywhere but in the encounter with the written Torah. But the writing down of exegeses of Scripture in a systematic way, signifying also the formulation of a program and a plan for the utilization of the written Torah in the unfolding literature of the Judaism taking shape, developed in a quite distinct circumstance.

Specifically, a fundamental aspect of the work of Mishnah exegesis began with one ineluctable question. How does a rule of the Mishnah relate to, or rest on, a rule of Scripture? That question demanded an answer, so that the status of the Mishnah's rules, and of the Mishnah itself, could find a clear definition. By itself, the Mishnah bore no explanation of why Israel should obey its rules and accept its vision. Brought into relationship with Scripture, in mythic language, viewed as part of the Torah, the Mishnah gained access to the source of authority by definition operative in Israel, the Jewish people. Accordingly, the work of relating the Mishnah's rules to those of Scripture got underway during the formation of the Mishnah's rules themselves. Collecting and arranging exegeses of Scripture as these related to passages of the Mishnah was first given literary form in the Sifra to Leviticus and in two books, both called Sifré, one to Numbers, the other to Deuteronomy. All three compositions accomplished much else, for even at that early stage, exegeses of passages of Scripture in their own context and not only for the sake of Mishnah exegesis attracted attention. But a principal motif in all three books was the issue of Mishnah–Scripture relationships.

A second, still more fruitful path emerged from the labor of Mishnah exegesis. As the work got underway in the third century, exegetes of the Mishnah and others undertook a parallel task. This was to work through verses of Scripture in exactly the same way – word for word, phrase for phrase, line for line – in which the exegetes pursued the interpretation and explanation of the Mishnah. To state matters simply, precisely the types of exegesis that dictated the way in which sages read the Mishnah now guided their reading of Scripture as well. And as people began to collect and organize comments in accord with the order of sentences and paragraphs of the Mishnah, they were stimulated to collect and organize comments on clauses and verses of Scripture. As I said, this work began in the Sifra and the two Sifrés. It reached massive and magnificent ful-fillment in Genesis Rabbah, which, as its name tells us, presents a line-for-line reading of the book of Genesis.

Beyond these two modes of exegesis, first on the Mishnah, then on Scripture, lies yet a third. To understand it, we once more turn back to the Mishnah's great exegetes, represented to begin with in the Yerushalmi. Whereas the original exegesis of the Mishnah in the Tosefta addressed the document by a line-by-line commentary, responding only in discrete and self-contained units of discourse, the authors of the units of discourse gathered in the Yerushalmi developed another mode of discourse entirely. They treated not phrases or sentences but principles and large-scale con-ceptual problems. They dealt not only with a given topic, a subject and its rule, but with an encompassing problem, a principle and its impli-cations for a number of topics and rules. This far more discursive and philosophical mode of thought produced for Mishnah exegesis, in some-what smaller volume but in much richer content, sustained essays on principles cutting across specific rules. And for Scripture the work of sustained and broad-ranging discourse resulted in a second type of exe-getical work, beyond that focused on words, phrases, and sentences.

Discursive exegesis is represented, to begin with, in Leviticus Rabbah, a document that reached closure, people generally suppose, sometime after Genesis Rabbah, thus in ca. 400–450. Leviticus Rabbah presents not phrase-by-phrase systematic exegeses of verses in the book of Leviticus, but a set of thirty-seven topical essays. These syllogistic essays take the form of citations and comments on verses of Scripture, but the compositions range widely over the far reaches of the Hebrew scriptures while focusing narrowly on a given theme. Moreover, they make quite distinctive points about that theme. Their essays are compositions, not merely composites. Whether devoted to God's favor to the poor and humble or to the dangers of drunkenness, the essays, exegetical in form, discursive in character, correspond to the equivalent, legal essays amply represented in the Yerushalmi.

Thus, in this other mode of Scripture interpretation, too, the framers of the exegeses of Scripture accomplished in connection with Scripture what the Yerushalmi's exegetes of the Mishnah were doing in the same way at the same time. We move rapidly past yet a fourth mode of Scriptural exegesis, one in which the order of scriptural verses is left far behind and in which topics, not passages of Scripture, take over as the mode of organizing thought. Represented by Pesiqta deR. Kahana, Lamentations Rabbati, and some other collections conventionally assigned to the sixth and seventh centuries, these entirely discursive compositions move out in their own direction, only marginally relating in mode of discourse to any counterparts in the Yerushalmi (or in the Bavli).

As I said at the outset, at the end of the extraordinarily creative age of Judaism, the authors of units of discourse collected in the Bavli drew together the two, until then distinct, modes of organizing thought, either around the Mishnah or around Scripture. They treated both Torahs, oral and written, as equally available in the work of organizing large-scale exercises of sustained inquiry. Hence, we find in the Bavli a systematic treatment of some tractates of the Mishnah, and within the same aggregates of discourse we also find (in somewhat smaller proportion to be sure, roughly 60 to 40% in my sample of three tractates) a second principle of organizing and redaction. That principle dictates that ideas be laid out in line with verses of Scripture, themselves dealt with in cogent sequence, one by one, just as the Mishnah's sentences and paragraphs come under analysis, in cogent order and one by one.

Chapters III through VIII: How We Read the Sources

The reason that the foregoing, somewhat protracted theory of the development and organization of the sources of formative Judaism requires attention is simple. If we are to trace the unfolding, in the sources of formative Judaism, of a given theme or ideas on a given problem, the order in which we approach the components, or books, of the entire canon gives us the sole guidance on sequence and context that we are apt to find. Why? Because we have no way of demonstrating that the authorities to whom ideas are attributed really said what is assigned to them.

The sole fact we have to guide us, therefore, is that the framers of a given document included in their book sayings imputed to certain named authorities. Are these dependable? It is unlikely, on the face of it. Why? Since the same sayings were imputed to diverse authorities by different groups of editors of different books, we stand on shaky ground indeed if we rely for chronology on the framers' claims of who said what. *What we cannot show we do not know.* Lacking firm evidence, for example, in a sage's own, clearly assigned writings, or even in writings redacted by a sage's disciples and circulated among themselves, we have for chronology only a single fact. A document, reaching closure at a given time, contains the allegation that Rabbi X made statement Y, so we know that people at the time the document reached closure took the view that Rabbi X made statement Y. We may then assign to statement Y a position in the sequence of sayings, defined by the location of the document in the sequence of documents.

Chapters III through VIII: Whose Judaism?

Now that we know how to gain access to unfolding opinion on emotions in the formative age of Judaism, we address one final question. Exactly whose views come before us? The answer is critical for framing a valid perspective on the whole, but a brief answer nonetheless serves. The entire literature derives from a single type of Israelite, a type represented in one continuous movement, with ongoing personal and institutional relationships beginning long before the closure of the Mishnah and continuing long after the conclusion of the Bavli.

This movement, with its traditions of learning, its continuities of institutions, leadership, and authority, its assured social position and substantial political power in the government of Israel, the Jewish people, in both centers of settlement in late antiquity, bears several titles. It is called "rabbinic," because of the title of honor accorded to some of its leaders, called rabbis. But "rabbi" meant simply "my lord," thus, in our context, not much more than "sir" or (pro domo) "professor." The term of honor occurs, with slight variation, in Christian Syriac sources (e.g., Rabban) and therefore does not have a distinctively Jewish, let alone Judaic, meaning at all. Another title is "talmudic," because of the principal document, the Talmud (meaning, the Bavli, the Talmud of Babylonia) produced at the end. Hence, people quite properly speak of "talmudic Judaism." Other, more theological titles circulate, for instance, "classical" or "normative," as in "classical Judaism" and "normative Judaism." Finally, within the system itself, the correct title would have to make use of the word "Torah," since the entire canonical literature forms "the one whole Torah of Moses, our rabbi," received from God at Mount Sinai. Accordingly, we could call this literature the canon of the dual Torah, and the movement, the movement of Torah sages.

From our perspective a single fact emerges from the multiplicity of titles. The canonical literature derives from a singular group of intellectuals, well-organized sages. These sages also formed a political class within Israel in the Land of Israel and in Babylonia. They further served as models for the nation at large, models not merely of virtue but of piety and holiness. So when we review what the literature of Judaism in its formative age tells us about the correct emotions and the proper modes and forms of the inner life of religious affections, what do we find? We find that singular vision that derives from men of intellect. (Not a single woman of consequence appears, in the early, middle, or late stages of the canon.) Here the message of a movement of intellectuals addressing issues of emotions finds exemplification. If, we ask, mind speaks of heart, what exactly does it say? Here we find the answer.

To summarize, since the components of the canon of formative Judaism derive not from named, individual authors but from collective decisions of schools or academies, we cannot take for granted the accuracy of attributions of sayings to individuals. We cannot show that a given rabbi actually said what he is alleged to have stated. We do not have a book or a letter that he wrote, as we do, for example, for Paul or Augustine or other important Christian counterparts to the great rabbis of late antiquity. Nor do we know whether the events related in a given story are accurately portrayed, or even whether they took place at all. Accordingly, we cannot identify as historical in an exact sense anything that comes down to us in the canon of Judaism. What is absolutely factual, by contrast, is that these books represent the views held by their authorship. That is why I do not allege we know what people were thinking before the point at which, it is generally assumed, a given document was redacted. Accordingly, if I wish to know the sequence in which views reached their current expression, I have recourse to the conventional order and rough dating assigned by modern scholarship to several documents. That accounts for the order of Chapters III through VII and the internal order of Chapter VIII.

Chapters III through VIII: Bibliography

Chapter III: The Mishnah

Neusner, Jacob. *Ancient Israel after Catastrophe: The Religious World-View of the Mishnah* (Charlottesville, 1983: University of Virginia Press).

A History of the Mishnaic Law of Appointed Times (Leiden, 1981–3: Brill), 5 vols.

A History of the Mishnaic Law of Damages (Leiden, 1983–5: Brill), 5 vols.

A History of the Mishnaic Law of Holy Things (Leiden, 1979: Brill), 6 vols.

A History of the Mishnaic Law of Purities (Leiden, 1974–7: Brill), 22 vols.

A History of the Mishnaic Law of Women (Leiden, 1979–80: Brill), 5 vols.

Judaism: The Evidence of the Mishnah (1981: University of Chicago Press).

The Mishnah: A New Translation (New Haven, Conn., 1987: Yale University Press).

Chapter IV: Tractate Abot

Neusner, Jacob. *Torah from Our Sages: Pirke Avot, a New American Translation and Explanation* (Chappaqua, N.Y., 1983: Rossel).

Chapter V: The Tosefta

Golden, Judah, trans., *The Fathers According to Rabbi Nathan* (New Haven, Conn., 1955: Yale University Press).

Neusner, Jacob. *The Tosefta, Translated from the Hebrew* (New York, 1977–86: Ktav), 6 vols.

Chapter VI: The Yerushalmi

Neusner, Jacob. *Judaism in Society: The Evidence of the Yerushalmi. Toward the Natural History of a Religion* (1983: University of Chicago Press).

Neusner, Jacob, trans., *The Talmud of the Land of Israel: A Preliminary Translation and Explanation* (1982–9: University of Chicago Press), 35 vols.

Chapter VII: The Bavli

Epstein, I., ed., *The Babylonian Talmud* (London, 1948: Soncino Press), 18 vols. Translations of passages of the Bavli that are not mine are identified by the name of the translator in the Soncino Press translation and the page of the appropriate volume.

Neusner, Jacob. *Judaism. The Classic Statement: The Evidence of the Bavli* (1986: University of Chicago Press).
The Talmud of Babylonia: An American Translation (Atlanta, 1984–5: Scholars Press for Brown Judaic Studies), Vols. 1, 6, 17, 18A–C, and 32.

Chapter VIII: Mekhilta, Sifra, Sifré to Numbers, Sifré to Deuteronomy, Genesis Rabbah and Leviticus Rabbah, and Pesiqta deRab Kahana

Braude, William G., and Israel J. Kapstein, trans., *Pesikta deRab Kahana: R. Kahana's Compilation of Discourses for Sabbaths and Festal Days* (Philadelphia, 1975: Jewish Publication Society of America).
Lauterbach, Jacob Z., trans., *Mekilta deRabbi Ishmael* (Philadelphia, 1949: Jewish Publication Society of America), 3 vols.
Levertoff, Paul P. *Midrash Sifre on Numbers* (London, 1926: Golub).
Neusner, Jacob. *Comparative Midrash: The Plan and Program of Genesis Rabbah and Leviticus Rabbah* (Atlanta, 1986: Scholars Press for Brown Judaic Studies).
Genesis and Judaism: The Perspective of Genesis Rabbah: An Analytical Anthology (Atlanta, 1986: Scholars Press for Brown Judaic Studies).
Genesis Rabbah: The Judaic Commentary on Genesis. A New Translation (Atlanta, 1985: Scholars Press for Brown Judaic Studies), 3 vols.
The Integrity of Leviticus Rabbah: The Problem of the Autonomy of a Rabbinic Document (Chico, Calif., 1985: Scholars Press for Brown Judaic Studies).
A History of the Mishnaic Law of Purities. Vol. 6: *Negaim Sifra* (Leiden, 1976: Brill).
Judaism and Scripture: The Evidence of Leviticus Rabbah (1986: University of Chicago Press).
Reading Scriptures: An Introduction to Rabbinic Midrash (Chappaqua, N.Y., 1986: Rossel).

Chapter IX: Exegesis, Torah, and Messiah

Neusner, Jacob. *The Foundations of Judaism: Method, Teleology, Doctrine* (Philadelphia, 1983–5: Fortress), 3 vols.

Where I Go from Here

The results of this book dictate three more projects. I have already completed the first: developing the thesis outlined in Chapter IX, about constancy and change, in its own terms. I have demonstrated, in the present volume, that the doctrine of affections remains constant and consistent in the unfolding canon of Judaism. But the same books show that other critical matters under went striking changes. Specifically, hermeneutics, teleology, and central symbol all reveal a remarkable shift, always marked by the same document, the Yerushalmi. Other works of mine have already shown that emotions are not the only point of stability in the canon. Doctrines of the "other," or outsider, remain impermeable to historical change, saying the same thing over and over again as the world goes from pagan to Christian and as Israel turns from autonomous nation within the Roman system to subject people. Views of the city or metropolis also retain their basic shape throughout the canon. Therefore, I have sketched a larger picture and speculated more systematically on persistence and change (see *Judaism in the Matrix of Christianity* [Philadelphia, 1986: Fortress]).

The results of the present volume as well as my work on the foundations of Judaism repeatedly point to the fourth century as the point at which Judaism as we know it emerged. My second project is, therefore, to read in a more systematic way principal documents of the fourth and early fifth centuries other than the Yerushalmi and Leviticus Rabbah. First among these is Genesis Rabbah. A new translation, one that permits systematic analysis of each of the units of thought of the composition and taxonomic study of the whole, is required. On that basis a new set of studies of the character, composition, and logic of the document parallel to my *Judaism and Scripture: The Evidence of Leviticus Rabbah* and *The Integrity of Leviticus Rabbah: The Synoptic Problem in Rabbinic Literature* must be worked out.

With the principal documents properly analyzed, my third project will be based on a fresh reading of the historical and literary facts of the fourth and early fifth centuries, on the side of both Judaism and Christianity. It appears that the definitive themes of Judaism at the end of late antiquity – hermeneutics, teleology, and symbolic form of doctrine – reached their now-familiar expression in particular in the Yerushalmi and closely related writings. One there, serendipitously, dealt with a principal challenge presented to Judaism by the Christianity of Constantine's successors.

To begin with the obvious, the Christians claimed that Christ in the person of Constantine and Constantine's heirs was triumphant, so what did Judaism have to say about the Messiah now? They held that the Hebrew scriptures had been proved beyond doubt to point to Christ, so where was the place for the authoritative writings of Judaism, such as the Mishnah? How otherwise was ancient Scripture to be read? And, of course, the cross had conquered, as Constantine had maintained, so what stood for the once-competing, now-vanquished faith?

The answers, in the form of the secure link between the writings of the sages and written Scripture, the symbol of the Torah, and the doctrine that the Messiah would come when the entire Torah of Sinai, written and oral, had been realized in Israel, had succeeded in Israel. Wherever Jews lived under Christian rule, they sustained a stable and spiritually secure, confident community. The sages' Judaism successfully met the challenge of Christianity. This meant that the system of Judaism for Israel, the Jewish people, had overcome the crisis of the triumph of Christianity in the Roman Empire, East and West. Why Judaism maintained itself so remarkably well in Islam is a separate question, and why Christianity did not meet the challenge of Islam, with the whole of North Africa going over to the new monotheism, also demands attention. It must follow that at the point at which Christianity confronted the sages of Judaism and presented a profound challenge, the sages met the crisis head on and, in hermeneutics, teleology, and doctrine, point to point. From this emerges a hypothesis worth exploring: In structure, in points of emphasis and of indifference, the Judaism that is fully formulated in the Yerushalmi and its contemporary and successor documents addresses the issues that it does because of specific points of conflict with the Christianity of that time and place. That same kind of Judaism ignores the issues that it does because they presented no challenge. Stated simply, although people commonly maintain that Christianity in the first century was born in the matrix of Judaism, in fact, Judaism in its most enduring form in the fourth century was born from the womb of Christianity. Thus, for both sustaining religious traditions of the West, the true *first* century was the fourth. These matters are dealt with in the following: *Judaism and Christianity in the Age of Constantine* (1987: University of Chicago Press); *Self-fulfilling Prophecy: Exile and Return in the History of Judaism* (Boston, 1987: Beacon); and *Death and Birth of Judaism: The Impact of Christianity, Secularism, and the Holocaust on Jewish Faith* (New York, 1987: Basic).

General Index

Abayye: prayers for individual use, 120; wrath of God, 112
Abba, wrath of God, 110
Abba B. R. Kahana: arrogance, 134; restraint and patience, 89–90
Abba Saul: display of emotions, 39; self-discipline, 50
Abin, wrath of God, 112
Abonah, hatred, emotion of, 85
Abun, love, emotion of, 84
Aha: love, emotion of, 82; messianic hope, 23; restraint and patience, 88
Aha b. Hanina: rejoicing, 109; wrath of God, 110
Aibu, arrogance, 135
Alexandri, arrogance, 105
alienation from God, 122–5
Ami, alienation from God, 122–3
Ammi, anger, emotion of, 79
anger, emotion of, 77–9, 100–101
Antigonos of Sohko, self-discipline, 48
Aqiba: death scene, 121–2; display of emotions, 30, 32, 64–5; humility and self-abnegation, 96; love, emotion of, 83; love of God/God's love, 138; restraint and patience, 83; self-discipline, 52; shame, emotion of, 70
arrogance, 104–8, 133–5
Ashi, arrogance, 106
Assi, alienation from God, 123
Averill, James R., 12–14, 20
Avira, arrogance, 105

Bar Kokhba, 17, 21–2
Bar Qappara, anger, emotion of, 100
Ben Azzai, display of emotion, 73
Ben Zoma, self-discipline, 53
Berekiah, love, emotion of, 87
Bibi, inadequacy, emotion of, 76

compassion of God, 112

Darwin, Charles, 9, 12
death scene, 121–2
deliberation and patience, 57–60
Dewey, John, 9, 12
display of emotions, 26–44, 61–74

Edwards, Jonathan, 9, 15
Eleazar: alienation from God, 122, 124–5; anger, emotion of, 78; arrogance, 105; faith and hope, 116; forbearance, 104; hatred, emotion of, 85; love, emotion of, 84; prayers for individual use, 119; restraint and patience, 93; temper, 132; wrath of God, 112
Eleazar b. Azariah, display of emotions, 32
Eleazar b. Jacob, love, emotion of, 83
Eleazar b. R. Sadoq, display of emotions, 64
Eleazar b. Shammua, self-discipline, 55
Eleazar of Modiin, messianic hope, 21–2
Eleazar the Modite, self-discipline, 52
Eliezer: death scene, 121; display of emotions, 29; hatred, emotion of, 85; love of God/God's love, 138
Eliezer b. Hyrcanus, self-discipline, 50–1
Eliezer Haqqappar, self-discipline, 55
Eliezer the Great, faith and hope, 116
Epes, humility and self-abnegation, 95

faith and hope, 116–17
forbearance, 102–4
Freud, Sigmund, 9, 12

Gamaliel: rejoicing, 108–9; shame, emotion of, 68
Gamaliel the Elder, display of emotions, 30
generosity, virtue of, 56–7

Haggai, love, emotion of, 83

Hama b. Hanina, alienation from God, 123
Hanin, inadequacy, emotion of, 76
Hanina, humility and self-abnegation, 95
Hanina b. Dosa, self-discipline, 51
Hanina b. Gamula, compassion of God, 113
Haninah, restraint and patience, 89
happiness, display of emotions, 29, 39–41
hatred, emotion of, 71–2, 85
Heer, M. D., 129–30
Hezekiah, arrogance, 105
Hillel, House of: self-discipline, 48; shame, emotion of, 68–9; traits of the heart, 118
Hillel the Elder, display of emotions, 63
Hisda: arrogance, 105; wrath of God, 110
Hiyya bar Abba, wrath of God, 110
Hochschild, Arline Russell, 12–13
humility and self-abnegation, 95–6, 135
Huna: alienation from God, 122; anger, emotion of, 78; love, emotion of, 83; temper, 132; wrath of God, 110

Idi, arrogance, 107
Ilai, display of emotions, 62
inadequacy, emotion of, 76–7
Isaac: arrogance, 107; forbearance, 102; restraint and patience, 89–90
Isaac bar Kahana, inadequacy, emotion of, 76
Isaac bar Nahman, love, emotion of, 84
Isaac b. R. Hiyya, mourning, emotion of, 80
Ishmael: display of emotions, 64; love of God/God's love, 130; mourning, display of emotions, 37; restraint and patience, 93; self-discipline, 52
Ishmael b. R. Sadoq, self-discipline, 54

Jacob bar Aha, hatred, emotion of, 85
Jacob bar Iddi, restraint and patience, 93
Jacob bar Idi: love, emotion of, 84; wrath of God, 110
Jeremiah, restraint and patience, 90
Jonathan: rejoicing, 109; restraint and patience, 88; self-discipline, 54
Joshua: arrogance, 107; display of emotions, 66
Joshua b. Hananiah, self-discipline, 50–1
Joshua b. Levi: alienation from God, 123; anger, emotion of, 100; arrogance, 106; mutual regard, one for another, 78
Judah: alienation from God, 125; display of emotions, 40–1, 62; mourning, emotion of, 80–1; shame, emotion of, 68–9; traits of the heart, 118
Judah b. Baba, display of emotions, 29–30

Judah the Patriarch: prayers for individual use, 119; self-discipline, 46

Kahana, restraint and patience, 92

Levi: arrogance, 107, 133, 135; messianic hope, 23; restraint and patience, 89, 94
Levitas of Yabneh, self-discipline, 54
love, emotion of, 82–5, 87–90
love of God, 113–16
love of God/God's love, 127–40
Luliani, love of God/God's love, 136

Mana: love, emotion of, 83; mourning, emotion of, 80
Mani b. Pattish, traits of the heart, 118
Mar b. Rabina, prayers for individual use, 120
marriage as social and public institution, 38
Mar Uqba, arrogance, 105
Matya b. Harash, self-discipline, 55
Meir: display of emotions, 41, 64; love of God/God's love, 114, 137, 139; mourning, display of emotions, 36, 79–81; restraint and patience, 93–5; self-discipline, 54; wrath of God, 112
Mephibosheth, arrogance, 107
messianic hope, 17–18, 20–5
mourning, display of emotions, 26, 28, 35–38, 78–82
mutual regard, one for another, 77

Nahman, arrogance, 104
Nathan, alienation from God, 125
Nehemiah, forbearance, 104
Niebuhr, Richard R., 9

Pappa: alienation from God, 124; arrogance, 108
patience and restraint, 57–60, 89–95
Phineas, arrogance, 135
prayers for individual use, 118

Rab: alienation from God, 124; forbearance, 103; humility and self-abnegation, 135; prayers for individual use, 119; traits of the heart, 118
Raba: alienation from God, 125; prayers for individual use, 119; wrath of God, 110
Rabbah, rejoicing, 108
Rabbah bar bar Hanah, death scene, 121
rejoicing, 108–9
Resh Lakish, traits of the heart, 118
restraint and patience, 57–60, 88–95

Sadoq, self-discipline, 54

Samuel bar Nahman: rejoicing, 109; restraint and patience, 88
Samuel b. Inia, alienation from God, 124
Samuel b. Isaac: alienation from God, 124; restraint and patience, 94
Samuel b. Nahmani, alienation from God, 124
Sehorah, wrath of God, 110
self-discipline, 45–60
selfhood, individual emotion and society, 9–16
shame, emotion of, 68–70
Shammai, House of, self-discipline, 48–9; traits of the heart, 118
Shema, recital of, 30–1
Sheshet, arrogance, 104
Simeon: mourning, emotion of, 80–1; self-discipline, 49
Simeon b. Abba, faith and hope, 116
Simeon b. Eleazar: love of God, 114; self-discipline, 55
Simeon b. Gamaliel, display of emotions, 65
Simeon b. Halputa, humility and self-abnegation, 95
Simeon b. Laqish: forbearance, 103; restraint and patience, 91; wrath of God, 111
Simeon b. Netanel, self-discipline, 50
Simeon ben Yohai, love of God/God's love, 136
Simeon the Righteous, self-discipline, 48
social foundations and emotional life, 11
Solomon, Robert C., 11–15, 19–20

Tanhum b. R. Hiyya: messianic hope, 23; restraint and patience, 88
Tarfon: display of emotions, 39; shame, emotion of, 68
temper, 132

traits of the heart, 117–18

Ulla, arrogance, 108
Ulla bar Abba, traits of the heart, 117

weeping, as display of emotions, 29–31
wrath of God, 110–12

Yannai, self-discipline, 55
Yohanan: alienation from God, 123; arrogance, 106, messianic hope, 21; prayers for individual use, 119–20; rejoicing, 108; restraint and patience, 88, 91, 93; wrath of God, 110–11
Yohanan b. Beroqa, self-discipline, 54
Yohanan ben Zakkai: death scene, 121; display of emotions, 29; self-discipline, 46, 49, 60; shame, emotion of, 68
Yohanan b. Torta, hatred, emotion of, 71
Yose, b. R. Halafta, mourning, emotion of, 79
Yose: display of emotions, 29; mourning, display of emotions, 36, 80–1; restraint and patience, 91–2
Yose bar Hanina, rejoicing, 109
Yose the Priest, self-discipline, 50–1
Yudan: arrogance, 135; love of God/God's love, 136; mourning, emotion of, 80
Yudan bar Hanan, love, emotion of, 87
Yudan the Patriarch, restraint and patience, 91–2

Zabedeh, restraint and patience, 94
Zakkai, arrogance, 135
Zeira, restraint and patience, 89–90, 94
Zeirah, hatred, emotion of, 85
Zira: arrogance, 106; prayers for individual use, 119

Index to Biblical and Talmudic References

Bible

II Chronicles
20:21	109

Deuteronomy
5:6	83
6:5	42–3, 114, 137
7:9	88, 114
7:15	83
13:17	88
14:1	52
14:29	136
16:14	62, 136
18:3	91
27:7	122
28:48	84
28:63	109
28:66	76
28:69	111

Ecclesiastes
2:2	134–5
7:1	120
7:2	64
7:20	122

Exodus
4:6	103
5:30	102
14:20	109
15:2	109
16:20	132
16:25	23, 132
20:6	114
20:7	138
20:20	88
20:24	63
23:17	122
24:1	135
24:10	130
34:7	113
34:8	113

Ezekiel
16:44	92
21:7	104
36:25	32

Genesis
9:6	52, 59
22:2	133
22:3	130
30:16	92
34:1	92
39:20	130
39:21	130
46:29	131
47:3	122

Hosea
2:5	92
5:1	91

Isaiah
1:2	122
1:11	122
1:25	108
2:14	106
13:5	89
21:11	23
22:8	85
22:12	124
25:8	37
26:19	105
26:20	112
30:15	23
33:7	124
41:8	114
50:2	111
53:10	110
54:10	87
57:20	105
58:3	70

61:6	131	10:22	79
63:10	130	11:10	109
66:10	67	15:1	120
66:23	105	16:32	53
Jeremiah		27:1	135
5:1	116	Psalms	
9:19	37	1:1	118
13:17	124–5	6:12	115
50:25	89	25:14	29
67:13	32	30:6	112
Job		31:20	115
11:3	123	35:10	138
15:15	123	37:11	107
29:8	93	44:22	137
Joel		50:23	106
2:13	88	51:19	106
I Kings		60:10	21
22:36	109	61:93	93
Lamentations		66:20	110
1:2	108	75:4	133
1:6	116	86:1	107
3:29	122	91:15	130
3:40	110	94:12	110
Leviticus		95:7	23, 155
2:13	111	96:6	124
11:34	39–40	101:5	105
11:36	39–40	104:31	134
13:18	106	109:22	82
14:56	106	119:46	107
16:2	134	119:62	107
16:16	131–2	119:99	53
16:30	32	119:175	137
Ch. 18	33	122:1	88
19:17	115–16	129:2	53
19:17–18	115	137:5–6	67
Malachi		137:7	85
2:7	131	138:6	105
Micah		149:2	133
6:5	112	I Samuel	
Nehemiah		2:30	53
9:8	82	2:36	106
Numbers		3:39	104
5:1	131	12:17	42
8:9	136	16:7	125
14:1	108	21:1	87
14:17	113	21:2	88
16:25	103	21:4	88
17:5	103	21:6	87
22:12	104	28:15	122
22:20	104	II Samuel	
22:21	130	19:2	80
23:8	112	Zechariah	
31:14	132	4:10	116
31:21–2	133	11:17	22
Proverbs		Zephaniah	
4:2	53	2:3	123
5:8	70	3:15	108
5:12	110–11		

Mishnah

Abot
1:1	48
1:1–18	46
1:2	48
1:3	48
1:5	56
1:6	56
1:7	56
1:10	56
1:12	48, 56
1:13	48, 54
1:14	49, 56
1:15	49, 59
1:17	49, 56
2:4	49, 56, 58–9
2:5	49
2:8	50
2:9	50, 57, 59
2:10	51, 56
2:11	51
2:12	51
3:9	51
3:10	52, 58–9
3:11	52
3;12	52
3:13	52
3:14	53, 59
3:15	53
3:16	53
4:1	53
4:3	54, 57
4:4	54, 57
4:5	54
4:7	54, 59
4:8	54
4:9	54
4:10	55
4:12	55
4:15	55
4:17	55
4:21	55, 57

Berakhot
5:1	30, 44
9:5	43–4, 137

Ketubot
7:4	38–9
7:5	38–9

Makhshirin
3:5	40
3:6	40
3:7	40–1

Moed Qatan
1:5	36
1:7	33
2:5	79
3:7	37–8
3:7–8	37

3:8	37

Sanhedrin
4:5	109
6:5	41–2
6:6	35

Sukkah
2:5	62
5:1	34
5:1–4	36
5:2	34
5:3	34
5:4	34–5, 63

Taanit
1:7	42
2:1	69
4.9	33

Terumot
11:10	80

Tohorot
2:1	125

Uqsin
2:1	125

Yebamot
16:7	30

Yoma
1:4	31
1:6	31
8:9	32

Tosefta

Berakhot
6:7	138

Hagigah
2:9	69
3:33	68

Ketubot
7:6	64

Kippurim
2:7	66–7

Makhshirin
3:1	62

Megillah
3:15	64
3:16	64

Menahot
13:22	71, 85

Moed Qatan
2:15	69
2:16	69

Sanhedrin
6:4	67

Shehit at Hullin
2:24	70

Sotah
15:6	65
15:11	66
15:12	66
15:13	66

15:14	67	**Babylonian Talmud**	
15:15	67	Arakhin	
Sukkah		16b	116
2:1	62	Baba Mesia	
4:1	63	59b	125
4:2	63	Berakhot	
4:3	63	4a	107
Taanit		5a	111
1:8	70	6b	111
3:12	65	7a	112
3:14	65	16b–17a	120
Yadayim		28b	121
2:16	67	39a	101
Zebahim		55a	103
2:17	67	61b	138
		Hagigah	
Palestinian Talmud		5a	123
Abodah Zarah		5b	124–5
2:2	85	Nedarim	
3:1	94, 96	22a	103
4:11	78	Niddah	
Berakhot		23a	101
1:5	138	Pesahim	
3:1	80	52a	138
5:3	78	66b	118
7:2	78	113b	103, 113
9:5	138	Qiddushin	
Erubin		40b–41a	118
3:2	78	49b	118
Horayyot		Sanhedrin	
3:2	78	39b	109
Moed Qatan		74a	114, 138
2:5	79	88b	117
3:7	93	98a	108
Sanhedrin		101a	122
2:6	92	104b	109
6:7	88	105a	104
10:1	87	106b	125
Shabbat		110a	103
6:1	96	111a	113
8:1	76	Shabbat	
14:1	84	31a	118
Sheqalim		32b	104
2:5	88	33a	118
Sotah		119b	116
1:4	95	Sotah	
5:5	83, 138	5a–b	106
Taanit		31a	114
1:1	23	48b	116
2:1	89	Sukkah	
3:9	22	29b	107
4:2	95	Taanit	
4:5	22	20a	117
Terumot		25a	124
3:10	90	Yoma	
11:10	81	9b	104
Yoma		19b	100
1:1	86	82a	138
6:4	83		

Leviticus Rabbah
XIII:I.3   133
XX:II   134
XX:III   135
XX:X   135
XXX:I   136
Mekhilta Beshallah
2   131
Mekhilta Pisha
14   130
Mekihilta Shirata
6:14   138

Pesiqta de R. Kahana
2   136
10   137
Sifre Numbers
1   131
80   132
119   131